RIGHT book RIGHT time

First published in 2007

Copyright © Agnes Nieuwenhuizen, 2007

All extracts quoted in this book are copyright © their respective authors.
All book covers are copyright © their respective publishers.

Allen & Unwin
83 Alexander St
Crows Nest NSW 2065
Australia
Phone: (61 2) 8425 0100
Fax: (61 2) 9906 2218
Email: info@allenandunwin.com
Web: www.allenandunwin.com

National Library of Australia
Cataloguing-in-Publication entry:

Nieuwenhuizen, Agnes.
Right book, right time : 500 great reads for teenagers.
ISBN 978 174114 883 1 (pbk.).
1. Best books. 2. Young adult literature – Bibliography.
3. Teenagers – Books and reading. I. Title.
011.625

Cover and text design by Ruth Grüner
Cover photographs: Mathieu Viennet/istockphoto.com (front),
Tanya Constantine/Getty Images (back),
Izabela Habur/istockphoto.com (spine)
Set in 9.8 pt Metaplus Book by Ruth Grüner
Printed and bound in Australia by Griffin Press

2 4 6 8 10 9 7 5 3

RIGHT book RIGHT time

AGNES NIEUWENHUIZEN

500 great reads for teenagers

ALLEN&UNWIN

Once upon a time...

contents

In memory of my son
John Nieuwenhuizen (Jnr)

24/04/1961–20/10/2006

introduction

You have to read a book at the right time for you, and I am sure this cannot be insisted on too often, for it is the key to the enjoyment of literature.

(Doris Lessing in *The Pleasure of Reading*, Bloomsbury)

To discover a book you love is not that different from discovering a person you love, and you can experience every emotion reading it . . .

(Jane Sullivan, *The Age*)

. . . if you're reading a book that's killing you, put it down and read something else.

(Nick Hornby, *The Complete Polysyllabic Spree*, Penguin)

Read! Read! Read! Read for pleasure, for thrills, for escape, for ideas. Read books that make you laugh and cry and wonder and think. Read for yourself and not for others.

But share books too, with friends, teachers and family. The best kind of recommendation is from someone whose opinion you trust or whose tastes are similar to yours. Many adults enjoy books written for younger people, just as teenagers like reading books for adults alongside those written specifically for them. 'Now, more and more adults acknowledge that some of the best writing today is in the YA field and find no shame or stigma in reading it.' (Jonathan Hunt, *Horn Book Magazine*, March/April 2007)

For all those voracious and eclectic teenage readers there are over 500 books to choose from in *Right Book, Right Time*. I haven't tried to provide a definitive or comprehensive selection but rather a large and enticing smorgasbord of mostly recent titles along with reminders of some older but still wonderful books. The quality, range and sophistication of books for teenagers today is astonishing, so the challenge was deciding what to leave out. There are quick reads, chunky reads, demanding reads and tantalising, innovative books with dazzling use of language. You will find scary books, funny books, sad books and some books that manage to be scary, funny and sad all at once. (Why are so many of the funny books Australian?)

Many of the writers included are famous (Pullman, Zusak, Provoost, Hartnett, McCarthy, Horowitz, Reilly, Cabot, Rowling, Crew, Marsden, Murray, Almond) but there are also exciting new ones, some with ambitious first books (Rosoff, Singleton, Shanahan, Green, Howell, L Wilkinson, Higgins).

The 200 main entries, in twelve thematic sections, are about recent books. There is one book per author, unless they have written in very different genres. This means readers are introduced to a rich variety of contemporary writers and voices. The many spin-off titles allow readers to follow their interests and to make those all-important connections: another book by . . . , another book like . . . , some earlier books about . . .

Alongside the outstanding Australian titles, there are great books from the USA, UK, Canada and Europe and even a few from Asia and Africa. Several European books have been translated from languages including French, Italian, German and Dutch. I have also ranged back in time to bring in earlier books – including classics – that amply repay a visit. Above all, I've tried to offer stepping stones, links, tangents, short-cuts and detours in the hope that everyone will find a reading trail that satisfies them.

Feel like some action and adventure? Or a crime novel or good mystery? Then the 'Action, Adventure, Crime' section is for you. In the mood for a realistic story about the lives of teenagers? Look under 'Life, Love & Loss'. After something more edgy? Go to the 'Extreme or Edgy' entries. The 'What if . . . ? ' section invites you to think about some *big* questions and includes exciting stories about genetic engineering, global warming, cloning and teleportation. (Why are so many of these from New Zealand and the UK?)

When you go on holiday, do you love getting lost in large, engrossing fantasy tales? You loved the Harry Potter books but you've read them all. What now? Well, dip into the 'Fantastic Worlds' section of over fifty titles. Fascinated by war stories or stories set in the past? Delve into the sections titled 'Been & Gone' and 'War & Conflicts'. Curious about the real or imagined lives of others? Explore 'Not Such Ordinary Lives'. Have you read Markus Zusak's extraordinary *The Book Thief*, a hit in the USA, the UK, and at home in Australia? You can find this, along with other best-sellers or much-loved and widely-discussed books such as those of JK Rowling, Margaret Mahy, Philip Pullman, Ursula Dubosarsky, David Almond, Mark Haddon and Sonya Hartnett, in a section called 'Outside the Square'.

The 'Fantastic Worlds' and 'This Sporting Life' sections were written respectively by Lili Wilkinson and Mike Shuttleworth my colleagues at the Centre for Youth Literature, where I worked for several years. I felt they knew more about these areas than me. For the same reason, a few individual entries have also been written by others. You'll find six Mini Essays scattered through the book. These encourage you to explore some lesser-known areas. Are graphic novels and pink books worth reading? Would we be lost without translation? And what do we think about verse novels, picture books for older readers, and the weird and wonderful non-fiction that some teenage boys love to read? Shouldn't all these be on library shelves?

As well as recent books I particularly enjoyed, I've included some older books I read and loved when I was a teenager, when there were no books written specifically for young adults. Many of these still enthral today's readers. The challenge, as Doris Lessing emphasised, is to find the right book at the right time.

AGNES NIEUWENHUIZEN

how to read
RIGHT book RIGHT time

Each book in *Right Book Right Time* is coded with a reading age.

Y = Younger Readers
YA = Young Adult
A = Adult

The order in which these codes appear indicates the primary audience for a book, or the audience for which the book was initially published. For example, YA/A means the book is primarily for young adults but is also of interest to adults. A/YA means the book was published for adults but is also appropriate for and of interest to teenagers. YA/Y means the book was published for teenagers but is accessible to younger readers.

The books are arranged alphabetically by title within thematic sections. You can also look up titles, authors or series in the index.

action, adventure & crime

Sometimes we want to read for thrills, action and escape, and to immerse ourselves in a breathtaking adventure. Crime fiction is a popular form of easy, absorbing reading for many teenagers, as it is for adults. There's nothing like that feeling when you can't wait to turn the page or find the time to get back to your book. The best action, adventure and crime fiction is often very up-to-date and uses recent developments in the real world of espionage, people smuggling, the drug trade, terrorism, cutting-edge technology and global events. Such books also delve into complex motives and methods of operating. If you love fast-paced action, being scared, or solving crimes from the comfort of your chair, your bed or the beach, here are some books for you.

The Alex Rider Adventures ➤ ANTHONY HOROWITZ

YA UK

The bomb had been timed to go off at exactly half past three.

So begins **ARK ANGEL** (2005), the sixth Alex Rider book. Leaping straight into the story with a sharp, short, high-octane opening is typical of this series, described by the *Guardian* as 'explosive, thrilling, action-packed'. Clearly you have to go on reading to find out how, why, what, who, when and even if. The *Daily Mirror* claimed, 'Horowitz is pure class, stylish but action-packed . . . Being James Bond in miniature is way cooler than being a wizard'. The reference is obviously to the Harry Potter series, and when Alex Rider nudged Harry Potter off the top of the bestseller list, the news made headlines. The Alex Rider series has sold over eight million copies world wide. *K-Zone* had this to say to the target audience of *Ark Angel*: 'You won't be able to put it down until you've read the very last page! – 4 stars: Cool as an ice cube in Eminem's glass of Coke.'

Pace, superb timing, big bangs, minimal description and dialogue, and an array of clever, teenage-friendly gadgets are what fuel these books. And at the centre of all the action is the quick witted, ever ingenious and never-say-die fourteen-year-old hero, Alex. Horowitz must enjoy creating the techie stuff as much as Alex revels in using it. Readers certainly enjoy all the zapping, crashing and flashing.

On each mission Alex faces huge challenges – even death – and finds himself in extraordinary locations (even once in the US President's plane, Air Force One). He also gets to meet gorgeous girls (but of course). But, for all the escapism, the books are grounded in reality. Horowitz gets most of his ideas from the news, and this, with careful research, adds a level of currency and credibility.

STORMBREAKER began the series and sets the tone. When Alex's uncle and guardian is killed in mysterious circumstances, Alex discovers that, far from being a staid Vice President of a bank, his uncle was a spy. Immediately, the government wants Alex (don't stop to ask why) to take over his uncle's mission investigating the makers of a revolutionary computer system, code-named Stormbreaker. Alex Rider is transformed from schoolboy to superspy within days, though a particular feature of these books is that Alex Rider, unlike James Bond, is a reluctant hero pressured into working for MI6. After each completed mission he's happy to get back to school and normal life.

Another reason for the popularity of the series is that while the books are not formulaic, they do follow a pattern. You know the kind of reading experience to expect, and you know you won't be let down. Also appealing is that you care about the hero and some of the other characters.

The plots and scenarios are clever and move fast enough for us not to dwell on exploits and escapes that can be pretty far-fetched. It's exciting, inventive, escapist fun. Above all, the reader is desperate to know what will happen. When you come to the end of one adventure you are ready for the next.

The Alex books in order of appearance are *Stormbreaker* (2000), **POINT BLANK** (2001), **SKELETON KEY** (2002), **EAGLE STRIKE** (2003), **SCORPIA** (2004) and **ARK ANGEL** (2005). **SNAKEHEAD** (2007), the seventh book, is partially set in Australia, where Alex touches down at the end of *Ark Angel*. Horowitz has promised his readers he will stop writing Alex Rider books when Alex turns fifteen, but in the world of fiction, time is stretchable. There is also a *Stormbreaker* movie, a graphic novel and a website for enthusiastic fans. « www.alexrider.com »

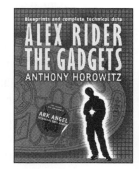

Horowitz is a prolific writer who also writes scripts for TV, movies and the stage. Adults will recognise his much-loved creations *Foyle's War* and *Midsomer Murders*. He has also written scripts based around Agatha Christie stories, including *Agatha Christie's Poirot* and *Murder Most Horrid*, and has created a dark, supernatural series for slightly older readers, Power of Five, and the popular Diamond Brothers series for younger readers.

Beast ➤ ALLY KENNEN

YA UK 2006

I decide that I'll take the pig back to the house and cut it up. Then I'll be able to manage it. This might sound simple to you, but it isn't really. You see my house isn't my home. At all, even though I've lived there for three years. And the family aren't my real family. I am what is known as a 'Looked After Child'. When I was younger they called it 'Being in Care.'

Beast is a scary book, full of menace. We rush and pant after Stephen as he tries to deal with *him* and to hold together his own complicated, rapidly disintegrating life. *He* eats a pig a week and *he* roars. So Stephen needs a pig to feed *him*. *He* has been living in a cage near a reservoir for four years. In that time *he* has grown.

Stephen's life is getting more difficult all the time. He's about to turn seventeen, so will no longer be fostered, and he's expected to move into a depressing hostel full of derelicts. His foster family is a mixed bag, including the apparently manipulative teenager, Carol. To make matters worse, Stephen has just lost his job and still has to deal with *him*.

Beast starts with a grim list of the nine worst things Stephen has ever done. They include bullying, vandalism, arson and even 'perversion, aged thirteen: nicked a neighbour's white, lacy bra from her washing line'. He imagines that number ten will read, 'murder, aged seventeen'. He hasn't done it yet, but Stephen knows he may have to kill *him*.

Stephen has had a very grim life, hence the foster homes. His father is around but pretty much a derelict. Even so, *Beast* is funny, compassionate and sad – a very well-paced and cleverly constructed first novel. Stephen's voice is strong and clear. He's surprisingly thoughtful and astute, and responds to situations in unexpected ways. Don't make your mind up about him (or anyone else in this book) too soon. As you read you may fear *Beast* will give you nightmares, but by the time you reach the end you may feel quite differently.

The Black Book of Secrets ➤ FE HIGGINS

YA/A UK 2007

By the time I staggered onto the bridge I was barely able to hold myself upright. Halfway across I saw a carriage outside the Nimble Finger. Just as its wheels began to turn, I clambered on the back, hanging on for my life. As the carriage pulled away the last thing I remember is the sight of Ma sinking to her knees. She was screaming at me from the river bank and the monster, Barton Gumbroot, was shaking his fist in rage.

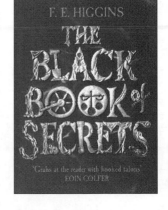

In this rollicking 19th-century pastiche, Ludlow Fitch's gin-soaked Ma rages because her 'diabolic plan' to allow Gumbroot to yank all Ludlow's teeth out for a good sum (before the days of anaesthetic, of course) is foiled. Ludlow, a nifty pickpocket who is constantly exploited by his parents, finds refuge with Mr Jellicoe, the mysterious pawnbroker who teaches him to read and write.

The owner of the carriage in the quote above is the evil, foul-smelling Jeremiah Ratchet, rich through blackmailing the poor of the remote hilltop village of Pagus Parvus. Just arrived in the village to open a pawnshop is the mysterious Joe Zabbidou. Ludlow becomes Zabbidou's trusty offsider and scribe.

Other wonderfully named characters in the village include gravedigger Obadiah Strang, baker Elias Sourdough, physician Samuel Mouldered, and Perigoe Leafbinder, the bookseller. All have terrible secrets. Zabbidou relieves them of guilt by inviting them to tell their stories. Ludlow duly inscribes these into the Black Book of Secrets. Joe even rewards each handsomely so they can pay off their debts to Ratchett, infuriating the latter. Dastardly deeds are revealed and the dire consequences lead to mayhem and catastrophe... Expect to hear more from this inventive, dashing new storyteller.

Cat's Mountain ➤ ALLAN BAILLIE

YA AUSTRALIA 2006

Cat could hear skittering round her and she realised she had never been on the mountain at night. She shivered. She had tramped around Mud Hut in the sun, rain, sleet, even snow, but never at night.

Allan Baillie cranks up the pace and tension of one of his best adventure stories yet.

Before Gramp died, he renamed Mount Foster 'Cat Mountain' because Cat (Catherine) was so at home in the remote bush eyrie. Now Cat has come to visit Gran, who also loves the mountain and refuses to leave. But where is Gran? There has been a huge storm. Has she had an accident? Is she lost? The storm has knocked out the phone connection so there is no way to call for help.

Cat has been terrorised at school by Brena and 'The Pack', so it takes her some time to shake off the conviction that she is useless. In fact, Cat is determined, practical and courageous. And she needs every bit of grit and wit once she finds the dead pilot in the crashed plane; the dying man Gran is trying to save; and the crazy, damaged gun-toting woman who is involved with him. Cat and Gran are caught up in a crime that has gone very wrong. Cat must 'read' the clues and act very, very carefully to avoid more disasters.

The Dark Ground ➤ GILLIAN CROSS

Y/YA UK 2004

High in the clouds, something slammed into Robert's sleeping brain and he woke suddenly, in a rush of adrenalin. His mind was churning with images of falling, of tumbling out of the sky in a roar of broken, burning metal. He smelt the scorching and felt the rush of air against his helpless skin as he fell . . .

'In a rush of adrenalin' is how you will read this story and its sequels. When we first meet Robert in some kind of jungle he is naked, lost, hungry and terrified. Neither he nor we have any idea what has happened to him or where he is. Is he the sole survivor of a plane crash? Is there anyone or anything else nearby? Why does everything seem so huge? He bravely sets about finding food and shelter. Soon he discovers that a girl is trying to help him, and he follows her to a cave where a group of others live a strange subsistence existence. They accept Robert but refuse to discuss their situation or to help him work out what happened. Their entire focus is on avoiding predators (there are some scary encounters with these) and on gathering and hoarding food. We are reminded of the lives of tiny creatures foraging to ensure survival through winter.

Without ever slackening the pace, Cross leads us to an understanding of Robert's situation. Step-by-step we follow Robert's dangerous and arduous quest to reach his family, but his troubles do not end there. They continue through the second book, **THE BLACK ROOM** (2005), the story of a girl locked in a pit by her parents, and eventually to the final book, **THE NIGHTMARE GAME** (2006). Gillian Cross never seems to run out of ideas that keep readers eagerly turning the pages.

Hunters and Warriors ➤ JUSTIN D'ATH

YA AUSTRALIA 2001

'I mean, it just kind of came out that it was the four of us. The fabju-lous foursome. Nobody actually said anything about you – at least, not . . .'
Jarrod suddenly stopped walking. He turned to Bass. 'Did you actually kill any?'
'Me? Of course I did.'
'Except for that one at the start?'
'There were two at the start,' Bass reminded him.
'One, two, who gives a shit? You were kidding around, right? That Luke Skywalker stunt!' Jarrod laughed. 'No one could say that was deliberate.'
'I . . .' Bass began.
'Not like us guys,' Jarrod came back over the top of him. 'We got right into it. It was fucking carnage! Guys!' Jarrod yelled.

A departure for an author best known for his wildly imaginative, humorous and adventurous books for younger readers. Based on a true story, *Hunters and Warriors* is a tough, uncompromising account of a school camp in Australia's beautiful coastal north that goes horribly wrong.

When we learn about horrific massacres during wars we may assume these are the result of wartime conditions and pressures. However, here, in idyllic surroundings and aware of environmental issues four teenage boys rapidly lose control and descend into hysterical group-barbarism as they massacre a whole colony of noddy birds.

D'Ath builds his story carefully and deliberately. He shows the pressure on the boys, especially the more gentle outsider, Bass, to belong and to conform to male expectations to perform in certain macho ways and assume the role of hunters – and of killers.

A confronting, important book that, due to its challenging subject matter and its realistic language, may not have had the commercial success it deserves.

Missing Abby ➤ LEE WEATHERLY

YA UK 2004

*When I had spotted Abby at the town centre bus stop that afternoon,
my first thought had been,* Oh, no! Hide!

*She was looking even stranger than usual, dressed in black combat trousers
and a black T-shirt with a screaming skull on it. Dozens of slithery silver
chains hung around her neck, like metallic snake-skin. She stood leaning
against the bus shelter, reading a paperback with a dragon on the cover.
Even from where I was standing I could see that her nails were long and
pointy, painted black.*

Abby goes missing. As police enquiries deepen, Emma, Abby's former best friend, realises she was the last person to see Abby before she disappeared. Reluctantly, Emma had boarded a bus with Abby. They had had an uneasy conversation and parted awkwardly. Gradually Emma uncovers the story of Abby's passion for a 'Goth' persona and for Dungeons & Dragons–inspired role-playing. This is painful territory for Emma to re-enter as she and Abby used to be teased and even seriously bullied for their 'uncool' pursuits and their fantasy creations. Now Emma finds that Abby was also willing to enter dangerous real worlds and take big risks.

Weatherly unreels a tight, page-turning tale, where nothing turns out as you might expect, and the startling ending, in the scary, half-lit bowels of an industrial plant, packs a punch.

The Road of the Dead ➤ KEVIN BROOKS

YA/A UK 2006

When the Dead Man got Rachel I was sitting in the back of a wrecked Mercedes wondering if the rain was going to stop. I didn't want it to stop. I was just wondering.

It was late, almost midnight.

A hard-edged, violent, spooky book in which Ruben follows his brother, Cole, in a quest to find the killer of their sister Rachel. Ruben's aim is to limit Cole's likely excesses. Cole has blank eyes and a capacity for violence. Ruben has the ability to see inside people; to 'be' with them when they are elsewhere. Usually he is only this way with Cole, sometimes with his mother, and only now, after she is dead, with nineteen-year-old Rachel. 'One moment she was with me . . . and then the moment suddenly cracked and I was with her, walking a storm ravaged lane in the middle of a desolate moor.'

Cole is determined to 'bring Rachel home'. Rachel had gone to stay with a friend who lives with her shadowy husband outside a village. The village men – silent, thuggish, threatening – all seem to be a part of some conspiracy. A shady property development is behind much of the menace and unbridled violence. Everyone is being stood over or has something to hide. Is there a link to the boys' father, a gypsy in prison for murder? Is this why beautiful Jess and the other gypsies are camped nearby?

Brooks creates a very scary set of characters, but also describes landscape brilliantly to build tension.

Brooks's next book, **BEING** (2007), is touted as his breakthrough title. It is a fast-paced science fiction crime thriller, but is not as tight or convincing as *The Road of the Dead*. *Being* has earned Brooks a nomination in the adult section of the Edgar Awards (a US prize organised by the Mystery Writers of America in memory of Edgar Allan Poe).

Smokescreen ➤ BERNARD ASHLEY

YA UK 2006

The soaking wet female running barefoot at her was more like a girl than a woman, and not much older than she was – but Chinese or Vietnamese. And in trouble. The girl grabbed at Ellie, pleading, 'Help me! You will help me? Please?'

'You fallen in?' Ellie asked, 'You want some dry clothes?'

'Hide! Hide me!' The girl turned, shivering, frightened, peering back through the tunnel. 'Bad people!'

Ellie is a 'pub kid' who has spent most of her life living, and helping out, in her parents' pub. Since Ellie's mother's death in a tragic accident, life has been tough for Ellie and her father, Chris Searle. Now Chris has inherited another pub by a canal and despite Ellie's reluctance to move Chris expects things to improve. He plans to refurbish the pub and start a cosy Italian restaurant. Ellie is befriended at school by the smart, sassy, black girl, Flo, and soon Flo's mother is helping out at the pub. But is Ellie ready for a new woman in her father's life? And why do the locals who run the seemingly innocuous Friday music evenings at the pub object more and more ferociously to any changes?

Bernard Ashley pulls a number of threads tighter and tighter to weave a gripping story. Gradually it becomes clear that there is a complex scam in progress, crossing many borders and even continents. Only then do we understand why the young Asian girl who Ellie found was so terrified and desperate, and why the canal location is so important. Can Ellie and her father win out or will the 'bad people' triumph?

more from bernard ashley ➤➤➤

EXCITING ADVENTURES FROM

bernard ashley

Bernard Ashley's lively, easy-to-read stories for teenagers deserve to be better known in Australia. The UK BookBox website says of Ashley, 'He likes to tell stories that are full of excitement and drama, but which also show how a child copes with a crisis point in his or her life.' «www.channel4.com/learning/microsites/B/bookbox/home.htm»

The biography of Ashley on the ACHUKA website «www.achuka.co.uk» tells us that his first novel, published in 1974, 'was followed during the 70s and 80s with successive novels which gained him the reputation as a 'gritty' writer in sympathy with the underdog. Strong characters and plots made Ashley's work the perfect vehicle for television and there have been several TV adaptations.'

Ashley has written more than two-dozen books, won numerous awards and twice been shortlisted for the Carnegie Medal. He has also written graphic novels, particularly the exciting Graphix series (which includes **RESPECT, RAPID** and **ROLLER MADONNAS**); picture books; works for younger readers and several other popular series. The latest series for teenagers is about intrepid investigative journalist Ben Maddox, who works in exotic locations. Meet Ben in **TEN DAYS TO ZERO** (2005), **DOWN TO THE WIRE** (2006) and **FLASHPOINT** (to be released in 2007). Several of Ashley's books also have a cross-cultural strand, picking up on contemporary themes.

TIGER WITHOUT TEETH (1998) is described as a 'thrilling story of survival, discovery and two sorts of love'. Philip Pullman wrote about this book, 'Bernard Ashley's great gift is to turn what seems to be low-key realism into something much stronger . . .'

LITTLE SOLDIER (1999) is about Kaninda, who is forced by circumstances to become a boy soldier in East Africa. But when he makes it to London he is drawn into equally ferocious urban tribal wars. Read it alongside Peter Dickinson's **AK**, also about boy soldiers in Africa, and the tough urban books of Bali Rai (see page 150).

FREEDOM FLIGHT (2003) is about Tom, who is dyslexic. He considers himself pretty worthless, but he's great with boats and maps, and when he rescues an immigrant girl he shows he can be clever and quick witted. But who is he really?

TORRENT (2004) is a highly illustrated adventure set in the French Alps.

Thunder Road ➤ TED DAWE

YA NEW ZEALAND 2003

For me it was an engine begging for mercy (there is no mercy), the steep rising pitch of the turbo, the screaming tyres and the curtain of white smoke hanging behind me: all the stuff that spells street racing.

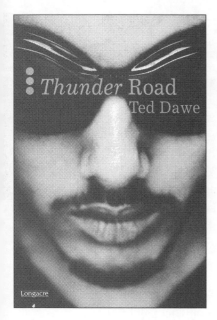

Country lad Trace, nineteen, hooks up with Devon, who wheels and deals with dangerous characters in increasingly dangerous goods. Then the big guys on the scene start showing who is really in charge, and Trace realises Devon is in big trouble and may even lose his girl.

A tough, no-punches-pulled kind of tale that rockets along as fast as the cars that scream and jostle (literally) along Thunder Road, 'where the street racers go to test their machines – and their nerve'.

Tokyo ➤ GRAHAM MARKS

YA UK 2006

*Adam felt totally spaced. It was now something like 2.35 am . . . he was . . .
being given the third degree by his parents . . . It also didn't help that he
hadn't quite got his head round the fact that Charlie had disappeared.*

'Don't judge a book by its cover', we're told. Yet it would be hard to resist *Tokyo*, with the title, the author's name, the words 'All alone in the big city' and some manga-style circular images scrolling down the red and black, Japanese-inspired front cover. The back is enticing too. It needs to be read horizontally. Design is all!

Between the covers is a racy, undemanding mystery with cute chapter headings that poke fun at 'Japanese English': 'I may be passed if you are speednuts and fooding space' and 'Have a nice day penguin duck'.

Charlie (Charlotte) and her best friend, Alice, are travelling. When Alice calls home in the middle of the night to say Charlie has disappeared, everyone is distraught. The police and the embassy are quickly on the case, but Adam and his parents do not think enough is being done. So Adam finds a way to fly to Tokyo to search for his sister. All he has is the name of the seedy bar where the girls were working as 'hostesses'. When he eventually locates this, he finds Alice and her boyfriend, Steve, have also vanished, and no one wants to talk. Adam hasn't considered how he'll manage alone in a city of 27 million people, unable to speak Japanese. But he's determined and will try anything, even if he is reckless and clueless. He has some classic hard-boiled detective style adventures with the gorgeous, sexy, available Aiko (too bad about Adam's girlfriend, Suzy, back home), and scarier ones with some pretty tough types. Nothing turns out as you might expect in this breezy story. Read also Marks's **ZOO**, described as a 'breathless thriller'.

Tomorrow When the War Began ➤ JOHN MARSDEN

YA/A AUSTRALIA 1993

There was a moment's silence. No one knew what to say.

'There's just no explanation that fits all this,' Robyn said.

'It's like UFO stuff,' Kevin said. 'Like aliens have taken them away.'
Then seeing the expression on my face, he quickly added, 'I'm not trying
to make a joke of it, Ellie. I know something bad's happened. I just can't
figure out what it could possibly be.'

As with the Harry Potter books, a great deal has been said about the hugely popular Tomorrow series of seven books. Readers, many of whom had never finished a book before, could hardly bear to wait for the next one. At the time of writing, the two millionth sale of a book from this series had just been announced. This first book has been translated and widely sold in Germany, Spain, Denmark, Holland, Belgium, Italy, Sweden, France, Korea, Japan, China and South Africa.

Clearly, the books have universal appeal and this stems partly from the action-driven nature of the stories. The main appeal to young readers, however, is the intimate and at times visceral involvement with a group of ordinary teenagers who, despite the terrible situations and dangers they encounter, take charge of their own lives. The intensity and complexity of their evolving relationships are also deeply engaging. It is, of course, Marsden's control of language and understanding of how teenagers function that achieves this empathy.

The seven friends come back from a camping trip in a remote bush hideaway called Hell to find all the local people are missing: they have been rounded up and placed in camps. Australia has been invaded. The intrepid teenagers fight fire with fire as they try to outwit the enemy and reclaim the country. The invaders are of Asian origin and appearance but we never find out who 'the enemy' is.

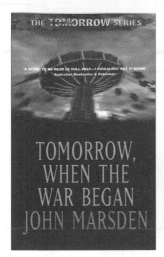

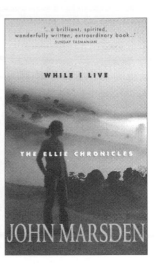

Marsden has won more awards internationally than at home, in countries such as Germany and Austria. Many European countries have Youth Choice Awards, so young people get a direct say in selecting their favourites. In Sweden, where a panel of teenagers selected this book as the one most teenagers were likely to read, a couple of hundred thousand copies were printed and given away free to encourage reading. The seven Tomorrow books were followed by three **ELLIE CHRONICLES** featuring Ellie, the key character from the first series. Despite the end of the war, the enemy is still out there, so more tension and action ensues.

more action, more adventure ➤➤➤

matthew reilly

Matthew Reilly is the author of the international blockbusters **CONTEST** (1996), **ICE STATION** (1998), **TEMPLE** (1999), **AREA 7** (2001), **SCARECROW** (2003) and **SEVEN ANCIENT WONDERS** (2005). He is a young man on a mission and is an inspiring example of what youthful determination can achieve. He wrote his first thriller, *Contest*, at nineteen, while in his first year of a law degree. After the book had been rejected by most major publishers, he decided to self-publish 1000 copies, which he successfully hawked around Sydney bookshops. He made sure that the book looked glossy, professional and like other blockbusters. His dream run began in 1997 when Pan Macmillan's commissioning editor for mass market fiction saw a copy of *Contest* in a central Sydney chain bookstore. After reading the book and being duly impressed, she contacted Reilly, who was already well into *Ice Station*, and offered him a two-book contract. Reilly was off!

Reilly writes the kinds of books he loves to read. They have lashings of action, very little description, exotic locations, plenty of hardware, state-of-the-art gadgets and plots that keep you turning the pages.

Says Reilly, 'I actually disliked reading in my early high school years. I was given very dry old classics in Year 7, and I still believe that put a lot of my classmates off reading for a long time. It was only after I read *To Kill a Mockingbird* and *Lord of the Flies* in Year 10 that I realised reading could transport you to another world. Once I figured that out, I went out and found all the action novels I could!'

In 2004, Reilly, always keen to try something new and develop his market, released his first free online novel, **HOVER CAR RACER**, specifically aimed at teenagers. Reilly's website « www.matthew reilly.com » is sophisticated, easy to negotiate and comprehensive.

Here he tells us that *Hover Car Racer* 'shot to a virtual number one with an estimated 180 000 readers (minimum) worldwide.'

Reilly is an enthusiastic, generous and engaging speaker, and he goes out of his way to promote reading, as well as his own books. He is also engaged in finding new forms for his ideas. He writes short stories, is keen to write for TV, and has had some of his books optioned for movies in the USA. He has written at least one screenplay. You can also find on his website a great list of his favourite books, reprinted here with his permission.

MATTHEW REILLY'S FAVOURITE BOOKS
(action, adventure and a few surprises)

JURASSIC PARK Michael Crichton 1990

RISING SUN Michael Crichton 1992

FATHERLAND Robert Harris 1992

THE SILENCE OF THE LAMBS Thomas Harris 1988

HONOUR AMONG THIEVES Jeffrey Archer 1993

THE FIRM John Grisham 1991

CLEAR AND PRESENT DANGER Tom Clancy 1989

THE DA VINCI CODE Dan Brown 2003

DUNE Frank Herbert 1965

SEARCHING FOR BOBBY FISCHER Fred Waitzkin 1988

A CIVIL ACTION Jonathan Harr 1995

THE SUBTLE KNIFE Philip Pullman 1991

ALL THE HARRY POTTERS JK Rowling 1997–2007

EATERS OF THE DEAD Michael Crichton 1976

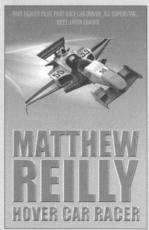

writers of
classic action,
adventure & crime

Most of these authors have had stories transformed into stage, film and TV productions many times over, featuring many great actors. Their books are still great reads!

EDGAR ALLEN POE USA
Poe is notable for his early detective and horror stories especially **THE FALL OF THE HOUSE OF USHER** (1839) and **MURDERS IN THE RUE MORGUE** (1841).

ALEXANDRE DUMAS FRANCE
Dumas wrote swashbuckling adventures with political contexts, including **THE COUNT OF MONTE CRISTO** and **THE THREE MUSKETEERS** (both 1844).

JULES VERNE FRANCE
Verne wrote many still-popular books, including **JOURNEY TO THE CENTRE OF THE EARTH** (1864) and **AROUND THE WORLD IN EIGHTY DAYS** (1873), and is considered the father of adventure science fiction.

H RIDER HAGGARD UK
Rider's **KING SOLOMON'S MINES** (1885) was the first full-length adventure novel set in Africa.

SIR ARTHUR CONAN DOYLE UK
Doyle was the creator of Sherlock Holmes and his partner in crime-solving, Dr John H Watson. Using careful observation, minute clues and logic, Holmes and Watson unravel murders and mysteries that stump even Scotland Yard. Starting in 1887, Doyle wrote four novels and fifty-six short stories featuring this pair. (See page 202)

ROBERT LOUIS STEVENSON UK

Apart from being a great action/adventure tale, **TREASURE ISLAND** (1883) set the fashion for portraying pirates: patched eye, hooked hand and one leg, with a parrot on the shoulder. It also created a trend for treasure maps and buried treasure. It has been illustrated by many artists, including Australia's Robert Ingpen (see page 233).

JACK LONDON USA

THE CALL OF THE WILD (1903) and **WHITE FANG** (1906) are rugged stories of man battling nature. London was industrious and prolific and became the highest paid and most popular American author of his time. He was also a great sailor.

EMMUSKA ORCZY (BARONESS ORCZY) HUNGARY/UK

THE SCARLET PIMPERNEL (1905) features a dashing, elusive hero who leads a secret society dedicated to rescuing people from the guillotine during the French Revolution.

CAPTAIN WE JOHNS UK

Beginning in 1932, ex-pilot Johns wrote ninety-eight books featuring the intrepid pilot hero Biggles.

AGATHA CHRISTIE UK

From 1920, Christie wrote sixty-six genteel crime novels. Hercule Poirot and Miss Jane Marple were her most famous sleuths. The books are still widely read, especially **MURDER ON THE ORIENT EXPRESS** (1934).

JRR TOLKIEN UK

Often seen as a precursor to the Lord of the Rings trilogy, **THE HOBBIT** (1937) follows the adventures of Bilbo Baggins on his quest to reclaim a stolen treasure from Smaug the dragon. He and his companions overcome many dangerous challenges. Not originally considered a children's book, but read by many.

poets raiding the novelists' shelves (that is, verse novels)

by Mike Shuttleworth

It is a truism in publishing that many people want to write poetry, but few people want to read it. Luckily, poets are nothing if not adaptable. (They have been with us since Homer, after all.) Recently poets have begun to raid the shelves usually reserved for novelists – those shelves that house plot, dialogue and (here's the point) action. Because, if it's true that poetry makes nothing happen, as WH Auden commented, the verse novel is a form seething with conflict and craft.

Verse novels can be funny, gritty, playful, sad or serious. They are a medium for all kinds of writing: diary, confessional, letter, travelogue, or documentary. And then there is the showbag of poetic tricks that writers bring to the telling: free verse, haiku, concrete, list poems, sonnets, he said/she said, stream of consciousness, interior monologue, parody, pastiche and more.

Steven Herrick said that he always wanted to write a story in which two teenagers are trapped at night alone in a cave. In **Lonesome Howl** (see page 125) Peter and Lucy are neighbours on struggling country properties who go in search of a fabled wolf. Herrick is one of Australia's best writers when it comes to portraying the lives of young, working class Australians. Catherine Bateson is another. **His Name in Fire** (see page 120) is like an antipodean **Under Milkwood**, so deftly does Bateson unpick the passions, fears and follies of a group of people in a country town. The arrival of a circus-skills trainer to create a work-for-the-dole project brings the chance for young and old to start again.

Surely one of the most striking verse novels, one that fully exploits the potentials of the first-person voice, is **Sold** by Patricia McCormick. **Sold** is the story of Lakshmi, a thirteen-year-old Nepali girl sold into sexual slavery in Nepal and imprisoned in a brothel. The story reads like a documentary, portraying the girls' enforced imprisonment, their ruthless exploitation and their slim hopes. The reader will be gripped and anguished by this haunting book.

In **Nine Hours North**, Tim Sinclair gives us verse novel as travelogue, with a dash of Nick Hornby-ish love-gone-wrong. Adam and Sarah are in Japan to teach English and see the world. But slacker-boy Adam is more interested in an older woman than grammar and his girlfriend. **Jinx** (see page 122) by Margaret Wild is unmatched as a story of failed love. Jen's first boyfriend takes his own life, her second dies in a freak accident. Wild wrings a powerful intimacy from the lives of Jen, her friends, and Jen's mother. Sonya Sones's **What My Mother Doesn't Know** is, by contrast, a light social comedy as Sophie finds Mr Right-and-a-Half, but at first fails to recognise him, and then fails to admit it when she finally does.

Verse novels are well suited to time-challenged teenage readers. They can go anywhere novels can, and then further. They can be a quick, easy read, but can also allow for dazzling technical skills, such as in **Love That Dog** by Sharon Creech. **Love That Dog** is a verse novel about—what else?—poetry.

been & gone

How different was life in the past? What was it like to experience the times and events that have been and gone? Life can be tough at any time, but was it tough or good or exciting at different points in history? In which of these periods would it have been best or worst to live? What do we learn from these stories? Is it easier to stand in someone else's shoes when reading a novel rather than a history book? What inspires writers to bring past times to life on the page? And why have so many authors been so enthralled by Venice and Troy that they keep writing books about them?

A Company of Fools ➤ DEBORAH ELLIS

Y/YA CANADA 2002

I, who had never been in the world beyond the abbey wall, was overwhelmed with sensation. The sights, the noise, the smells! Open sewers ran down the center of the street. People shouted and moved without order. I saw a dead donkey rotting on a street corner, with big black rats scrambling over it. I saw men wearing velvets and big hats with feathers, and urchins in rags fighting over scraps of garbage tossed out a window.

From the war in Afghanistan (the Parvana series) to medieval France, Deborah Ellis ranges far and wide. This time she transports us to France in 1349. Henri is a small, shy, student choir boy at the Abbey of St Luc near Paris.

Wild, mischievous Micah arrives and draws Henri into adventures and escapades. When plague breaks out, wreaking death and havoc, the monks decide that the boys can make a contribution by amusing and entertaining the frightened and suffering populace, or what is left of it. Micah revels in the challenge.

Ellis celebrates the resilience of children and their capacity to create joy and laughter even in the direst of situations. She also shows how terrible events and experiences can bring out the worst, but also the best, in people of all ages and circumstances. And like Laurie Halse Anderson and Catherine Jinks, Ellis also paints a vivid picture of the times and makes us think about what is different and what is the same.

Coram Boy ➤ JAMILA GAVIN

YA/A UK 2000

It was true that a lucrative part of his father's business as a travelling man was to collect abandoned, orphaned and unwanted children – many from local churches and poorhouses – and take them to the ever increasing number of mills that were springing up throughout the country. Otis always called the children 'brats' – as if like rats, they were really vermin – but he made money out of them.

Otis takes babies and money from desperate mothers, promising to deliver them to the Coram Foundling Hospital in London. Instead, he murders them and buries them by the roadside – to the horror of his son, Meshak, who is 'not quite of this world'. It is 1741 and the beginning of the Industrial Revolution in England. The grand Mr Gaddran rears Toby, the son of an African slave, as his plaything. Toby becomes inseparable from Aaron, the illegitimate son of a nobleman. (Aaron is supposed to be dead, but Meshak saved him.) When Meshak realises whose son Aaron is, he tries to rescue both boys, now thirteen. But someone close must die first. An engrossing tale of fathers and sons, rich and poor, greed and cruelty; a tale that shows that wealth and social standing do not determine how parents treat their children.

The Coram Foundation was established to save children from such circumstances and still functions as The Coram Family. And in case we think such things don't happen any more, Jamila Gavin reminds us that 'One only has to look at countries today – from India to Brazil, from China to Romania – and see how children fare there.'

This dark, rich and often scary book has been favourably compared to the works of Dickens and is equally absorbing for adults and teenagers.

Daughter of Venice ➤ DONNA JO NAPOLI

YA USA 2002

*Unless I marry, a convent lies ahead of me, too. . . . Thus far Laura
and I have escaped such a fate merely because of the accident of our
birth order – because a second daughter just might, with luck get a
marriage offer.*

Imagine living in a large, wealthy, noble family where, to preserve
the family fortune, only one son and one daughter can marry. The
remaining boys must become traders, industrialists, scholars or
statesmen. For the girls it is the convent, though one daughter
can stay home to look after the small children. The boys in the
distinguished Mocenigo family are fortunate to have a learned
tutor. The girls learn musical instruments, but the focus is on dress,
deportment, suitor-hunting and decorum. They don't learn to read.
This is Venice in 1592.

But Donata, fourteen, is highly intelligent and a rebel. She
persuades her father to allow her to sit in on the boys' tutorials,
but that is not enough. She needs to see the world, to learn, to
escape her sheltered life. So she disguises herself as a boy and
roams around town, including into the Jewish Ghetto, with near-dire
consequences for herself and the reputation of her family. This book
is an utterly beguiling glimpse into another time and place. It is also
an insight into the very particular and timeless joys of family life,
alongside the constraints and sacrifices accepted in those times.

venice also features in . . .

DEATH IN VENICE Thomas Mann A/YA GERMANY 1912

Mann was one of Germany's greatest writers. This small
classic draws on a visit to Venice by Mann, who uses both
the beauty and the decadence of Venice as a backdrop.
Mann explores the relationship between life and art, beauty
and death, chaos and order.

The disciplined, restrained writer Von Aschenbach finds
himself in the grip of a chaotic and overwhelming passion
for Tadzio, a beautiful boy of fourteen. A cholera epidemic
engulfs the city. The ageing Aschenbach dies on the beach
but the young boy escapes. *Death in Venice* was made into a
classic film in 1972 by the famous Italian filmmaker Visconti.

EVA'S ANGEL Garry Disher YA AUSTRALIA 2003

An unusual novel that weaves the magic and beauty of Venice
into a story of art, intrigue and exploitation. Eva Hicks
visits Italy as a tourist but decides to stay and study art. She
meets the shadowy, creepy Nye, who is supposed to mentor
students. Eva's life also intersects with Matt, who works in a
crypt below Venice, cleaning some ancient frescoes. Both are
questioning life and relationships.

THE MERCHANT OF VENICE William Shakespeare A/YA UK

Written between 1596 and 1598, *The Merchant of Venice*
is both a comedy and a study of the triumph of good over
evil. It also pits the superficial attraction of gold against the
Christian qualities of mercy and compassion. The villain is
the Jewish merchant/moneylender, Shylock, who literally
demands a pound of flesh from his Christian counterpart,
the generous Antonio. Presenting the play has become
problematic because of its stereotypical caricature of a
money-obsessed medieval Jew.

▶▶▶

NIGHT LETTERS Robert Dessaix A AUSTRALIA
Constructed as a series of sophisticated, erudite letters from
Venice to an anonymous correspondent in Melbourne, the
writer, a man recently diagnosed as having a fatal disease,
decides to take an adventurous, open-ended journey. In
twenty letters he reflects on his experiences and the places
he visits, on humanity, on life and on his diagnosis and its
implications.

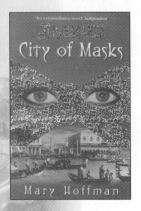

**STRAVAGANZA SERIES: CITY OF MASKS, CITY OF
STARS, CITY OF FLOWERS** Mary Hoffman Y/YA UK
In an alternative time Hoffman has created a
Venice-like alternative world called Bellezza.
It has all the physical beauty, gorgeous
buildings and people, the political intrigues,
the sumptuous balls and masquerades that
might have been found in the Venice of the
Medicis. The stories, spiced up with wonderful,
believable characters and lashings of mystery
and adventure, are hugely popular.

THE TITIAN COMMITTEE Iain Pears A/YA UK
A murder mystery set in Venice, and part of an art history
mystery series.

THE WINGS OF THE DOVE Henry James A/YA USA
A classic love triangle set in Venice in the early 20th century,
told in James's characteristic, gorgeously convoluted,
sophisticated and leisurely style. *The Wings of the Dove* was
made into a movie with beautiful scenes of Venice.

THE WORLD OF VENICE Jan Morris A/YA UK
Written in 1974 by the famous travel writer, this is a richly
detailed and insightful exploration of the past and present of
Venice. The book was revised in 1995.

Edward Britton ➤ GARY CREW & PHILIP NEILSEN

YA AUSTRALIA 2000

Edward Christopher Britton. No. 2380. Ordered to serve eighteen months probation at Point Puer Boys' Penal Establishment. Transported for stealing from his employer, Mr Randolph Ballyntine, owner of the new London Theatrical Company Ltd., goods, value fourteen pounds, viz: one silk-lined cape, one pair trousers, one gold embroidered jacket, one felt hat. No misconduct while in custody awaiting trial.

Edward Britton, now seventeen, was a juvenile Shakespearean actor in London in the mid 1800s. He is well educated and good looking, but he has allegedly been stealing costumes and is transported.

Izod Wolfe couldn't be more different. Dark and brooding, he is desperate to get revenge on the brutal commander of Point Puer, who earlier drove Izod's destitute family off their Irish farm. (Many Australians of Irish descent came here after being similarly thrown off their farms during the famine).

The teenagers are thrown together. Edward is favoured; he avoids hard labour, and is allowed to put on a play for the officials and to start a romance with the commander's daughter (though in this he fares badly at the hands of the girl's jealous stepmother). Izod gets the worst jobs, laying out the dead bodies and cleaning the pigsties. Both struggle and suffer in their own ways to deal with horrific conditions and cruelty.

Although many people have heard of the notorious convict prison at Port Arthur in Tasmania, they may be unaware of the boys' prison, Point Puer, across the bay, where this story is set. Even boys as young as ten were brought all the way to Australia, supposedly to be reformed.

Life wasn't easy for many people, young or old, back then. Novelist Crew and poet Neilsen create a powerful mix of adventure, romance, violence and revenge.

a **classic convict** story

FOR THE TERM OF HIS NATURAL LIFE Marcus Clarke A/YA AUSTRALIA

Published in installments between 1870 and 1872, and in book form as *His Natural Life* in 1874, this has become an Australian classic. Written in the manner of the large 19th century English novels (for example, those of Dickens and Thackeray), the story follows the life, times and trials of Rufus Dawes, who was transported to Australia for a crime he didn't commit. Clarke used this central fictional character to portray many aspects of colonial life and the horrific excesses of the convict system. Perhaps Australia's most famous and significant 19th-century colonial novel, it has been translated into many languages including German, Dutch, Swedish and Russian.

Emil and Karl ➤ YANKEV GLATSHTEYN

Translated by Jeffrey Shandler

Y/YA/A POLAND/USA 1940/2006

My God,' [the teacher] said, raising her hand to her head, 'What is this?'

'We were beating up Emil, he's just a filthy Jew, and now Karl is taking his side', the children squealed.

The circle opened up, but Karl and Emil stayed where they were . . .

'We're just practicing on Emil, so we can take care of grown-up Jews when we're bigger . . .'

What made Lebanese Australians and other Australians clash in Sydney in summer 2006? It seems to take little to foment tension and violence between ethnic or religious groups even when they have been peacefully coexisting sometimes for generations. Think of Christian Serbs and Muslim Albanians in Kosovo, goaded into nationalism and religious hatred in the pursuit of power. The persecution of Jews, before and during World War II, is one of the most extreme and horrific examples of neighbours and friends turning against each other. Adolph Hitler used anti-Semitism as a major tool to gain power.

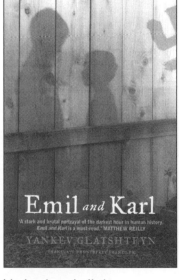

Emil *and* Karl

'A stark and brutal portrayal of the darkest hour in human history. Emil and Karl is a must-read.' MATTHEW REILLY

YANKEV GLATSHTEYN

Set in Vienna, *Emil and Karl* is a remarkable book and all the more so because it was written in 1940 before the full extent of the Holocaust was known. Glatshteyn lived in the US but visited family in Poland in 1938 and saw what was happening. He wrote his book for Yiddish speaking American children so they might understand and hopefully learn tolerance. Despite this aim, *Emil and Karl* is not didactic and tells a powerful story. Only recently translated ▶▶▶

into timeless English, it is a book of its time but equally for today. Karl's father was killed for being a Socialist and now, his mother is suddenly and brutally dragged away, leaving Karl totally alone. He has nowhere to turn except to his best friend, the Jewish Emil. Emil's father is also gone and when his mother falls apart, the two terrified nine year-olds, run, hide, starve but somehow find adults who look after them as best they can. The boys are temporarily rescued by Matilda and her apparently crazy husband, Hans. It turns out both are engaged in highly dangerous work to undermine Hitler and smuggle children out of the country. Did Karl and Emil make it? We certainly hope so. The book has an excellent explanatory afterword from the translator, a US academic. (See War & Conflicts for more stories of the Holocaust.)

Fever 1793 ➤ LAURIE HALSE ANDERSON

Y/YA USA 2000

A week later, sixty-four people had died, though no one seemed quite sure what killed them. Rumours of a fever near the docks snaked through the city. People avoided the shops by the river and came to our end of High Street, where the air smelled cleaner.

Anderson tells a grim (but not gruesome) and engrossing story boldly and well. The outbreak, rapid spread and deadly impact of Yellow Fever in Philadelphia in 1793 is seen through the eyes of Mattie. She watches, comments, works hard and suffers, and like others is often confused. She survives the illness then struggles valiantly to hold the remains of her family together and to help others. The infrastructure in the prosperous city soon disintegrates as those who can escape – the wealthy – do. Food and other necessities, including proper burials, become scarce. There is also a terrific struggle between those who believe in quackery (using leeches, for example) and others who understand the importance of hygiene, fresh air and getting rid of rats.

This is outstanding historical fiction with a lively, likeable heroine. It also has a contemporary resonance, as the fear of epidemics (SARS, AIDS, bird flu) is ever-present.

Girl with a Pearl Earring ➤ TRACY CHEVALIER

A/YA USA 1999

I turned my head and looked at him over my left shoulder . . . He seemed to be waiting for something . . .

'Griet', he said softly. It was all he had to say. My eyes filled with tears I did not shed. I knew now.

'Yes. Don't move.'

He was going to paint me.

A famous, seductive, mysterious painting captures the imagination of a hugely talented writer and so a magical bestseller comes to be. How often do we gaze at a marvellous portrait and wonder about the sitter and the story behind the painting? Here Tracy Chevalier has not only brought the model to life but has also painted a vivid word picture of life in the Delft of mid-17th century Netherlands.

At sixteen, Griet becomes a maid in the busy household of the painter Johannes Vermeer. Protestants and Catholics are suspicious of each other, so Griet, from a loving Protestant family, knows she must tread carefully in Vermeer's Catholic household. She must also subtly manage the demands of Vermeer's wife, Catharina, the six children, the shrewd mother-in-law and the loyal maid. At the same time, Griet contends with the attention of a young local butcher (she rather likes him!) and a wealthy Vermeer patron. When the master notes Griet's painterly way of seeing things he soon has her mixing colours and helping him in other ways. Then he decides to use her as a model, causing anger and jealousy in the household and scandal beyond. But Vermeer also produces a gorgeous painting that has intrigued people for centuries.

Who was the girl with the pearl earring? Do we believe Chevalier's version? Does it matter how true or accurate her version of events is, or is it enough that she has created an enjoyable, believable book and brought many new people to Vermeer's painting? There is also a lovely movie of the same name.

Ivy ➤ JULIE HEARN

YA UK 2006

The name Paradise Row did not exactly suit the collection of houses that lined the alley the way rotten molars fill a smelly mouth. Hell's Hovel would have been better. Or Purgatory Place at the very least . . . And that was when he saw her . . . A stunner. An angel. A pearl among swine.

Ivy is the 'stunner' and this is how the pre-Raphaelites, a particular group of artists of the 1860s, labelled unexpectedly lovely girls discovered in the seething slums of London. Tiny, fragile, an orphan and unable to read, but with ethereal looks and an extraordinary tangle of red hair, Ivy is passed around for the benefit of whoever finds her or can make money out of her. Ivy's aunt and uncle and their rough, lewd family are all thieves and con artists, out for what they can get.

Hearn creates a cast of Dickensian characters. One of the most vivid is the formidable Carroty Kate, who is not quite who she seems. With her murderous accomplice 'Fing' Nolan, Kate and her gang of 'skinners' lure, then strip victims of clothes and valuables. The innocent Ivy is a handy decoy. She is kept passive with doses of addictive laudanum (opium), another challenge she must face if she is to take control of her life. Then Ivy is spotted as a perfect model by the wonderfully pretentious would-be painter Oscar Aretino Frosdick. Ivy's greedy cousins smell riches and do a deal that nearly costs Ivy her life.

Ivy is a delicious romantic adventure with many twists. It provides a rich portrait of the times and of an unforgettable heroine, as resilient as she is lovable and lovely. Look out for the sequel, **HAZEL** (2007), and read also Hearn's earlier book, **THE MERRYBEGOT** (2005), about a girl believed to have powers of witchery. Hearn is a dazzling new talent.

Land of Milk and Honey ➤ WILLIAM TAYLOR

YA NEW ZEALAND 2005

There are them as would give eye-teeth for the chance you're getting.
A farmer's life for you, young fellow me-lad. You'll be living off the fat
of the land and the pig's back, and don't you forget to show how grateful
you are!

As in Ruth Starke's **ORPHANS OF THE QUEEN** (see page 41), a brother and sister are arbitrarily and cruelly separated, but in this case it's on arrival in New Zealand. William Taylor presents an angry and savage account of UK children sent out to 'the colonies' during and after World War II.

Jake, fourteen, and his little sister are not orphans, as their father is still alive, though he is poor and has been seriously injured in the horrific bomb attack by the Germans on Coventry, England. After Jake is separated from his sister he is dumped with farmers from hell. He is not only exploited, but also brutalised, mainly by the farmer's sadistic son and the son's mates. Jake makes a heroic escape and falls (literally – he stumbles into their garden) into a loving, caring home where a bright future becomes possible.

Taylor is a major NZ writer who has not always received due acknowledgement. This is a powerful and significant book about a less-than-glowing episode in the history of New Zealand. Clearly, though, the underlying intentions were good, as they often are when dealing with displaced people.

mixing fact & fiction
australian history for younger readers

Australian author Kirsty Murray says: I *love writing historical fiction; every story leads you to another story. History is woven together by so many incredible strands. When you discover one beautiful coloured thread, you can be sure that if you follow it through, it will lead you to a vast and complex tapestry of stories.*

THE BAMBOO FLUTE Garry Disher 1992
Disher drew on his family's history in rural South Australia to write the moving, gentle, award-winning *The Bamboo Flute*, set during the Depression.

BLACK SNAKE: THE DARING OF NED KELLY Carole Wilkinson 2002
Was Kelly a villain or a hero fighting for the rights of the poor? From an early age Kelly was in trouble. He stole horses and cattle, and became a bank robber and murderer. Yet, when he was to be hanged, thousands wanted his life saved. Kelly has become a national hero and parts of his famous homemade armour and slotted helmet can be viewed at the State Library of Victoria and in a world famous series of paintings by Sidney Nolan. One of Black Dog Books's The Drum series that mix fact and non-fiction to bring history to life.

THE CHILDREN OF THE WIND QUARTET Kirsty Murray
This quartet starts in the 1850s and ends in the present day. It vividly evokes how the mix of origins and cultures evolved to create today's Australia. Each book focuses on the dramatic story of one child in a particular period. In **BRIDIE'S FIRE** (2003), Bridie O'Connor, like many others of the time, sails to Australia for a new life after losing her family during the Great Hunger in Ireland. **BECOMING BILLY DARE** (2004), set around the time of Federation, is the story of an Irish boy who runs away to Australia and becomes an actor. The third book, **A PRAYER FOR BLUE DELANEY**

▶ ▶ ▶

(2005), follows the outback adventures of orphaned Colm, who runs away from the cruelties of Bindoon Boys' Home to search for a family of his own. The final book, **THE SECRET LIFE OF MAEVE LEE KWONG** (2006), is the story of sad, confused Maeve, who, when her mother is killed in a car crash, is caught between the expectations of her Hong Kong Chinese grandparents, her previous life in Australia, and her Irish origins. What will her future be like and where does she belong? Read also Kirsty Murray's earlier **MARKET BLUES** (2001), a time-slip adventure taking us back to the early days of the Victoria Market.

FLY A REBEL FLAG Robyn Annear 2004
Another of Black Dog Books's lively The Drum series. During the gold rushes, the diggers of Ballarat, Victoria, decided to take a stand against what they saw as unfair licence fees. They built a stockade and swore to fight for their rights. The short but fierce battle came to be known as the Eureka Stockade.

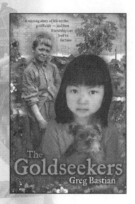

THE GOLDSEEKERS Greg Bastian 2006
When we think of the Asian presence on the gold fields, we usually only think of the Chinese. Here, alongside the Chinese, we meet two Korean children who have been kidnapped and forced to work on the NSW goldfields in the 1850s. They must work to survive, and to save for their passage home. Many adventures and disasters follow, which reveal how tough life was, especially for small children torn from their families and cultures.

THE LONG WALK Kerry Greenwood 2004
Mining family history, Greenwood writes about children walking the Great Ocean Road in search of their father during the Depression in the 1930s, when thousands were out of work and destitute.

MY STORY SERIES
Scholastic's popular, engaging series, written by top Australian authors, presents fictional characters telling their stories during critical times and events in Australian history. Writers include Libby Gleeson,

Nadia Wheatley, Alan Tucker, Christopher Cheng, Anita Heiss, Jenny Pausacker and many others.

ORPHANS OF THE QUEEN Ruth Starke 2004

During World War II, orphans and homeless children were brought to Australia, ostensibly for a better life. But they were often put into orphanages, badly treated or put to work in harsh conditions. This story, based on one such orphanage in Adelaide, tells of a feisty young girl fighting to survive and determined to be reunited with her tiny brother, Egg, separated from her on arrival. In her quest to find Egg, Hilly cleverly and very publicly exploits the visit of Queen Elizabeth II to Australia in 1952. (See *Land of Milk and Honey*, page 38, for a New Zealand version of the practice of sending children to the 'colonies'.)

THE RABBITS John Marsden and Shaun Tan 1998

An award-winning but controversial picture book for any age. Told from the point of view of native animals, it is a bold and angry take on colonialism. It shows the lack of understanding or sympathy of the colonisers (the British) for the inhabitants of the land (the Aboriginal people) and also the impact of imported food, plants and diseases. Shaun Tan's powerful illustrations carry much of the story and established him as a highly significant and original artist. (See page 198 for Shaun Tan's latest, **THE ARRIVAL**.)

VALLEY OF GOLD Jackie French 2003

French lives in the Araluen Valley in NSW. Via a series of snapshots, she threads her way through significant periods and events. She looks at the gold rushes, asks who may have killed the last thylacine, considers how returned soldiers coped with injuries and building a new life, and glances at the development of hippie communes. Being a noted gardener, her focus is on the impact of human habitation on the land. Read also French's **SOLDIER ON THE HILL** (1997) about life in country Australia in World War II, when our hero, Joey, finds a Japanese soldier, but no one believes him.

Pagan's Daughter ➤ CATHERINE JINKS

YA AUSTRALIA 2006

'She's sixteen years old, Holy Father. Sixteen years old! And for all those years I have striven to make her a Good Christian, according to her mother's wishes. But she is a crooked stick. She will not obey God's law. It's the priest's blood, I'm certain – her mother was never like this.'

For those who know the four earlier Pagan books, the tone will be familiar. Babylonne has certainly inherited her father's feisty character, sharp wit and even sharper tongue. She is the illegitimate daughter of the now-dead Archdeacon Pagan Kidrouk and Lady Mabelia, his Cathar heretic lover.

Ten years after the first Pagan book was published, Catherine Jinks hasn't lost her love for the Crusades or medieval history, or her ability to make real the lives and times of her characters through sparkling dialogue and often gorgeous, gruesome detail. *Pagan's Daughter* is rich in historical, military and religious detail and well-placed, snappily labelled, amusing drawings.

Despite every kind of cruel punishment, Babylonne will not 'behave', so she is to be married off to an ancient man. Of course, she won't yield and is desperate to flee. When she finally makes her escape she meets a mysterious red-headed priest. Though wary, she understands she has little choice but to trust the gentle, highly educated man. He turns out to be Isidore, her father's faithful scribe, come to find her. On the road, life becomes increasingly dangerous and soon Babylonne is in the thick of action, danger, death, and her seventh bloody siege. Babylonne realises she wants a new life and her best chance is to follow Isidore. As they head off 'into the rolling green countryside beyond' we sense there will be more adventures.

The Pagan series
PAGAN'S CRUSADE 1993
PAGAN IN EXILE 1994
PAGAN'S VOWS 1995
PAGAN'S SCRIBE 1996

Powder Monkey ➤ PAUL DOWSWELL

YA/Y UK 2005

*When I ran back to my cartridge box, I immediately noticed how much
hotter it had become on the gun deck. All around was frantic activity.
Every gun was at various stages of reloading. Barrels were being swabbed,
burning fragments hooked out, cartridges and cannonballs loaded, and
wads rammed home. I had been gone barely sixty seconds, and already our
crew were needing my cartridge . . .*

When, at just fourteen, Samuel Witchall announces
he wants to become a sailor, his father tries to
dissuade him. But Sam is determined to have
adventure. Eventually his parents agree, but only on
the condition that he joins a merchant ship, which is
supposed to be safer. Sam joins the *Lady Franklyn*,
learns the ropes and enjoys himself. But this is 1800
and Britain is at war with France and Spain, and out
on the high seas he is 'pressed' (forced) to join a
Royal Navy frigate. Sam gets the most dangerous
job of a powder monkey.

This lively account of the perilous life at sea includes storms,
battles and vicious punishments. When asked what inspired him
to write this book after writing mostly non-fiction, Dowswell said,
'I was researching a piece on naval warfare and was struck by how
young many of the sailors in Nelson's time were. Then I saw *Master
and Commander* [the popular movie starring Russell Crowe], which
really drove the point home. Boys whose voices had not yet broken
were being sent to kill and be killed. I also thought it would be
interesting to write the story from the point of view of a boy at the
bottom of the ship's hierarchy rather than someone at the top.'

PRISON SHIP, the sequel, finds Sam wrongly accused of a
crime and transported to Australia. Susan Cooper's time-slip tale
VICTORY is another engaging look at the life of a powder monkey
during the time of the Napoleonic Wars.

Set in Stone ➤ LINDA NEWBERY

YA/A UK 2006

Samuel Godwin: *Dearest Mother: . . . This is a most unusual house, not at all what I imagined . . . It stands in a very isolated spot . . . clearly Mr Farrow is a man who enjoys seclusion, although of course he could not have imagined that he would live here as a widower . . .*

Crammed with secrets and shocking twists, this is a great saga to get lost in, sitting by a fire on a cold winter's day. *Set in Stone* is told in the style of 19th-century stories by Charlotte Bronte, Wilkie Collins and others. Linda Newbery loves exploring what may have happened inside and outside the walls of beautiful old buildings.

Impoverished young artist Samuel Godwin is invited by the widower Mr Farrow to his imposing home, Fourwinds, to become art tutor to his daughters, Marianne and Julianna, under the supervision of their admirable governess, Charlotte Agnew. Samuel is intrigued from the moment he arrives, in the dark, and is greeted by the wild, beautiful, hysterical Marianne. She is seeking the West Wind. He is confronted with his first mystery. Little does Sam realise that by asking questions and snooping he will uncover terrible deeds and much pain. Why did Gideon Waring and the previous governess leave under a cloud? Why is Julianna so sad and withdrawn, and Marianne so often distraught and sleepwalking? Why is Mr Farrow trying to push Julianna and Sam together? Who is the mysterious little boy in the nearby village? And above all, is Mr Farrow the charming, loving father he seems? What really happened to his wife? And is even the ever-patient Charlotte who she seems to be? Unravelling the truth becomes even more fun and challenging as the narrative is shared between Samuel Godwin and Charlotte Agnew.

The book was a controversial winner of the 2007 Costa (formerly Whitbread) Prize. Read **THE SHELL HOUSE** for another foray into the possible dramatic impact of architecture and landscape on lives.

Troy ➤ ADÈLE GERAS

YA UK 2000

[Xanthe] *prepared the pallets, and the water, and the bowls of oil used for cleaning the worst wounds, and when all was ready, she left the Blood Room . . . Xanthe hated war. Every day, the huge wooden gate they called the Skaian Gate . . . opened wide, and the chariots poured through, filled with armed soldiers.*

The siege of Troy lasted ten years. In *Troy*, Geras retells the *Illiad* through the experiences of two orphaned sisters, Xanthe and Marpessa. Previously, most writers have focused on the battles and deeds of the men, but Geras explores the lives of the girls and women.

As well as working in the Blood Room, Xanthe is nursemaid to Hector's son, so she is close to the action and the main players. Everyone is suffering and people's lives are made worse by the meddling of the gods, who are often bored and fighting among themselves. Eros, the god of love, makes Xanthe fall in love with one of the soldiers she nurses. Aphrodite, the goddess of desire, decides it would be fun to make the sisters fall in love with the same man. Geras's long, detailed story brings to life this ancient epic and, because there is a lot of action and the emotions and predicaments are universal, it makes for an enthralling story.

ITHAKA (2005), the follow-up book, re-imagines the *Odyssey*. Here our sympathies are with Penelope, who has been waiting and pining for her husband, Odysseus, for ten long years. Again the focus is on the women left behind, including a young servant girl, Klymene, caught in the huge, grim events of the time. Klymene has to deal with the fraught, chaotic situation at home when hordes of suitors, full of evil intentions, want to claim Penelope's hand and her lands. Everyone becomes embroiled in a tense waiting game. And, once again, the gods and their games add to the volatile brew, as does Klymene's secret passion for Odysseus's son, Telemachus. But all bets are off when a naked, half-drowned man washes up on the beach.

This is another great saga with a contemporary feel.

more trojan tales ➤➤➤

trojan tales

ACHILLES Elizabeth Cook A/YA UK 2001
The Atlantic Monthly described this short, somewhat eccentric take on the deeds of Achilles as, '[A] poetic masterpiece, a psychologically acute portrait . . . *Achilles* is also unfailingly modern: swift, cinematic, sexually explicit, and ravishingly beautiful.'

BLACK SHIPS BEFORE TROY Rosemary Sutcliffe Y/YA UK 1993
A classic retelling of the *Illiad*, told with all the skill of a master storyteller and with wonderful illustrations by Alan Lee. It offers younger readers an introduction to the heroes of ancient Greece while providing the complete story of the siege of Troy. One of the last books by one of the greatest and most prolific writers of historical novels for children.

DATELINE: TROY Paul Fleischman Y/YA USA REVISED EDITION 2006
Fleischman's book cleverly juxtaposes resonant newspaper clippings of events – from World War I to the 'War on Terror' – with his evocative retelling of the story of the Trojan Wars. The clippings are beautifully laid out as collages. Described in the *Kirkus Review* as 'perhaps the ultimate model for making history relevant . . . A superb and often inspiring work.'

THE MOON RIDERS Theresa Tomlinson Y/YA UK 2003
An unusual book that reveals the part played by the Amazon women (the Moon Riders) in the battle of Troy.

Who were these legendary Amazon women? A fascinating combination of research, myth and storytelling. The *Financial Times* said, 'Theresa Tomlinson is among the strongest of a younger generation of historical novelists.'

Followed by **THE VOYAGE OF THE SNAKE LADY**.

ODYSSEUS Ken Catran YA NZ 2005
Catran seems to be able to turn his hand to any genre. This story is made immediate through a great deal of dramatic action and its lively first-person narrative, as Odysseus tells his own story to a poet (Homer?). Odysseus relives his ten-year journey after the battle in Troy, during which he was desperately trying to find his way home to his beloved Penelope, and Telemachus, the son he did not know. Read also Catran's equally exciting **THE GOLDEN PRINCE**, about Pyrrhus, the son of Achilles, as he leads his troops at the Siege of Troy.

THE WAR AT TROY 2004 and **THE RETURN FROM TROY** 2005
Lindsay Clarke A/YA UK
Myth and history intersect in a gripping retelling of the epic tale of the siege and its aftermath. The lives and passions of Paris and Helen, Agamemnon and Clytemnestra, Odysseus and Hector seem startlingly contemporary in these lively books.

The Wings of Kitty St Clair ➤ JAMES ALDRIDGE

YA/A AUSTRALIA 2006

They were looking up to see Fay's small white figure suddenly plunge into the empty air, and when that happened Kitty sucked in her breath. She hated to see that first moment of the jump, particularly when Fay's fall seemed too free and too long before the parachute opened.

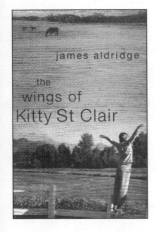

To fully appreciate this story you need to enjoy the slow, quiet build-up of details about places, events, situations, characters and subtle interactions. This is how Aldridge cleverly builds drama and tension.

The book falls into two halves. Since World War I, Kitty, almost fourteen, Jock, her war-damaged pilot father, and Fay, her aerobatic mother, have been leading a nomadic life, doing aerial stunts at fairs and shows in country towns. They return to their hometown St Helen for the annual fair, but change is in the air. Jock's Besterman plane is showing signs of wear, as are Fay's Gypsy Moth and parachute – and audiences are dwindling. As well, Kitty, who has grown up in a cockpit and done most of her lessons there, should be attending a regular school.

The family stays with Billy, who used to fly with Jock. Billy's very French wife, Claudette, runs a boarding house, and their daughter Louise is Kitty's best (only) friend. There is to be one final show, but we sense we are heading for a tragedy.

For a long time after her mother's death, the shocked and devastated Kitty loses her voice. How Kitty is helped to recover makes up the powerful second half of this sad, engaging story, which also beautifully evokes Australian country life in the 1930s as well as the joy, daring and danger of flying in those tiny planes.

The Wings of Kitty St Clair is the seventh book in the St Helen series, which James Aldridge began forty years ago. The books share a particular tone and outlook, and cast a sharp eye over the tensions and constraints of small town life. All feature feisty young people struggling to find their way, often in difficult circumstances. The stories are actually set in and around Swan Hill in north-western Victoria where Aldridge grew up, though he has lived most of his life in Europe. Here he worked as a journalist and wrote many other books.

The St Helen series
MY BROTHER TOM 1996
RIDE A WILD PONY 1975
THE UNTOUCHABLE JULIE 1975
THE TRUE STORY OF LILLI STUBECK 1984
THE TRUE STORY OF SPIT MACPHEE 1986
THE TRUE STORY OF LOLA MACKELLAR 1992

extreme & edgy

Not all children are loved and cherished. Many children and teenagers find themselves in extreme family, social and political situations. Life can be so extreme some may be driven to murder or suicide or crazy behaviour, or even imprisoned. Others struggle with violence, bullying, battles with drugs, body image, crime, fear, poverty, friends, school or illness. Writing about extreme situations can produce challenging, edgy fiction because the writer's imagination, control of language, empathy and craft can lift the book above the merely bleak and grim and beyond any single 'issue'. Here are a few of the best.

All Rivers Flow to the Sea ➤ ALISON McGHEE

YA USA 2005

*Your sister Ivy and you had an accident. The world should have
stopped, but it didn't. The world kept on going . . . How can the world
just keep on going?*

Finding an answer to this question that Rose, seventeen, can accept is the subject of this sad, absorbing book. Following a car accident involving both sisters, Ivy is now on life support. The doctors recommend the life support be turned off, but the girls' mother can't bring herself to agree. This makes letting go even harder for Rose, and her grief, survival-guilt and confusion drive her to some risky, desperate sexual adventures in the hope of forgetting what happened, even for a moment. While she finds no quick or easy answers, Rose is able to draw on the quiet wisdom of an older neighbour, William T. Her growing relationship with childhood friend Tom Miller also brings her solace and allows her to stop reliving what happened.

Set in a small community in the Adirondacks this is a haunting and poetically written novel. A book to read and ponder that gently explores what makes life worth living and how we can keep on going in trying circumstances.

Chanda's Secrets ➤ ALLAN STRATTON

YA CANADA 2004

The real reason the dead are piling up is because of something else.
A disease too scary to name out loud. If people say you have it, you can
lose your job. Your family can kick you out. You can die on the street
alone . . . Thank god nobody whispered 'AIDS' when Esther's parents
got sick. Her papa had a cough and her mama had a bruise.
It started as simply as that.

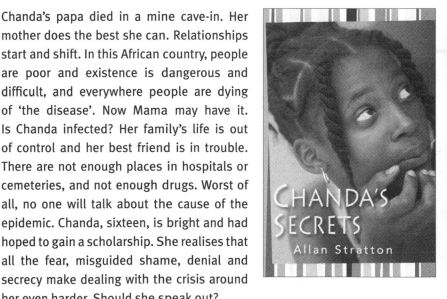

Chanda's papa died in a mine cave-in. Her mother does the best she can. Relationships start and shift. In this African country, people are poor and existence is dangerous and difficult, and everywhere people are dying of 'the disease'. Now Mama may have it. Is Chanda infected? Her family's life is out of control and her best friend is in trouble. There are not enough places in hospitals or cemeteries, and not enough drugs. Worst of all, no one will talk about the cause of the epidemic. Chanda, sixteen, is bright and had hoped to gain a scholarship. She realises that all the fear, misguided shame, denial and secrecy make dealing with the crisis around her even harder. Should she speak out?

The statistics of those, many of them children, infected by the AIDS virus in African countries are horrific. Yet a work of fiction can often be much more direct, personal and powerful than mere statistics. So it is with *Chanda's Secrets*. Chanda's grim, brave, sad story is unfailingly gripping and moving, but also frightening in its portrayal of ignorance, neglect and an apparent lack of political will.

Come Clean ➤ TERRI PADDOCK

YA/A USA 2004

'Fear of, and anxiety for, teenagers reached a political peak last week with both Tony Blair and David Blunkett condemning violence and truancy and a £12.5 million lottery fund driving an expansion of summer camps. With new court orders known as ASBOs (Anti-Social Behaviour Orders) parents, who feel increasingly unequal to the struggle of keeping children of all ages safe and off the streets . . . may feel the solution is to use US-style institutions to sort out problems with discipline, drunkenness and drug abuse.' (Amanda Craig in a review of *Come Clean* in the *Sunday Times*, August 2004)

Based on her sister's experiences in one of the real-life chain of US closed 'facilties', called Straight Inc (here, Come Clean), Paddock has written a very angry and frightening book.

Justine, fifteen, wrote in her diary about liking a boy who had been drinking at a party. This was her 'crime'. She is then tricked into attending the facility where her sister is already locked up. Punishment, isolation, starvation, betrayal of others, brainwashing and humiliation – mostly by peers – in regular AA-type Seven Step programs, are routine. Innocence or guilt seem irrelevant. Staff members are presented as exploitative, sadistic or self-serving; and parents as ineffectual, complicit or uncaring. We keep turning the pages, hardly able to believe these situations and events could exist.

The big questions are: how did the Straight Inc facilities become so successful, and, if this way of dealing with supposedly 'difficult' teenagers is becoming popular in the US and UK, could it happen here?

The Fearful ➤ KEITH GRAY

YA UK 2005

He hated these mornings when he was forced into helping his father with the collecting . . . He'd do anything to stop it from happening. Anything. He'd change his name; he'd leave home if he had to. He just had to do it soon, because in only a few days he'd be sixteen and then, for what it was worth, the rest of his life would be over.

At the next weekly gathering of 'The Fearful', Tim Milmullen will celebrate his sixteenth birthday with a 'Carving', when he will be designated the thirteenth 'Mourner'. Like most in his small lakeside town, Tim is struggling to believe in the legend of the 'The Mourn'. It is told that in 1699, when Tim's ancestor William Milmullen took his six pupils to the lake, a monster rose from the depths and only William returned. Since then the family has guarded against the return of the creature by daily collecting small farm animals and rowing them out into the lake for its supposed voracious inhabitant. Milmullen's descendants continue to carry out this responsibility in the face of increasing derision and disbelief. They hold that it is only because of their efforts that others can enjoy recreational activities on the lake.

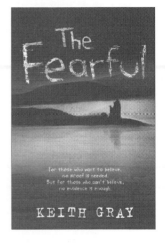

Tim is mercilessly bullied by the local youth for his family's beliefs and the almost cult-like behaviour of their followers, 'The Fearful'. How can Tim determine what is relevant and what is self-interest in others? Can progress be stopped? Can you, or should you, believe in something you have never seen? Where is the line between science and faith? Big questions, posed within an easy-to-read, fast-paced story for our times.

more about bullies ➤➤➤

boys (and the odd girl) who bully

BAD BAD THING Julia Lawrinson YA AUSTRALIA 2005
Boys might threaten physically, but girls can do as much harm with words and just plain nastiness – like Bonnie, who steals school lunches and makes the lives of girls, large and small or any size, hell.

BRUISES Archimede Fusillo YA AUSTRALIA 2004
Forced to attend a school camp, Falco, averse to conflict and distracted by his brother's terminal illness, is a reluctant bunkhouse leader. Ape bullies others to gain the approval he craves from his older, delinquent brother. The disparate group also includes the new, needy kid Brad, the weak Cannucia and 'fat boy' Singh. They create an edgy mix. Can they survive the camp?

THE CHOCOLATE WAR Robert Cormier
YA USA 1974
See page 65.

FAT BOY SWIM Catherine Forde YA UK 2004
An easy-to-read, punchy book showing how, under the tutelage of the priest and trainer dubbed GI Joe, a very fat boy learns to swim, sheds kilos, regains his self-respect and confronts those that bully him. Jimmy Kelly also has a 'secret gift': his ability to cook.

HOLD ON Alan Gibbons YA UK 2005
Annie wants the bully-boys she believes drove her friend John to suicide brought to justice. But not even her family or friends will support her. She also realises people's motives

and behaviour, including her own, are more complex than she imagines. A tense, challenging, but ultimately compassionate, story.

SHADOWS IN THE MIRROR Cameron Nunn YA AUSTRALIA 2006
For five years, David has lived by his boarding school rule that 'you never dob. Not on anyone. Not about anything. Unless you want the crap kicked out of you.' Now he must decide whether to stand with the bullies and the 'in' crowd or with his seriously bullied room-mate. In the process he uncovers a horrific age-old culture of intimidation and brutality.

a couple for
younger readers

THE EIGHTEENTH EMERGENCY Betsy Byars Y USA 1976
Mouse Fawley has a lively imagination. He also likes drawing. When he draws an arrow pointing to the school bully as a neanderthal he is bound to create an 'emergency'. To avoid the situation, Mouse thinks of seventeen other likely (very funny) emergencies. But ultimately he needs to confront his demons.

THE PRESENT TAKERS Aidan Chambers Y UK 1983
Note: Girls involved here. An unusual, clever, thoughtful response by children to two girl bullies who demand daily 'presents' from Lucy. Chambers shows that being clever may work better than trying to be tougher. Perhaps a challenge to the Byars book, as the children in this story are actually reading *The Eighteenth Emergency*.

Firestarter ➤ CATHERINE FORDE

YA UK 2006

Reece petrolled Mario's.

He's a firestarter.

He's dangerous.

He can't tell right from wrong.

I had him in this house last night.

I've let him play with Annie.

He thinks we're mates.

And I can't help feeling sorry for him.

Is Keith weak and hopeless? If he isn't, why doesn't he make Reece go away, or tell his dad, or call the police? *Firestarter* is a tense, short, thought-provoking book. It is also subtle and complex in the way it presents and explores how Keith and others react to Reece.

Keith is a responsible, loving boy. He has persuaded his mother to let him look after his small sister, Annie, for a week during the school holidays while Mother attends a short course and Dad goes to work. Reece shows up suddenly with 'matted blue hair, all spiked up and red at the tips. Like flames on a match-head'. Fire imagery is everywhere. Threatening. From the moment we meet him, we know that Reece is trouble and also extremely troubled. He was sent to a children's home when he was four and has now been brought to stay with his great aunt, next door. His grim history is gradually revealed. He is dramatic and unpredictable but also charming, especially with Annie. He is also very hard to get rid of. Keith is at once repelled, frightened, sympathetic and mesmerised. The signs mount that Reece poses a real risk. Reece is a sad, terrible example of neglect by those who should have loved and cared for him, and by authorities, who seem unable to act until it is almost too late.

Gravity ➤ SCOT GARDNER

YA/A AUSTRALIA 2006

I was wedged in a family that was eating me alive. Stuck at a school I didn't like doing my last year of study so that I could fall into a job I loathed in a town I absolutely hated.

Where can Adam go from here? And why does he feel so bad about every aspect of his life that he drinks far too much and then drives? His anger and pain are highlighted when we discover that his older brother, Simon, almost died in an alcohol-fuelled car crash that killed his best friend. Simon now lives with acquired brain injury. Lately, he has been cared for by Adam and his father. It is a tough, relentless assignment, previously managed single-handedly by their mother, who eventually left, needing a break. Adam decides to do the same.

He finds his bitter mother and escapes again into some wild city adventures. He also reignites his love for working with wood (he hails from a tiny timber town). But he is haunted by the past and by his confused, inarticulate feelings for Tori and her small son, fathered by Simon before the accident. When Simon disappears, it is the catalyst for all the players in this drama to reappraise their lives and relationships, and for Adam to find a clear path forward. There is a lot going on in this story, including a searing glimpse of the destructive force of sibling rivalry.

I'm Not Scared ➤ NICCOLÒ AMMANITI

Translated by Jonathan Hunt

A/YA ITALY 2001/2003

At the bottom of the hole there was a boy.

He was lying on his side. His head was hidden between his legs.

He wasn't moving.

He was dead.

I stood looking at him for God knows how long. There was a bucket too. And a little saucepan.

Maybe he was asleep.

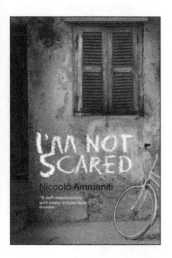

An enthralling, but devastating, story about two small boys trapped in a nightmare. It is 1978, in the scorching heat of summer, when bored children from a tiny, poor, rural Italian village head out across the wheat fields on dilapidated bikes to see some famous pigs. While exploring an abandoned house, Michele, nine, discovers what he believes to be the body of a boy his own age. Then he realises the boy is alive but a prisoner; the victim of a local mafia-like struggle. Unable to tell anyone, Michele brings the imprisoned boy food and water, gradually uncovers his terrible story and finds that most of the adults in his community are implicated. Despite his fear and confusion, Michele persists in helping the boy. His actions lead to a heart-stopping climax.

Written in spare prose, beautifully rendered in the translation, the book captures Michele's voice and shifting emotions. This is a hard book to bear, but also impossible to put down. Made into a well-received movie of the same name in 2003.

Inexcusable ➤ CHRIS LYNCH

YA USA 2005

'The way you make things look is not the way they really are, Keir,'
Fran said, leaning forward to try to put a hand on my knee. I pushed her
hand away. 'You make things up to be what you want them to be.
And Ray lets you.'

'Shut up, Fran. Don't say anything bad about Ray.'

It is typical of Keir to neither listen nor respond to what someone says, particularly when it's something he doesn't want to hear. Some critics have reduced this startlingly original and profoundly disturbing book to being 'about' date rape. Yes, Keir brutally forces himself on the gorgeous Gigi Boudakian. However, Keir's story is a much more complex and sinister exposé of how so many young people are allowed to live their lives. The rape is one horrific, but quite logical, progression of the consistently self-centred and self-indulgent behaviour considered acceptable by many of Keir's circle – and largely ignored by his father. Football, drugs, alcohol, girls and money, accompanied by few expectations from adults about consequences or responsibility, lead to toxic situations.

Keir and his sisters, Fran and Mary, have been lovingly brought up by their father. Now Fran and Mary have left for college and Keir has had a wonderful year of being buddies with his dad, who drinks a lot of beer and whisky but is never late for work. When Keir realises his dream of winning a football scholarship to the same college as his sisters, he assumes they must be delighted. After all everyone loves him, don't they? But when Keir's plans for a surprise reunion with his sisters are thwarted, he spins out of control.

Lynch never makes excuses for Keir. He remains focused on the story, but continues to shine his spotlight on the society which has bred Keir (and Gigi) and allowed him to become so self-deluded. This goes well beyond the 'me generation' and is all the more scary and compelling for that. Born in the US but living in Scotland, Lynch is a powerful, confronting new voice.

Junk ➤ MELVIN BURGESS

YA/A UK 1996

A boy and a girl were spending the night together in the back
of a Volvo estate car . . .

Tar said, 'Come with me.' . . .

'You must be crazy, said Gemma.

'Why?'

'What have I got to run away from?'

Gemma, fourteen, is merely bored, but Tar is an easy target for his alcoholic, abusive family, so he does have a real reason to run away. Tar loves Gemma. Eventually, without any thought of consequences, Gemma does take off with Tar.

Melvin Burgess is not one to shirk a tough topic or avoid the grimmest realities. At first Tar and Gemma play at being runaways, finding room in a squat and enjoying the freedom and endless parties. But in this environment, drug-taking rapidly becomes a habit. The intensity of the book comes from the matter-of-fact way Burgess details the very rapid downward spiral engulfing both young people. Whether either will survive will depend on their personal strengths and insights.

Set in Bristol in the 1980s, where Burgess then lived, *Junk* is arguably the best novel written about teenage drug-taking and has a powerful sense of veracity and authority. Perhaps this, as much as its subject matter, led to the considerable controversy surrounding the book, particularly after it won both the Carnegie Medal and the Guardian Prize. While Burgess never preaches, he makes clear the likely consequences of drug-taking. The controversy once again highlighted the inability of many who comment on writing for young people to acknowledge that writing about a tough topic like drugs doesn't equate to promoting or condoning the practice. Burgess shows respect for his readers by refusing to sensationalise, titivate, trivialise or sugar-coat. (See page 116 for Melvin Burgess's equally edgy **DOING IT**.)

Looking for Alaska ➤ JOHN GREEN

YA USA 2005

There were so many of us who would have to live with things done and
things left undone that day. Things that did not go right, things that seemed
OK at the time because we could not see the future. If only we could see
the endless string of consequences that result from our smallest actions.
But we can't know better until knowing better is useless.

Looking for Alaska is divided into 'the number of days before' and 'the number of days after'. Before and after create the tense drama and pace of this remarkable, much-admired first novel.

Set in a co-ed boarding school in Alabama, apparently not unlike the one Green attended, the story fizzes with the intensity of its characters, their dialogue and their frequent craziness. The focus is on four teenagers: Miles (to be called Pudge, because he's skinny); his new roommate, Chip (the Colonel); Takumi; and Alaska. Drinking (sometimes to oblivion), smoking, pranking and some illicit sex do not prevent intense study. All are extremely bright, great readers and ambitious students. Alaska's room is stacked with books from garage sales. Pudge has a passion for biographies and people's last words. Rebellious, impulsive, inventive Alaska is the ring-leader. The others are loyal and love her in various ways.

There are many ideas and a lot of philosophy, learning and hard thinking in this book. But there are also strong emotions, sadness, risk-taking and unresolved pain that lead to tragedy. Green writes with such verve, conviction and involvement that the reader is with the characters every minute: thinking, wondering, laughing, crying and finally coming to some level of understanding, as do the characters. *Looking for Alaska* well deserved its prestigious US Michael Printz award for Young Adult fiction. We need such an award in Australia.

Looking for JJ ➤ ANNE CASSIDY

YA UK 2005

Everyone was looking for Jennifer Jones. She was dangerous, the newspapers said. She posed a threat to children and should be kept behind bars. The public had a right to know where she was. Some of the weekend papers even resurrected the old headline: A Life for a Life!

Alice Tully read every article she could find. Her boyfriend, Frankie, was bemused. He couldn't understand why she was so fascinated.

For six happy, if tense, months, JJ – well supported by the relevant authorities – has lived as Alice Tully in the home, and under the protection, of the warm but tough Rosie. But the media are relentless, so Alice must change her identity and location again. What is JJ's story?

Cassidy cleverly and tensely assembles the bleak story of a child's rage after being largely abandoned by her single mother. JJ killed her best friend and spent six years incarcerated. As damaged as her daughter, JJ's feckless and immature mother never accepts responsibility, nor does she admit she has become a prostitute rather than a model. The mother's delusional desire for security even leads her to profiteer from her daughter's misfortunes.

Cassidy's book was obviously inspired by some notorious UK cases of children murdered by other children, and by the media and community responses those murders generated. She tells a gripping, heartrending story that avoids clichés and pushes the reader beyond crude assumptions about good and evil. Perhaps most chilling is the community's lust for revenge, opportunistically fanned by the media. This book won the 2004 UK Booktrust's Teenage Book Prize, an award aimed at 'bringing books and reading to as wide an audience as possible.'

enduring edgy stories

THE CHOCOLATE WAR Robert Cormier YA/A USA 1974

Archie Costello, leader of the high-school gang the Vigils, aims for absolute control of other students through initiation tests, victimisation and humiliation. Honest, straightforward new boy, Jerry Renault, is targeted as a non-conformist. A chocolate-selling fundraiser becomes the catalyst for some very nasty action involving an ambitious, corrupt priest in the Catholic school.

An important book that reflected the way groups, businesses and even countries exert power, this book launched Cormier as a fearless writer who believed no subject was taboo. He also believed that the truth, as he saw it, about the lives of many young people needed to be told. Cormier remained a practising Catholic. He was widely celebrated and read but also regularly banned and condemned for being too edgy and extreme – and also too political. Other outstanding, edgy books by Cormier include **I AM THE CHEESE** (1977), **AFTER THE FIRST DEATH** (1979), **THE BUMBLEBEE FLIES ANYWAY** (1983), **FADE** (1988) and **WE ALL FALL DOWN** (1991). Cormier died in 2000. See page 121 for **FRENCHTOWN SUMMER**, a verse novel.

A CLOCKWORK ORANGE Anthony Burgess A/YA UK 1963

The protagonist, fifteen-year-old Alex, is the leader of a gang that steals, rapes and bashes people in a lawless and violent future. Eventually, other gang members decide that Alex is becoming too powerful and cocky, and they betray him. Two years into his fourteen-year prison term, Alex undergoes a new brainwashing treatment and he emerges docile. But Alex's old mates haven't finished with him and more violence and dramatic reversals follow.

Responses to the book were polarised. Many people were hostile and dismissive, though most acknowledged the inventive and brilliant use of language. Burgess denied that his book was science fiction but considered it an allegory on free will. The book and the equally confronting 1971 movie are now considered classics.

▶▶▶

FOREVER Judy Blume YA USA 1975

Like Robert Cormier, Judy Blume is one of the most banned authors but also the recipient of many awards. From its publication, every teenage girl has had to read this book, but probably also had to hide it. It tells of two older teenagers who fall in love and decide to have sex, as they believe their relationship is serious. Before Judy Blume, no one had written so frankly for teenagers about sex. This book also realistically examines the couple's conviction that their love is 'forever'. It demonstrates Blume's unerring ability to speak directly to young people's experiences and emotions, even though the situations and writing in her books are often simplistic.

FRANKENSTEIN: OR, THE MODERN PROMETHEUS
Mary Shelley A/YA UK 1818

There is still debate about whether this is a horror story or not. The monster is born from experiments in electricity and assembling body parts. Once the doctor realises what he has produced, he abandons his creation. The devastated, sad, rejected monster vows revenge on his creator. This story continues to inhabit the imagination of readers. Mary Shelley wrote *Frankenstein* when only twenty and in Switzerland with husband, poet Percy Bysshe Shelley, with whom she ran away at sixteen. Kenneth Branagh made the 1994 film *Mary Shelley's Frankenstein*.

GO ASK ALICE Anonymous YA USA 1971

With over one million copies sold, debate still rages over whether this was a diary or not. Still in print, it is now sold as fiction. Many believe it was written to be a powerful cautionary tale at a time when drug-taking was becoming fashionable and even accepted.

Like *Forever*, this became a must-read book, and it was equally controversial. Does it glamorise drug-taking? Perhaps, but it still makes compulsive reading. The so-called diary starts with its fifteen-year-old writer's first drug experience and ends with her death just after her seventeenth birthday. The book 'documents' a rapid decline into addiction and misery.

LETTERS FROM THE INSIDE John Marsden YA AUSTRALIA 1991
Two girls answer an ad and start a correspondence. They get to know each other and seem to be confiding in each other. Or are they? Mandy has a creepy brother. When Mandy's letters stop, Tracey is angry and worried by turns. She keeps writing for a while from 'the inside'. But why is she in prison? Marsden lets the reader work this out, and what might have happened to Mandy. The clues are all there, but do we want to face the likely truth? Two other excellent, edgy books from Marsden are his first and best-selling **SO MUCH TO TELL YOU** (1987) and **CHECKERS** (1996).

LORD OF THE FLIES William Golding A/YA UK 1954
Published not long after the end of World War II, this classic partly explores our ability to work together for the common good. It also shows how quickly the trappings of so-called civilised society can disappear. At first, the schoolboys whose plane crashes on a deserted island try to pull together. But power struggles and conflicting desires soon undermine sensible Ralph's attempts at order. It does not take long for the boys to descend into savagery and barbarism. This is a chilling, haunting story that never loses its relevance. William Golding wrote many other fine books and received the Nobel Prize for Literature in 1983.

THE STRANGE CASE OF DR JEKYLL AND MR HYDE Robert Louis Stevenson A/YA UK 1886
In this classic gothic horror story, a wealthy doctor and scientist named Dr Jekyll creates a potion, drinks it and unleashes a monster that is his other, more evil, half. The story is told from the point of view of Jekyll's lawyer friend, John Utterson, who is, at first, merely curious about a recent incident where a little girl is apparently attacked by a 'fiend'. He is then utterly horrified by what he uncovers.

No Worries ➤ BILL CONDON

YA AUSTRALIA 2005

Mum reckoned I was a quitter. Quit the job. Quit school. So that marked me a quitter for life. No question . . .

She blazed like a sunflower until she virtually fell asleep where she stood. Then she'd wake up refreshed and blaze again. But gradually her energy levels dropped and her frustrations grew, until the tiniest thing stressed her out . . .

From anywhere in the house I could hear her bellyaching. And I couldn't talk to her without her yelling at me. She was like a plane spinning out of control. I knew she couldn't pull out of the dive. I knew the crash was sure to come, just didn't know when.

In a discussion following the film *Three Dollars*, the director, Robert Connolly, commented on the difficulty of portraying a good man in engaging and interesting ways. Bill Condon succeeds admirably in making us care about kind, gentle Brian Talbot. Seventeen, a school dropout in his first real job – doing night shift among laconic, rough men in a dairy – Brian is also struggling to manage life with a mother suffering a bipolar disorder. While his medical understanding is patchy, his insight and tolerance are deep and are presented in honest, realistic ways. Shiftless Dad has withdrawn to his shed, consoling himself with alcohol and escaping on fishing trips with his mates. Brian must hold things together, which is not easy, as his mum spirals out of control. But Brian is intelligent as well as sensitive, and knows when and where to find help in extreme situations. A warm, humorous, unflinching book that would be of great interest to many teenagers and their parents at a time when mental illness is often in the media.

Sexy ➤ JOYCE CAROL OATES

YA USA 2005

*Girls liked to say about Darren Flynn that he was sexy, but shy.
Or he was shy but sexy.*

Darren is confused. Why does he feel the need to be one of the jocks? 'A guy's guy. A jock. Meaning you didn't study, much. You didn't aim for high grades.' And what should Darren do about girls? Above all, why does he allow himself to get drawn into a stupid, nasty situation targeting Mr Tracy, the best English teacher he has had? At home, Darren's under-educated father and older brother despise intellectual pursuits, so-called 'weakness', but above all they despise the idea of homosexuality. At home, as at school, there is an atmosphere of crude homophobia and no distinction between being gay or being a paedophile. In this overheated environment, tragedy is almost inevitable, and police attitudes are part of the problem. However the scary, chaotic, all-too-real party near the end of the book takes Darren in unexpected directions.

Oates, a professor of English, is an extra-ordinary and prolific writer, best known for huge numbers of enthralling adult novels and for many articles and reviews. Now she is also writing terrific, tough, fast-paced novels for teenagers. *Sexy* followed **BIG MOUTH & UGLY GIRL** (2002) and **FREAKY GREEN EYES** (2003). In each, Oates probes the so-called American Dream to reveal in-tolerance, conformity, hypocritical 'family values' and bullying.

Shooter ➤ WALTER DEAN MYERS

YA USA 2004

I remember when I was six and marched to the beat of a child.
Over the last decade of my life I have lost the cadence and de-generated
into de-cadence. That is what the decades are about, the slow march
to de-cadence.

Printz Award–winning Author of MONSTER
WALTER DEAN MYERS

SHOOTER

This is the voice of Leonard, as reproduced in his diary, or, as he writes 'die-ary'. Now dead by his own hand, following a shooting spree in his school, Leonard was clearly troubled. He was also fascinated by guns, which he introduced to various friends. His best friend, Cameron, and ex-girlfriend, Carla, are so alienated and desperate for friendship that they cannot allow themselves to see how disturbed Leonard is, until it is too late.

Told from multiple perspectives, *Shooter* is an astonishing feat of imagination and writing, based on, and inspired by, the Columbine shootings of 2004. The first two sections are in the form of interviews with Cameron and Carla, one of whom is white, the other black. One interview is with the Senior County Psychologist and the other is with an FBI Threat Assessment Analyst. These are brilliant so-called reconstructions. Newspaper reports are also included.

The tense, pared-down writing exposes the fine lines between interview styles, preconceptions and attitudes, and how difficult all this can be for fragile and already traumatised teenagers. The final section is a tour de force of insightful and imaginative writing as Myers invents the diary of the final days of the killer: a clever, witty, articulate, but damaged and hugely bitter and angry young man.

walter dean myers

Walter Dean Myers was born in West Virginia in 1937 but spent most of his childhood and young adult life in Harlem. He writes in tough, realistic and compassionate ways about the experiences of black youth in the USA. His inventive, dazzling use of language and innovative structures make his over-seventy books both accessible and highly literary. He has won many awards, including the inaugural Michael L Printz award for young adult fiction, for the book **MONSTER**. When asked if whites should write about blacks, Myers replied 'Of course . . . you should write about anybody you want to write about . . . But what very often happens is that, when you're writing about a culture that's not your own, you may hit large areas of it, but there are so many areas that you miss.'

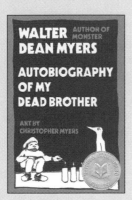  

As well as young adult novels, Myers writes picture books, short stories, poetry and non-fiction, including black history and biography.

FALLEN ANGELS 1988
Still one of the best books about the Vietnam War. (See War & Conflicts for more about the Vietnam War.)

▶▶▶

SLAM 1996

A book with lots of basketball action but also much more. 'Slam' Harris, seventeen, has total control on the basketball court. But when he moves to a new, more-academic school his tough street talk only gets him into trouble. He struggles to find his way, to keep his girlfriend and to cope with the possibility that his dad is dealing drugs.

MONSTER 1999

The owner of a convenience store is shot in a robbery gone wrong. Steve Harmon, black and sixteen, is there. Was he the lookout? He is arrested and put on trial. He could face a twenty-five year sentence and he is scared. The story is relayed through Steve's journal entries, the movie script he writes while sitting for hours in court, and astute observations from his prison cell. Who is telling the truth, Steve or the authorities?

THE GREATEST: MUHAMMAD ALI 2000

'A story about a black man of tremendous courage, the kind of universal story that needs a writer as talented as Myers to retell it for every generation.' (*Booklist*/ALA) In his usual direct style Myers covers every aspect of this sporting legend's difficult life.

HERE IN HARLEM: POEMS IN MANY VOICES 2004

Inspired by Edgar Lee Masters's *Spoon River Anthology*, and by his love of Harlem, Myers writes poems in different styles to match the distinctive voices of various Harlem residents. Each provides a story, a reflection or a memory to create an inspiring and revealing collection.

Skin ➤ AM VRETTOS

YA USA 2006

This is what I feel like: I'm trying to keep my balance in a cold, hard wind, standing on the tip of a gigantic metal cone that towers over everything in my world . . . if I lose my balance, I'll go flying off the tip of the cone, and the whole world will come apart.

Skin is really fourteen-year-old Donnie's story. It starts with a list of 'the things you think when you come home to find that your sister has starved herself to death'. From there it travels backwards and forwards. Throughout the time leading up to Donnie's return from school to find Karen as 'flat as a board', life in this household is almost unbearable for Karen and Donnie, but also for the reader. Vrettos's extraordinarily assured first book is grimly absorbing. It is directly written and presents a clear, unsentimental portrait of a family in distress. Vrettos is too clever to create a simple cause-and-effect story that links the relentlessly bitter battle waged between the parents to Karen's anorexia. Rather, she shows a brother and sister experiencing their domestic situation in different, yet similar, ways. Both want to disappear. Donnie's aim at home and school is to render himself invisible, and Karen uses every possible strategy to avoid food. Mom clumsily tries to normalise life. Dad, who moves in and out, can't seem to help picking fights. If the makings of an ice-cream sundae are not in the fridge when he decides that is what is needed to create a 'family night', the fight is on. For years, the siblings have escaped by huddling in blankets on the front step. Karen tries to protect Donnie, but as they grow older these simple childish tactics are not enough.

However, the parents do care, and make hapless attempts to look after their children. They force Karen into hospital a couple of times, but they are repeatedly overwhelmed by their own immaturity and power struggles. Their inability to let each other go and focus on their children leads to tragic consequences for Karen. For Donnie, some balance and a new life may be possible.

Sleeping Dogs ➤ SONYA HARTNETT

YA/A AUSTRALIA 1995

Jordan and his sister go into town to do the weekly shopping . . . People in shops lift their heads to watch them walk by, but the Willow children look at and talk to no one. Michelle walks quickly and Jordan slinks after her and the lady behind the counter of the antique shop . . . makes a comment about a witch and her white cat.

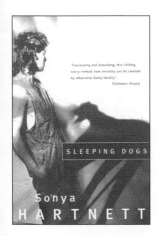

'I feel Sonya Hartnett is a brilliant writer and goes where no other author would dare.' (Alex, aged fifteen)

Isolated and anti-social, the Willow family (which included five children, some now adult) run a ramshackle caravan park on their desolate property. Their brutish, punitive father and fragile mother have forced the children to look inwards and to each other. Their loyalty to each other is obsessive and destructive. Griffin, also given to violence, regularly targets Jordan, a talented artist who is considered odd and therefore fair game. When Oliver, the youngest, allows blow-in Bow Fox, an aspiring painter attracted to elder sister Michelle, a glimpse into their lives and family secrets, events and emotions are unleashed that inexorably spiral into tragedy. Hartnett subtly and cleverly leaks telling facts about the characters and how they react to the dire family situation. The snarling tangle of dogs on the property heightens the sense of foreboding.

Dazzling in its grim vision, its clarity and control of language, *Sleeping Dogs* garnered much praise but also criticism for its uncompromising bleakness. The book won the inaugural Victorian Premier's Award for young adult literature.

sonya hartnett

ALL MY DANGEROUS FRIENDS 1998

The young people in this book deliberately and determinedly chose to live a life of drugs and lawlessness. A disturbing look into a world where there seem to be no rights or wrongs, and the high price paid by some is considered worthwhile.

THURSDAY'S CHILD 2000

Set at the time of the Great Depression, in a landscape as dusty and desolate as the existence of the people in it, the book covers six years in the lives of the Flute family. Harper, now an adult, mostly remembers the strange activities of her small, mute brother, Tin, who disappeared into the burrows and mazes he tunnelled underground. Gradually, Harper comes to understand that her family's life disappeared as well, and she begins to get some sense of herself. Hartnett won the UK Guardian Prize for this book.

FOREST 2001

Told entirely from the point of view of cats, *Forest* never slips into anthropomorphism, despite the cats and other animals being able to communicate. When his mistress dies, a city-bred tomcat is dumped in the forest with two kittens. The cat is determined to get back home and he survives against all odds. We also meet bush animals and see how much destruction cats have wrought on the environment. Yet our sympathies are always with the tomcat. A strange, beautiful, brilliant book, and a deserving Children's Book Council of Australia award winner.

SURRENDER 2005

Published as an adult novel, this is one of Hartnett's darkest works. Set, as many of Hartnett's books are, in an isolated country town, it tells the sad, cruel, tragic story of a boy whose parents destroy his, and his mentally disabled brother's, childhood. One boy dies and the other must endure an endlessly painful and lonely life. (See page 219 for Hartnett's multi-award-winning book **OF A BOY**.)

The Song of an Innocent Bystander

> **IAN BONE**

YA/A AUSTRALIA 2002

At precisely 2.45p.m., a man stood on one of the small tables near the service counter. He had a black sports bag clutched to his chest. Nobody noticed him until he spoke in his unremarkable voice, until his words echoed across the near-empty expanse of fake wood below him.

'It's time to pay your dues, Family Value,' he said. 'You've been sucking the life-blood of the masses for too long, peddling your lies, your poisons.'

This complex, tense, sharply written thriller about urban terrorism has not received the attention or accolades it deserves. It would make an excellent, thought-provoking text for senior school study. But is it too demanding, too close to how big chains do business, too confronting? It is both a forensic investigation of how advertising, consumerism and a voracious media permeate contemporary society and a complex psychological portrayal of the realities of being a witness. It asks the question, Can anyone claim to be an innocent bystander?

The book throws up important and fascinating moral dilemmas. It looks at the endless ramifications on the life of nineteen-year-old Freda and the others involved in a terrifying thirty-six-hour siege in which two people die. Then aged nine, Freda unwittingly allied herself with the one person who could save her: the deranged gunman. Since then, Freda has carried this guilt and other secrets. She also struggles to free herself from the mother who has made her life revolve around protecting Freda. Then a young man claiming to be a reporter appears. He seems to know more than he could or should. We urgently need to know what happened in that basement and what Freda really knows.

Stone Cold ➤ ROBERT SWINDELLS

YA UK 1993

You can call me Link. It's not my name, but it's what I say when anybody asks, which isn't often. I'm invisible see? One of the invisible people. Right now I'm sitting in a doorway watching passers by. They're afraid I want something they've got, and they're right. Also they don't want to think about me. They don't like reminding I exist.

There was uproar when Swindells won the Carnegie Medal for this tough, scary, angry book. What are we feeding our youth? As Link says above, '[People] don't like reminding I exist.' Yet it was clearly a book of its time, a time when England was still suffering the consequences of Thatcher Government policies that increased the gap between the haves and have-nots in a supposed effort to make people self-reliant.

Link has escaped his mother's brutal boyfriend. He tries to find work, but living on the streets rapidly leads to disconnection from society and denies him access to resources that might make him employable. At first, he is supported by the streetwise know-how of Ginger. But when Ginger disappears, Link becomes easy prey for the psychotic, brutal Shelter, the ex-army man determined to rid society of 'druggy dossers whose activities are dragging the country down'. *Stone Cold* is riveting to read and still highly relevant, especially in Australia, with its rising numbers of homeless.

The Story of Tom Brennan ➤ JC BURKE

YA AUSTRALIA 2005

'We leave these words with all of you, the words of a respected citizen of this town, words that seem to represent what many of us feel – Daniel Brennan was an accident waiting to happen. What a shame his accident happened to others.'

Daniel Brennan is drunk, angry and out of control. His girlfriend, Claire, has just dropped him. When Daniel leaps into a car, the results are predictably catastrophic. He kills two teenagers, and his cousin Fin is left a quadriplegic. How often do we get media reports of teenagers dying or being seriously injured when a car driven by another teenager crashes? What is day-to-day life like and what really happens to the lives and families of those left behind? There is disbelief, pain, fury, gossip and chaos as people try to make sense of what happened and why. The letter in the quote above was sent to Daniel Brennan's family by the Munroes, whose daughter, Nicole, was one of the two killed.

The story is told from the point of view of Daniel's brother, Tom. Tom and Daniel were close and their greatest bond was football. The testosterone and alcohol-fuelled desperation to win at any cost, coupled with the inability of most of the boys to communicate or express emotion, is shown to be a lethal mix in the country town, all-boys Catholic school environment. As everyone waits for the court case, the situation for the Brennans becomes intolerable. Mum takes to her bed, sister Kylie fights for some normality, and Tom can't face anyone. Dad puts their house on the market and moves the family in with eccentric Grandma in a much larger town.

While Daniel awaits sentence, Fin must deal with a near-death experience and what follows. Tom loves them both but struggles to deal with them. Yet gradually, Tom, his mother and even Daniel begin to see how life can be lived differently.

This clear-eyed, tough, compassionate book won the 2005 CBCA Book of the Year Award for older readers. All football-loving boys (and their teachers and parents) should read it.

Under the Wolf, Under the Dog ➤ ADAM RAPP

YA/A USA 2004

*I'm currently in residence at this place in the middle of Michigan
called Burnstone Grove. There are about thirty-five kids here. About half of
us are drug addicts, and another half have tried to check out of this world
in one way or another. Probably a third of us have dabbled in both pursuits.
I don't entirely fit into either category, so I'm what they call
a Gray Grouper.*

Adam Rapp: 'My plays and novels constantly involve people trying to find refuge in chaos.'

Most of this story is Steve Nugent's gruelling account of falling apart and drifting onto the streets and into petty crime following his mother's death from cancer, his older brother's suicide and his father's depression, expressed in blank inertia. Rapp does not spare the reader the horrific details of the brother's suicide by strangulation, as it is Steve who finds his brother's body. Yet, despite his confusion and pain, Steve cannot help making astute, honest and, at times, humorous observations about his fellow inmates in Burnstone Grove, and about his own situation. He struggles valiantly to get himself out from under the dog of despair. He even manages to re-establish contact with his father.

Rapp's books are not for squeamish or timid readers. The language is blunt, stark and dazzling, and the vision of abused, neglected and desperate children and young people is bleak. Rapp is a formidable, uncompromising talent who has been compared to JD Salinger. That his books – including the equally extraordinary, if horrifying, **33 SNOWFISH** – are widely published and praised (if also widely banned) demonstrates that US publishing is much bolder than is often suggested in Australia. Rapp is also a musician and director for stage and film.

Vernon God Little ➤ DBC PIERRE

A/YA AUSTRALIA 2003

I'm a kid whose best friend took a gun into his mouth and blew off his hair, whose classmates are dead, who's being blamed for it all, who just broke his mama's heart . . .

Did dirt-poor Vernon Gregory Little, fifteen, really kill sixteen of his school mates in Texas? Vernon insists, 'Everyone knows Jesus is ultimately to blame.' His best friend, the Mexican teenager Jesus Navarro, that is. Unfortunately, Vernon returns from an errand (he's too embarrassed to say what) to find Jesus about to shoot himself. As the only survivor, Vernon becomes a scapegoat. The small-town police and hapless justice system can't cope. But the hysterical locals need to be pacified, the police need a 'result' and the frenzied media needs ever-more gruesome and far-fetched material to report. The result is grim, excruciating mayhem. Vernon is desperate and infuriating in his stupidity, but endearing as well. He can't help rolling out the cynical wisecracks. It's his voice that hooks you.

This is tragic satire that is laugh-aloud funny. It has a lot to say about many aspects of Western, but particularly American, society, with its love of guns and its confused, alienated, uncared-for teenagers; its dysfunctional families and its rabid but powerful media. A clever, funny, crude, horrific, angry book that won its Australian-born, first-time author the prestigious British Booker Prize. One reviewer wrote that it left him 'dazed and stunned'. A deliberately confronting book with lashings of very 'bad' language.

The Wild ➤ MATT WHYMAN

YA UK 2005

*You need faith to believe a sea was once here . . . the ruling party . . .
decided to play around with the rivers . . . had they left the water flows
alone, we might still be netting sturgeon and harvesting orchards, but that's
how it is. We are the children of Aral, not her relics . . . She may be cruel,
but she has raised us to be tough.*

Matt Whyman likes to write about extreme situations faced by
young people in wild, lawless places. His earlier book **BOY KILLS
MAN** (2004) is located in Mexico, where twelve-year-olds become
proxy killers because they can't be prosecuted. *The Wild* is mostly
located in desolate Kazakhstan. Existence is a struggle. The area
is hugely toxic. Many have died or are sick, including Alexi's nine-
year-old brother, Misha, who suffers seizures from a brain tumour.
Their mother is dead and their father has largely given up. To survive
and seek medical help for Misha, Alexi makes money by salvaging
debris from crashed or discarded space shuttles. After each crash,
his small crew of bold teenagers race to beat the opposition. This is
dirty, dangerous work.

When Misha alerts them to a 'big one', there is a tense battle
for the spoils. They return to find that a grenade has exploded in
their apartment. Father stirs himself to help them flee by train, but
on reaching Moscow their plight only gets worse. It is freezing and
chaotic, and nothing can be achieved without 'papers' or a lot of
money. The brothers' great love for each other provides the only
softness, but can Alexi save Misha's life?

It is hard to believe this story is not science fiction. It is in equal
parts hard to take and impossible to put down.

fantastic worlds

Even if you are the most devoted Harry Potter fan, you should know there are many, many other fabulous books that transport you to fantastic worlds: to the future, to new visions of our world, to completely alien worlds and even to other versions of the past. It's all about imagination and world building!

ENTRIES SELECTED AND WRITTEN BY LILI WILKINSON

Across the Nightingale Floor ➤ LIAN HEARN

A/YA AUSTRALIA 2002

Water trickled from the cistern where you washed your hands and mouth to purify yourself on entering a shrine. Earlier, when the world was normal, someone must have lit incense in the great cauldron. The last of it drifted across the courtyard, masking the bitter smell of blood and death.

Set in a world that is very much like feudal Japan, the Tales of the Otori quartet tells the stories of Takeo, an orphaned boy seeking vengeance, and Kaede, a young woman with a thirst for power. These two are destined to fall in love, and it's pretty clear from the beginning that it's not going to be the happy-ever-after sort of love, more the star-crossed kind. Embroiled in a treacherous and deeply political world of honour, revenge and betrayal, Takeo and Kaede must fight for their freedom and identities. There are assassins, spies, outcasts, forbidden romances and exactly the right amount of magic.

This series appeals for a number of reasons: the uniqueness of the setting, the grand-epic plot, the beautiful presentation of the books. Hearn blends new (to a Westerner) stories with old, creating characters and situations that are unique, yet at the same time strangely familiar. Takeo is the one person who can unite the three warring factions of his world: he was born of the Tribe, raised by the Hidden and adopted by the Otori (people in charge). Kaede has the same aura of prophecy about her: they say that every man who falls in love with her will die.

Published in thirty-two countries and with movie options, this has become a runaway bestseller. Book Two: **GRASS FOR HIS PILLOW** (2003), Book Three: **BRILLIANCE OF THE MOON** (2004), Book Four: **THE HARSH CRY OF THE HERON** (2006).

Alyzon Whitestarr ➤ ISOBELLE CARMODY

YA AUSTRALIA 2005

'Good,' the woman yelled, leaning nearer and touching my hand.
The smell of roses and wet earth pressing on me, along with a feeling
of terrible exhausted grief. 'Alyzon, you're in the hospital.
Do you remember what happened?'

Those of you who are desperately waiting for the final Obernewtyn book (it's coming) will have to temporarily ease your suffering with this latest tome from Isobelle Carmody. *Alyzon Whitestarr* is reminiscent of *The Gathering*; it's also set in the real world, and features strange gifts and sinister happenings. Alyzon has always considered herself to be the 'normal' one in her bizarrely eccentric family. But that changes when she has an accident and falls into a coma. When she awakens, Alyzon finds herself with remarkably heightened senses. Her father's anxiety smells like ammonia, her

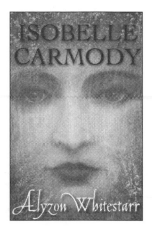

sister's depression like aniseed. She can smell people's feelings and essences, and some people smell very, very wrong. Do they have some kind of sickness? What is this strange disease? And can it sense her, just as she can sense it?

Like all of Carmody's books, *Alyzon Whitestarr* is not limited to the fantasy world, but makes comment on our own world and the challenges that face us. The issues of refugees and asylum seekers are given voice in Alyzon's story, as are notions of depression, love and disability. It's a complicated and powerful story that manages to be both thought-provoking and a page-turner.

more isobelle carmody ➤➤➤

isobelle carmody

OBERNEWTYN YA 1987

Now an Australian fantasy classic, *Obernewtyn* is the story of Elspeth, a Misfit with strange powers. It is followed by **THE FARSEEKERS**, **ASHLING** and **THE KEEPING PLACE**. The fifth and sixth books are eagerly awaited.

THE GATHERING YA 1993

One of the scariest books I've ever read. Nat moves to a strange new town, and it doesn't take long for him to realise that something is horribly wrong.

DARKFALL YA 1996

Sisters Glynn and Ember are swept from an Australian beach through a portal to the strange watery world of Keltor, where they are hailed as magical saviours. *Darkfall* was followed by **DARKSONG**, with the promise of a third book.

BILLY THUNDER AND THE NIGHT GATE YA 2000

Rage Winnoway has to travel to Valley to find a cure for her mother's illness. Accompanied by her animal friends, she encounters forbidden black magic in the sinister dark city.

LITTLE FUR Y 2005

This series is based on stories Carmody told her daughter in Prague, where they have been spending alternate years. Aimed at a much younger audience, the beautifully produced books include charming black-and-white illustrations by the author. Little Fur is an elf-troll and a healer. When her secret wilderness is threatened, she must venture forth into an ancient city and face the greatest danger – the humans.

The Amulet of Samarkand ➤ JONATHAN STROUD

YA UK 2003

The sulphur cloud contracted into a thick column of smoke that vomited forth thin tendrils . . . There was a barely perceptible pause. Then two yellow staring eyes materialized in the heart of the smoke.

Hey, it was his first time. I wanted to scare him.

Set in a parallel London controlled by magicians, this is the story of Bartimaeus, a 5000 year old djinni, and Nathaniel, a young apprentice with a cold heart. When Nathaniel is publicly humiliated by powerful magician Simon Lovelace, Nathaniel swears revenge and summons Bartimaeus. Nathaniel is an extremely unlikeable protagonist, and we immediately find ourselves siding with the smart-mouthed, sarcastic Bartimaeus, who is an outrageously unreliable narrator. Stroud's skill lies in the way he handles the screamingly funny asides of Bartimaeus without compromising the seriousness of the overall plot.

The series is less about magic and orphaned-boys-with-wands, and more about political intrigue. The second book in the Bartimaeus trilogy, **THE GOLEM'S EYE** (2004), delves much more deeply into the political world of the magicians, and unlike *Harry Potter*, criticises the apartheid that exists between the ruling magicians and the commoners. In the final volume, **PTOLEMY'S GATE** (2006), any previous alliance between commoners, magicians and demons is destroyed. New allegiances are formed, making way for an amazing, unexpected and moving conclusion. The Bartimaeus trilogy established Stroud as a major voice in fantasy for young people. Read also **THE LAST SIEGE** (2003).

Blaze of Glory ➤ MICHAEL PRYOR

Y/YA AUSTRALIA 2006

Aubrey blinked. 'Nonsense?'

'Politicians and diplomats. They love a chance to scheme and plot away from the eyes of the public. They're more excited than a class of schoolboys on a field trip.'

Aubrey Fitzwilliam is very far from being your typical orphan-peasant-makes-good fantasy hero. He's the son of an ex-prime minister and cousin to the Prince Regent. He's got a lot to live up to. When Aubrey and his friend George stumble across a dastardly plot at a weekend shooting party, Aubrey seizes on the perfect chance to prove himself worthy of his father. Set in an alternate Earth called Albion, in what seems like the early 20th century, *Blaze of Glory* has a precise and refreshing magic system. There is no esoteric wand-waving here, but rather difficult, systematic processes that must be learned and studied. Pryor's well-rounded characters and deft, gentle sense of humour make for a cracking good read. This book is the first in the Laws of Magic series and is a welcome return from one of Australia's most committed fantasy practitioners.

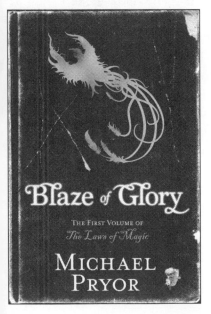

Century ➤ SARAH SINGLETON

YA UK 2005

Mercy could see ghosts, the echoes of people who had died. The dead moved on to another world, to heaven perhaps, or Valhalla if you were a Viking. Sometimes they left threads of themselves behind, like a piece of cloth snagged from a dress, or strands of hair caught on a nail.

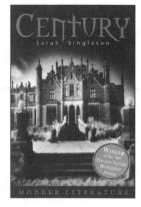

When Mercy awakens one morning to find a snowdrop on her pillow, she begins to wonder about her way of life. She and her sister Charity live in a sort of twilight world. They get up at sunset and live only in the wintry darkness, while their widowed father works away in his study. Then things start to change. Mercy meets a man called Claudius – the first stranger she has encountered for as long as she can remember. Claudius is strange and mysterious, and, for the first time in a long while, Mercy thinks about her mother. How did she die? Did Mercy go to the funeral? Where is her mother's grave? With Claudius's help, Mercy starts to unlock the past, exploring her family's history through a magic book – the book that keeps the house trapped in a perpetual darkness. In order to break her father's spell, Mercy has to rewrite her family's story in a new book, giving it the happy ending it's been waiting for. A beautiful, haunting book that would work well with Ursula Dubosarsky's **ABYSSINIA** or a film like *The Hours*. *Century* won the 2005 UK Booktrust Prize.

Dogboy ➤ VICTOR KELLEHER

YA AUSTALIA 2005

He didn't weaken and die. On a steady diet of dog's milk, he flourished. His cheeks took on a ruddy glow, and his limbs grew brown and sturdy in the summer sun.

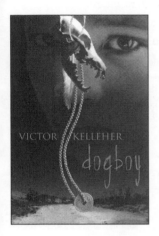

A baby is abandoned on a mountainside and suckled by a wild dog. He is marked by the wild – fire, water, a wild bear, a soaring eagle. Surely he must be destined for great things. The wild dog brings the baby to a village nestled under the mountain. The Great Dry hangs heavily over the villagers – nothing will grow. They are suspicious and wary of this strange baby – this Dogboy – and leave him to die. But Magda, the poorest of the poor villagers, takes pity on him. Dogboy grows up – a strange child who is somewhere between human and wild animal. When a pedlar comes to the village, Dogboy becomes fascinated by the idea of wealth and power, and sets out to seek his fortune. He will be a great shaman. He will find water.

This is an extraordinary coming-of-age story, set in a beautiful, mythic, primitive world. The setting, characters and themes would not be out of place in a chapter of the Bible. This is a book that asks the big questions. What does it mean to be human, and is it a desirable thing? Or would we all be better off as wild animals? A powerful, gritty and, at times, horrifying book. Victor Kelleher at his finest.

Dragonkeeper ➤ CAROLE WILKINSON

Y/YA AUSTRALIA 2003

The blade dug deep into the flesh of the dragon. Thick purple blood oozed from the wound. Lan cut out the dragon's heart and liver and put them in a bowl. From the pit the howl of the other dragon grew louder. The slave girl covered her ears, and prayed for the soul of the dragon.

Set in Han Dynasty China (141 BCE), this is the story of Ping, a slave-girl. Ping saves the life of the last Imperial Dragon, and flees from her mountainous home in China's far West. The dragon convinces her to help him travel to Ocean, a far-off land where he can be healed. Danzi, the dragon, makes Ping carry a mysterious stone which must be protected from a pursuing dragon hunter. Ping's journey is really an emotional one, as she grows from a lonely slave-girl not worthy of a name to realising her own power and potential as a true Imperial Dragonkeeper. The historical detail is meticulously researched and beautifully presented, with a great deal of heart and humour – particularly from Ping's pet rat, Hua. The sequels are **GARDEN OF THE PURPLE DRAGON** and **DRAGON MOON**.

Carole Wilkinson has written a considerable amount of non-fiction, often laced with fiction. She has always been fascinated by China and dragons, and loves to research. These passions have combined here to create a hugely popular and award-winning series, now sold into many countries, including China. Wilkinson has clearly found her voice.

Dreamhunter ➤ ELIZABETH KNOX

YA/A NEW ZEALAND 2005

The sandman released the ranger, who saw the monster's bitten fingers reform, grow from a trickle of sand running like veins down the surface of its arm. He saw the fingers lengthen, till the hand was whole.

The creature was holding a fragment of the letter.

The Place is described as being like a fold in a map. Most people just walk straight over it, but a very select few can enter. These people are dreamhunters. In the Place they can catch dreams, and perform them to the public or use them for other, more sinister purposes. Set in a 1900-ish sort of world, the book is about young cousins Rose and Laura, who come from two very famous dreamhunting families. Tensions rise when shy Laura is chosen to be a dreamhunter, and confident Rose is not. When Laura's father disappears, Laura becomes determined first to find out what happened, and then to complete his great work.

True to its title, *Dreamhunter* has a floaty, ethereal tone that moves very quickly from the richly beautiful to the darkly sinister. It is a lushly detailed flight of the imagination. Fans of Ursula Dubosarsky and Philip Pullman will devour this book and clamour for the sequel, **DREAMQUAKE** (2007), but more action-driven readers may not be engaged. This is Knox's first foray into high fantasy and young adult-friendly territory. So far she has been best known and much praised for **THE VINTNER'S LUCK**, her 1998 breakout book.

Ferren and the Angel ➤ RICHARD HARLAND

YA/A AUSTRALIA 2000

So strange, so perfect, so incredible! He didn't even know if she was beautiful, she was so different to the People's idea of female beauty. By the standards of the tribe, she was abnormal and misshapen. But to Ferren she seemed like a miracle come down upon the Earth.

It all started in 2010, with the Invasion of Heaven. Human psychonauts figured out how to travel to heaven and the angels fought back. Now it's the year 3000. The Millennial Wars rage overhead in the night sky. The Earth is ruled by the Doctors, and the terrifying semi-mechanical Humen. The last real humans, the primitive Residuals, cower in the ruins of their once-great race. Ferren is a Residual. Every night he watches the lights from the battles in the sky. One night, something comes hurtling down and crashes to the ground. It's an Angel. Miriael. She and Ferren are thrown together, unwillingly at first, but a friendship inevitably develops. Together, the two of them start to uncover some startling truths about the War, and those who orchestrated it.

This series is an amazing combination of fantasy and science fiction. The mythology of the angels is woven seamlessly with descriptions of technology and warfare, creating an epic, sweeping sense of history. The series is also expertly laced with action, romance and humour. The next two books in the Heaven and Earth trilogy are **FERREN AND THE WHITE DOCTOR** (2002) and **FERREN AND THE INVASION OF HEAVEN** (2003).

Firebirds: An Anthology of Original Fantasy and Science Fiction ➤ SHARYN NOVEMBER (ed)

A/YA USA 2005

Alice May looked at them from a weird and forbidding place inside her own head. She knew them, but felt no remorse. Butcher, baker, ne'er do well and ore-washer. All men of the town. – Garth Nix, 'Hope Chest'

Firebird is a Penguin imprint which publishes fantasy and science fiction that appeals to both adults and teenagers. *Firebirds* is an anthology of sixteen short stories by writers connected to the imprint. The book is edited by Firebird Editorial Director and general children's and young adult fantasy powerhouse, Sharyn November. Anthologies can often be tricky, but this one has been crafted and shaped beautifully. The stories themselves are all original works – there is no recycled material here. The writing is fresh, skilled and varied – from writing about cats by Diana Wynne Jones to hunting foxes in Emma Bull and Charles Vess's short story in comic-book form. My personal favourites include Delia Sherman's 'Cotillion' – a modern retelling of the Tam Lin story; Lloyd Alexander's deliciously out-of-character fable 'Max Mondrosch', about an ordinary man looking for a job; and Garth Nix's story 'Hope Chest', which really is beyond description, but is a kind of western-meets-fantasy-meets-thriller, political assassination, alternate universe kind of thing.

First Test ➤ TAMORA PIERCE

Y/YA USA 2000

Joren hit Kel hard and fast, raining blows on her. 'Do you like this?'
he demanded breathlessly as he pressed her. 'Do you think you can
keep up? Why don't you go home?'

'I belong here,' Kel said grimly.

Kel is the first girl in Tortall to officially apply to train as a knight.
(Readers of the Alanna series will know all about girls unofficially
training as knights). But Lord Wyldon, the training master, doesn't
believe in Lady Knights. So he puts Kel on probation for a year. Kel is
picked on and bullied, but she is determined to succeed. The series
follows Kel through her training years, until she is a fully fledged
knight. Alanna fans will feel a bittersweet happiness when reading
these books – the famous Lady Alanna is present, sort of. She is
around, but forbidden by Wyldon to have anything to do with the
fledgling Kel.

Pierce has been winning devoted followers to
her tales of female knights for over twenty years,
and she's still churning out good reads. This series
is packed full of typical Tortall action: incredibly
detailed and gripping sword fights, magic, animal
familiars, crushes and love.

Foundling ➤ DM CORNISH

Y/YA AUSTRALIA 2006

People were only ever marked with a monster-blood tattoo if they had fought and slain a nicker. The image of the fallen beast was pricked into the victor's skin with the dead monster's own blood.

Rossamünde Bookchild has spent all his life at Madam Opera's Estimable Marine Society for Foundling Boys and Girls. He wants nothing more than to be a vinegarroon (sailor), but instead he is offered a job as a lamplighter. Rossamünde sets out for his new workplace, which is in a different city. Nothing goes right; he is first swindled by a corrupt bargeman and then attacked by ettins and grinnlings. He falls into company with Europe, a mysterious and beautiful lahzar – a monster-fighter, with dark and sinister powers.

Foundling, book one of the Monster Blood Tattoo series, adeptly blends the familiar trope of the orphan boy in a strange new world with some amazing, unique worldbuilding. Extra levels of complexity are introduced in the hundred page Explicarium – a kind of glossary – listing word-meanings, historical references, the Half-Continent's calendar and days of the week, diagrams of barges and uniforms, and some truly beautiful maps. You get the feeling that you are only skimming the surface of a wholly realised world. With its brooding, gold-embossed cloth hardcover, two place-marker ribbons and gorgeous pencil illustrations, *Foundling* is a piece of artwork in itself. Everyone will want to be seen reading a copy.

Jonathan Strange and Mr Norrell

➤ **SUSANNA CLARKE**

A/YA UK 2004

'Can a magician kill a man by magic?' Lord Wellington asked Strange. Strange frowned. He seemed to dislike the question. 'I suppose a magician might,' he admitted, 'but a gentleman never would.' Lord Wellington nodded as if this was just as he would have expected.

It is 1808, the middle of the Napoleonic Wars. Magic has become an entirely theoretical practice. But fusty, ambitious Mr Norrell is a practical magician. He is trying to use magic to win the war. He conjures amazing illusions, and becomes a highly influential man. His apprentice, Jonathan Strange, is different in every way. Where Norrell is stuffy and traditional, Strange is glamorous and experimental. The two inevitably clash, and drama ensues. The book is peppered with sumptuous 19th-century detail and epic footnotes about the history of magic.

This 800 page, Tolkien-meets-Austen doorstopper made considerable waves in the world of publishing. Neil Gaiman described the book as, 'unquestionably the finest English novel of the fantastic written in the last seventy years'. A bestseller, the novel was long-listed for the Booker Prize, and shortlisted for the Whitbread and the Guardian Prizes. Ten years in the writing, Susanna Clarke's debut shows a masterful use of style, control and humour as she details her story of professional envy, betrayal, revenge, madness and despair. This is an important book; it has allowed fantasy to join the echelons of 'real literature'. But above all, it is an engrossing and fascinating read: you can lose yourself in Clarke's wonderfully detailed fictional history of England and wander around in there for many weeks. It is a classic in the making. Clarke's next book is described thus on the Bloomsbury website: '**THE LADIES OF GRACE ADIEU** (2006) takes the reader deep into the world of Faerie and some stories feature characters from *Jonathan Strange and Mr Norrell*, including some from the footnotes.'

Magic or Madness ➤ JUSTINE LARBALESTIER

YA AUSTRALIA 2005

Fibonaccis are my favourites. They can take you a long way. Forever, in fact. Fibonaccis are numbers, special numbers that keep getting bigger and bigger as you go. The Fibs are kind of like lies—they keep creating more Fibs endlessly or until you get tired of the whole thing.

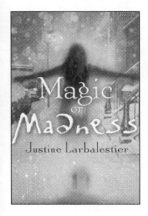

Reason Cansino has always been taught to fear her witch-grandmother, Esmerelda. But when Reason's mother is committed to a mental institution, Reason is sent to live with Esmerelda in Sydney. Reason has been brought up to respect mathematics and science: there is no such thing as magic. But when Reason opens the back door of Esmerelda's house and finds herself in a wintry New York, she is forced to reconsider everything she has ever believed in. Larbalestier's magic is steeped in science, making it entirely credible. But magic is not a gift or an easy solution to a problem. It can achieve amazing things, but it is also a burden and a responsibility. Reason's discovery and exploration of her two options are beautifully juxtaposed with her discovering two cities for the first time – her 'home' town of Sydney, and far-off New York (the author herself splits her time between these two cities).

Larbalestier has fun with confusions caused by even the slightest variations in language. Some of the best moments of the book involve the clash of the two cultures, and there is even a glossary at the back of the book to explain the unfamiliar US terms (in the USA, the book is published with an Australian glossary). **MAGIC LESSONS** (2006) and **MAGIC'S CHILD** (2007) are the sequels.

more **travel between worlds**

DARKHENGE Catherine Fisher YA UK 2005
Rob's sister Chloe looks as though she's in a coma, but she's really in Darkhenge, kept prisoner by a King with a mask of leaves. But does she want to be rescued?

THE EYRE AFFAIR Jasper Fforde A/YA UK 2001
Thursday Next is a literary detective in a world where, instead of blowing up buildings, terrorists steal first editions of Dickens. For lovers of literature and the absurd.

THE KEYS TO THE KINGDOM SERIES Garth Nix
Y AUSTRALIA
Arthur Penhaligon is the rightful heir of the House. But first he has to defeat the seven custodians (one for each day of the week). For the Harry Potter crowd, but this is better! The series begins with **MISTER MONDAY** (2003).

THE NEW POLICEMAN Kate Thompson
Y IRELAND 2005
JJ promises to get his mother more time for her birthday. So he travels to Tír na nÓg where people have too much time. Beautifully Irish and musical.

QUENTARIS SERIES Paul Collins & Michael Pryor (eds)
Y AUSTRALIA
A traditional shared-world fantasy series. Quentaris is a city on the edge of caves that lead to other worlds. Contributing authors have included many of Australia's best such as Isobelle Carmody, Gary Crew and Margo Lanagan.

The Merlin Conspiracy ➤ DIANA WYNNE JONES

YA UK 2004

I thought I knew then. I was sure this was one of my dreams about getting into another world and that it had got mixed up with the sort of dream where you're on a bus with no clothes on, or talking to a girl you fancy with the front of your trousers missing. So I wasn't particularly bothered.

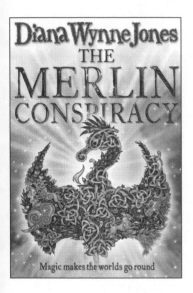

Magic makes the worlds go round

A great, fun, sprawling fantasy novel which links our world to another that is almost the same, but where the Merlin is still an important political position and magic is common. Roddy and Grundo are children at the travelling court, and when they realise that something is not quite right about the new Merlin they try to find help. Nick Mallory is sucked out of his world and into a strange adventure that starts with his desire to be a Magid, and ends up closely linked to Roddy and Grundo. British mythology and geography are very important to this story, and Jones effortlessly winds these elements into her narrative. Roddy, Nick and Grundo are amazing characters. They have flaws and we know that they are capable of some very unheroic actions, but we love them unreservedly.

Diana Wynne Jones is possibly the world's finest living fantasy writer, and she never fails to deliver a cracking read with intricate plot construction, well-rounded, lovable characters and plenty of humour and sparkle.

diana wynne jones

CHARMED LIFE Y 1977

Cat and his sister Gwendolyn are sent to live with their magician relatives. Here Gwendolyn is determined to prove herself a great witch – by being as irritating as possible. Winner of the Guardian Children's Fiction Prize in 1977, this is the first of the Chrestomanci series.

FIRE AND HEMLOCK YA 1986

When ten-year-old Polly crashed a funeral, she met Tom Lynn and suddenly the line between make-believe and reality didn't seem to exist any more. Then Polly did something terrible ... but what was it?

HOWL'S MOVING CASTLE Y/YA 1986

Sophie is transformed from a pretty girl into an old woman and finds herself thrown into a strange adventure which features walking castles, living scarecrows and talking fire. Recently given new life with the Miyazaki animation.

DEEP SECRET A/YA 1997

Junior Magid Rupert Venables has to recruit a new Magid. He never thought it would be this difficult. He contends with a depressing list of candidates, a crumbling Empire on another world, and a science-fiction convention – not to mention falling in love. A sort-of prequel to **THE MERLIN CONSPIRACY**.

Mimus ➤ LILLI THAL Translated by John Brownjohn

YA GERMANY 2003

A chaotic jumble of images danced behind his closed eyelids: Duke Bonizo sprawled on the floor; his father kneeling before Theodo; the maidservant wielding the scissors; Mimus capering round his father like the devil incarnate; Mimus with a bunch of steaming intestines in his hands; Mimus . . .

Not so much fantasy as a kind of alternate-history. There is no magic here, just a medieval kingdom full of malevolence and scheming inhabitants. Florin, the only son of the King of Moltovia, is summoned by his father to Vinland – a rival nation that is close to reaching a peace treaty with Moltovia. On arriving in Vinland, Florin is eager to see his father, but realises too late that he has walked into a trap. His father is imprisoned, and Florin, the only heir, is to be murdered. But Theodo, king of Vinland, has a twisted sense of humour, and instead of killing Florin he apprentices him to Mimus, the court jester. Florin is forced to live on cold stones in the tower where the King's animals are kept, where he is fed with occasional scraps and beaten into submission. Mimus is a hard master, displaying the kind of cruelty that only those who are themselves treated cruelly can achieve. He is bitter and full of hate and spite, yet he also protects and instructs Florin. This is an extremely complex book of courtly intrigue and treason. The plot is watertight, and although Florin's character seems at times to be a little thinly drawn, Mimus is enigmatic enough for both of them.

Mortal Engines ➤ PHILIP REEVE

Y/YA UK 2001

It was a dark, blustery afternoon in spring, and the city of London was chasing a small mining town across the dried-out bed of the old North Sea.

Try not to be put off by the term 'postapocalyptic steampunk'. The Hungry City Chronicles are set in the future, after a nuclear holocaust referred to as the 'Sixty Minute War'. What followed was a strange new world, where cities are mounted on wheels, and run around the planet chasing smaller cities and towns in order to survive. This is known as Municipal Darwinism. Tom Natsworthy is a fifteen-year-old apprentice living in London. When Tom meets his hero, the adventurous and debonair historian Thaddeus Valentine (not to mention Valentine's beautiful daughter Katherine), he thinks that, for once, things are looking bright. That is, until Valentine pushes him down a waste chute and Tom finds himself stranded in the barren Great Hunting Ground, watching London rumble away into the distance. His only companion is Hester, an angry, deformed girl with a mysterious past. *Mortal Engines* is one of the most original, fascinating and gripping speculative fiction books of recent years. It is succeeded by **PREDATOR'S GOLD** (2003), **INFERNAL DEVICES** (2005) and **A DARKLING PLAIN** (2006). It is worth noting that the series – particularly the later books – becomes incredibly complex, with some fairly gruesome violence. Not for the very young or the fainthearted.

Sabriel ➤ GARTH NIX

YA/A AUSTRALIA 1995

The wind was stronger and colder, too, out on the ridge, and the oilskin seemed less comforting, as its memories of her father brought back remembrance of certain pages of The Book of the Dead and tales of horror told by little girls in the darkness of their dormitory, far from the Old Kingdom.

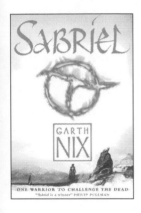

When Sabriel's father, Abhorsen, goes missing, she leaves the comfort and security of her boarding school and journeys into the Old Kingdom – a world full of ice, danger and death. When she reaches Abhorsen's house, Sabriel is greeted by Mogget, a white cat that is more than it seems. Mogget informs her that her father is dead, and that she is the new Abhorsen – a title, not a name. The Abhorsen is a necromancer, but instead of raising the dead, the Abhorsen returns the half-dead back to Death. Sabriel sets out to recover her father's body before it gets taken over by an undead monster. The Old Kingdom is a violent, cruel and terrifying world, and Sabriel will encounter untold challenges before she truly understands her destiny.

Sabriel is a gripping and demanding combination of high fantasy and horror. The first in the Old Kingdom trilogy, it's followed by **LIRAEL** (2001) and **ABHORSEN** (2003), as well as **ACROSS THE WALL** (2005), a book of short stories some of which are set in the Old Kingdom. These books have built a considerable reputation for Nix in the USA and more recently in the UK. Nix is thoroughly professional in all he does and takes both his writing and its promotion seriously.

On his comprehensive website Nix tells us that this trilogy has been translated into twenty-eight languages and that *Sabriel*, *Lirael* and *Abhorsen* are going to be full-colour graphic novels.

The Seeing Stone > KEVIN CROSSLEY-HOLLAND

YA UK 2000

When I stared at the stone, I could see myself inside it. It was black of black, and deep, and very still. Like an eye of deep water.

'A mirror,' I said.

'Not really,' said the Merlin.

It could be said that the Arthurian myth has been done to death. Once there has been a Disney cartoon, a Marion Zimmer Bradley feminist retelling and an overblown Hollywood epic starring Keira Knightley, where else is there to go? Kevin Crossley-Holland has a pretty good stab at giving the Arthur story a fresh coat of paint, and the results are impressive. It is 1199. Arthur de Caldicot is thirteen years old, the second son of a knight living in an English manor house. Because he is the second son, he won't inherit anything, so he has to train to be a knight and earn his own land. Except he's not very good at fighting. He's left-handed. And he's good at reading and writing, which would make him more suited to being a scribe. But scribes don't get manor houses. The story really begins when Merlin gives Arthur a stone – the Seeing Stone of the title – and makes him promise not to tell anyone about it. Inside the Stone, Arthur watches the life of another Arthur unfold – the mythical King Arthur. Is Arthur de Caldicot seeing his own future? Or the past? Or is he seeing a sort of parallel world that mirrors his own? *The Seeing Stone* won the Guardian Children's Fiction Prize, the Tír na nÓg prize and the Nestle Smarties Book Prize Bronze Medal, and was shortlisted for the Whitbread Award. It is followed by **AT THE CROSSING-PLACES** (2001) and **KING OF THE MIDDLE MARCH** (2003).

The Taste of Lightning ➤ KATE CONSTABLE

YA AUSTRALIA 2007

As a tiny child, Skir had been struck by lightning. He had no memory of it, though his body seemed to remember: his hair crackling, the taste of metal in his mouth. He did have a vague memory of his mother singing, to comfort him. It was all he could recall of his mother.

Kate Constable's brand of fantasy is very traditional, but never feels generic. This new book is set in Tremaris, the same world as her successful Chanters of Tremaris trilogy, but in a different, mercenary country, deeply suspicious of magic and even of writing. Tansy is a serving girl, blackmailed into stealing an item of clothing from a young man for sinister Lady Wanion's spell. The young man in question is Skir, the Priest-King of Cragonlands – or at least he would be, if he wasn't being held hostage by the Baltimaran King. After a botched rescue attempt, Skir and Tansy find themselves fleeing from the Baltimaran army, along with Perrin, a soldier with the Power of Beasts – the ability to control and communicate with animals. As they flee across the border to Cragonlands, all three of them must come to terms with who they really are – and what they really want.

In this deeply political book, Constable has moved away from the magic-and-adventures brand of girl-fantasy that characterised **THE SINGER OF ALL SONGS** and its sequels, and ventured into something more complex and adult. *The Taste of Lightning* is about trust, responsibility, deception and truth.

Temeraire ➤ NAOMI NOVIK

A/YA USA 2006

A single leap, and they were airborne, the broad wings thrusting in great sweeping arcs to either side of him, the whole long body stretched out like an arrow driving upwards into the sky.

Another Napoleonic Wars fantasy (see **JONATHAN STRANGE AND MR NORRELL** page 97). It is 1805. Armies clash, and the Royal British Navy is desperately trying to turn the tide. As is Britain's Aerial Corps – the dragons. Captain William Laurence captures a French ship, and claims its prized cargo: a dragon egg. When the baby dragon hatches, it immediately attaches itself to Laurence, who is forced to leave the Navy and join the airforce to be an aviator, training his dragon, Temeraire, to fight. Laurence is an unwilling recruit to the Aerial Corps, having to sacrifice both his naval career and the woman he loves in order to start again as a flyer. But despite his misgivings, he soon learns to love the feeling of flying, and he and Temeraire develop a deep bond.

The first of a series of at least three, Temeraire is a masterful combination of history, fantasy and interpersonal relationships. An amazing amount of research has gone into this book; there are times when you completely forget that it is fantasy. The relationship between Laurence and Temeraire is touching, and the battle scenes are thrilling. Using the Napoleonic Wars as setting and inspiration seems to be in fashion. Read also Susan Cooper's charming recent parallel worlds story, **VICTORY** (2006), and Paul Dowswell's **POWDER MONKEY** (2005) (see page 43).

Valiant: A Modern Tale of Faerie ➤ HOLLY BLACK

YA USA 2005

'Nevermore,' Lolli said. 'That's what Luis calls it, because there're three rules: Never more than once a day, never more than a pinch at a time, and never more than two days in a row.'

When Valerie runs away from home, she finds herself hanging around with a bunch of kids who live in an abandoned New York subway station. These kids survive by running errands ... for faeries. The faeries that live in New York are not the pink, sparkly critters that immediately spring to mind. They are dark and mysterious. And sick. The iron in New York makes them sick, and the street kids are ferrying around their medicine. Well, most of their medicine anyway. They siphon off some and shoot up, heroin-style. It gets them high, bestows a faerie-like glamour on them where people will do anything they want – give them money, humiliate themselves, anything. But can Val escape the lure of the Nevermore for long enough to figure out what's poisoning the faeries? Is it Ravus, the hideous troll to whom Val is strangely attracted? Or is it one of her street-kid friends?

This sort-of sequel to **TITHE** (2004) is a creepy, disturbing book that contains some graphic drug references. It has a gripping plot and solid, well-rounded characters. Good for those who like their fantasy dark and twisted. Read also **IRONSIDE** (2007).

classic fantasy

THROUGH THE LOOKING GLASS Lewis Carroll Y/YA/A UK 1871
This sequel to **ALICE IN WONDERLAND** (1865) is full of hidden
allusions and mathematical problems. For extra fun, read **THE
ANNOTATED ALICE** (1960) by Martin Gardner.

THE PHOENIX AND THE CARPET E Nesbit Y UK 1904
The often-overlooked sequel to **FIVE CHILDREN AND IT** (1902),
this is the story of the Phoenix, a proud, vain creature that takes
Cyril, Robert, Anthea and Jane on many new adventures.

THE LORD OF THE RINGS TRILOGY JRR Tolkien A/YA UK 1954–1955
You don't get much more fantastic than Tolkien. Middle-earth is
under threat by the evil Sauron. It's up to Frodo to destroy him
by casting the One Ring into the fires of Mordor. Tolkien not
only created a whole world and peopled it with extraordinarily
imagined creatures, but he even created a whole language for
them. Often selected as the most popular fantasy novel ever, and
a book some fans claim to re-read almost every year! It was made
into an equally amazing Oscar-winning series of movies by Peter
Jackson, a New Zealander with a Tolkienesque vision.

WEIRDSTONE OF BRISINGAMEN Alan Garner Y/YA UK 1960
Colin and Susan are on holiday in Cheshire. Things begin to spiral
out of control, and the children are being hunted by the forces
of evil. The novel draws on Celtic, Norse and Arthurian legends.
Garner also wrote the extraordinary **THE OWL SERVICE** (1967),
ELIDOR (1965) and **RED SHIFT** (1973) and is arguably one of
the greatest, most imaginative and most sophisticated writers of
complex allegorical fantasy.

THE DARK IS RISING Susan Cooper Y/YA UK 1999
On his eleventh birthday, strange things start happening to Will
Stanton. He learns that this is because he is an Old One, and must
find and join together pieces of a Thing of Power. This is actually
the second book in the sequence of the same name, but they don't
need to be read in order.

life, love & loss

Different ways of loving and being. Different times. Different kinds of relationships. Tears, rage, family, work, illness, friends, school, death, love, sex, money, music, girlfriends, boyfriends, exams, accidents and alcohol. How can you think and talk about all this? How does it all fit and make sense?

Bird and Sugar Boy ➤ SOFIE LAGUNA

Y/YA AUSTRALIA 2006

The sun, the willow leaves, the slow water went right inside me.
All the sounds were going right inside me too . . . All those sounds went
into where the bird thoughts were.

When James Burdell (aka Bird/Birdy) finally allows himself to cry
he says, 'The ball bearings came out then, rolling up from my gut,
past my throat.' You, too, might struggle at times with those ball
bearings. Bird's mother 'shot through' when he was tiny, and he
is brought up in a country town by his ex-bikie father. Dad owns
a struggling car repair place and 'can fix anything' but is not too
good with words. Birdy is trying to understand the past and himself.
Increasingly a 'behaviour problem' at school, he has no idea why he
says and does the crazy things that get him into trouble. His love of
birds and drawing them (and flying away with them in his head when
things get really tough), and his friendship with Sugar Boy sustain
him. Then Sugar's father gets a job in Broome. Bird makes a wild
plan to run away to the Blue Mountains, where the author of his one
precious possession, *Birds: A Field Guide*, is said to live. Disaster is
just averted with help from Dad's mates.

This is not an action-driven story, but it is carried by Sofie
Laguna's poetic language and her ability to inhabit James and
portray his frustration and pain. Laguna offers an acute insight into
some possible causes of so-called 'bad behaviour' in school. She
also shows how badly the 'perpetrators' and their teachers may deal
with such behaviour. A rare bird this!

Boy Meets Boy ➤ DAVID LEVITHAN

YA USA 2003

I've always known I was gay, but it wasn't confirmed until I was in kindergarten. It was my teacher who said so.

'Fiction for the OC generation'

'Utterly absorbing'

david levithan

BOY MEETS BOY

'Outrageously quirky and romantic'

'Intimate, feel-good and quick-fire'

'Move over Will & Grace'

'Rating: 5/5'

Who said same-sex affairs need to be fraught and kept in the closet? This book is 'out'! The whole community in this story is 'cool' and warmly supportive. That's just the way they are. This is a cheeky and, I suspect, deliberately romanticised book, but all the more engaging and important for that. One of the funnier highlights and stereotype-busting segments is the role of the glamorous transgendered star football player. But this is Paul's story, and his matter-of-fact voice reinforces the book's attitude: that it's normal to be gay. Paul says, 'There isn't really a gay scene or a straight scene in our town. They got all mixed up a while back, which I think is for the best.'

Levithan, a publisher and editor with Scholastic USA, works with the likes of Garth Nix, Markus Zusak and John Marsden. In his own writing he is keen to show another side to the gay experience. He said, 'As a reader and editor, I was extremely dissatisfied with the way gay teen characters were portrayed in teen literature. For much of teen literature's history, the gay characters had to die, be harmed, be miserable, be abused or be outcasts.'

In the lively *Boy Meets Boy*, the teenagers lead rich, normal lives with the usual tensions and frustrations, with friends, school and family. Levithan says, 'It's not as if I'm claiming that this is reality. It's what reality should be.' (Interview from CYL newsletter, May 2005)

more YA gender benders ➤ ➤ ➤

YA gender benders

BAD BOY Diana Wieler CANADA 1992
In the tough macho world of ice hockey, no one could possibly be gay or be a gay person's friend. No wonder AJ is so angry and disoriented when he discovers where Tulsa's real interests lie.

THE BLUE LAWN William Taylor NZ 1994
Two quite different types of teenager are drawn into a relationship that neither completely understands. David, fifteen, a star rugby player and edgy outsider, and Theo, sixteen, find an unlikely friendship growing into something more. A controversially award-winning book.

DANCE ON MY GRAVE Aidan Chambers UK 1982
Hal, sixteen, and Barry fall in love. After Barry dies in a motorcycle crash, Hal is arrested for dancing on his grave. The focus is on Hal's state of mind and on the intensity of first love. An early, challenging 'gay' young adult book, innovatively constructed and told.

HANGING ON TO MAX Margaret Bechard USA 2002
A perfect companion to Joanne Horniman's **MAHALIA**. Another young father looking after baby and making tough choices.

MY HEARTBEAT Garret Freymann-Weyr USA 2002
Siblings Ellen and Link and their friend James are inseparable. Then someone asks if James and Link are a couple. Link's father needs to believe his son is not gay. Ellen loves both boys. So many silences, secrets and shifting emotions. A sophisticated story.

READY OR NOT Mark Macleod (ed) 1996
and **HIDE AND SEEK** Jenny Pausacker (ed) 1996
Two groundbreaking Australian collections, published
in tandem, containing stories from leading Australian
writers exploring gay and lesbian experiences.

A TRICK OF THE LIGHT Susanna van Essen AUSTRALIA 2004
Josie's very normal life includes two loving, gay
fathers (she's the biological child of one). The main
game is cantankerous Josie's determination to wreak
revenge on her much hated teacher. She is saved by
her doppelganger!

Doing It ➤ MELVIN BURGESS

YA UK 2003

'OK,' said Jonathon. 'The choice is this. You either have to shag Jenny Gibson – or else that homeless woman who begs spare change outside Crammer's bakers.'

If anyone takes literally this crude opening conversation between friends Jonathon, Dino and Ben, they either deserve to be shocked or know very little about how teenage boys think, feel or operate. It is a very clever rendering of how boys hide behind verbal sparring. Nevertheless, Burgess is setting out to challenge and tell it like it is.

Doing It is hilarious and deadly serious at the same time. Burgess bores into the fears, hopes, glories, longings, fumblings and expectations of older teenage boys. They are desperate and yet terrified about 'doing it'. They also want to 'do it' right. Each has secrets, particularly Ben, in the throes of an affair with a teacher, which is rapidly running out of control. Ben wants out, but how can he extricate himself? Jonathon worries that other friends will hassle him for his interest in Deborah because she is larger than the magazines stipulate. And why won't Jackie come good for Dino?

Burgess brilliantly captures the anxieties of these sex-obsessed young men, but also shows them to be clever, witty students with a lot on their minds. Some much older males have said they wish they could have read something like this in their youth, to show they were neither alone nor freaks. Girls also love to read this book so they might understand those weird, lustful, inarticulate creatures in their lives.

boys' stuff
hopefully helpful hints

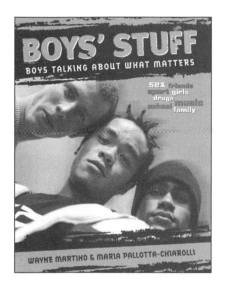

BOYS' STUFF: BOYS TALKING ABOUT WHAT MATTERS Wayne Martino and Maria Pallotta-Chiarolli AUSTRALIA 2001
Two academics asked teenage boys to tell them what they think about growing up, friends, sex, sport, drugs – no holds barred.

SECRET MEN'S BUSINESS
John Marsden AUSTRALIA 1998
John Marsden says, 'Becoming a man is the biggest challenge you'll ever have. There are twelve things you need to do, if you are to reach manhood.' Warning: May be challenging for some adults.

THE 'S' WORD: A BOYS' GUIDE TO SEX, PUBERTY AND GROWING UP James Roy AUSTRALIA 2006
Simply and humorously presented responses, mostly in the form of extended email questions and answers, to questions many boys may not be quite prepared to ask.

XY 100: ONE HUNDRED STRATEGIES FOR LIFE
Matt Whyman UK 2004
Mike Shuttleworth says, 'A frank, compact guide to essential life skills . . . *XY 100* offers reassurance without the sermon'.

Falling from Grace ➤ JANE GODWIN

YA AUSTRALIA 2006

I worry about lots of things. Big things and little things. I worry that terrorists will blow something up in Australia. I worry about the future, the drought, and global warming . . . I worry that I'll never get a girlfriend. I worry that I can't be bothered doing things like I used to.

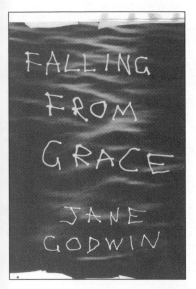

This is principally Kip's story, but it also belongs to Grace and her sister Annie. Kip feels suddenly directionless and 'lost'. Why has this rising swim-star lost the drive to swim? Grace really gets lost and the subsequent search and police investigation power the story along. How does Ted, the drunk, clapped-out musician, fit into their story, and who is little David? The setting, during a storm and king tide at the treacherous Cheviot Beach on Victoria's Mornington Peninsula, adds more drama. The introduction of so many characters and apparently unrelated strands is disconcerting at first. But as the story builds, we see that this is what might happen: the police are looking for clues, wanting results and joining the wrong dots; witnesses are getting confused, intimidated or hiding something, or doing things for reasons they can't themselves understand. In tense, chaotic circumstances, trivial snippets and coincidences can be misread or missed. Cleverly woven together, the strands create a powerful tale where eventually everything fits together and life starts making sense again for Kip and the others.

The Happiness of Kati ➤ JANE VEJJAJIVA

Translated by Prudence Borthwick

Y/YA THAILAND 2006

Mother never promised to return

Kati waited every day for mother

Kati no longer remembered mother's face

No one knew how much time mother had left

These tiny chapter headers gently lead the reader towards the truth about the absence of Kati's mother. We see Kati's life by the river with her grandparents through finely etched domestic detail that also show the ageless rituals of Thai life, including the importance of food preparation and domestic order. Grandpa and Grandma spar constantly and this provides touches of much-needed humour. They used to be high-powered professionals but have retired, probably to look after Kati. But despite all the love and care there are silences and great sadness. Eventually, the time comes for Kati to learn why her mother is absent. She is taken by her grandparents and close relatives to be with her mother for her mother's last days. Here the tone of the book changes dramatically as we are provided with clear, even blunt information about the stages of motor neurone disease. Despite the distress and sadness of the characters, the situation is thoughtfully and graciously managed to provide everyone with time, space and whatever beauty possible. Kati is also helped to fit together the story of her past. Flowers – their colours, scents and arrangement – are constants in the story. There is one final mystery to solve: who is Kati's father? It is left to Kati to decide how to deal with this. The cultural setting and the delicately structured style make this luminous, lyrical gem a special reading experience.

His Name in Fire ➤ CATHERINE BATESON

YA AUSTRALIA 2006

I got the job, Seb, I'm off
to start a circus.

The town has:
The abattoir, four pubs
Safeway, the racetrack,
A dawdling river –
What else do you need?
A job.

Mozza says:
As if a circus can help.
What do they think we
are?
Kinder kids?
I've got a missus –
practically –
we've got a kid
no jobs no money
no way out.

There are others in town. Emma is sad and silent about her mad, unavailable mother. Matt and Emma love each other but can't speak or reach out. And there is Emma's dad, who loves her and loves his snakes, too.

Gradually Mollie gets the locals going, gets the circus happening and frees up lives and emotions. As in earlier verse novels, Bateson captures places, teenagers, adults, relationships, love, loss and longing in short bursts of verse. Even the music that they start to make finds expression in lovely bluesy poetry. Mollie is terrific at uniting and galvanising the community. She's proud of her success, but still sad and lonely. After the grand performance and the wild party, it seems the circus might go on without Mollie.

Read other Catherine Bateson verse novels, especially **A DANGEROUS GIRL** (2000) and **THE YEAR IT ALL HAPPENED** (2001).

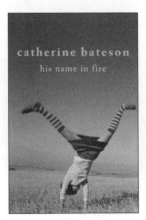

verse novels make great easy reads

THE BRIMSTONE JOURNALS Ron Koertge USA 2001
Fifteen US high school students chronicle their tough lives. Will one of them have the courage to blow the whistle on Boyd and the arsenal in his basement? Guns and violence in US schools, this is similar territory to the Booker Prize winning **VERNON GOD LITTLE** by DBC Pierre (see page 80).

BY THE RIVER Steven Herrick AUSTRALIA 2004
A gentle father-and-son story of growing up and love and loss by a river. Read also Herrick's **A SIMPLE GIFT** and **LOVE, GHOSTS AND NOSE HAIR**.

LOVE THAT DOG Sharon Creech USA 2001
A tiny gem about a small boy, a dog and an inspiring teacher. Jack reluctantly learns to write and love poetry. It changes his life, and how he remembers his dog.

THE REALM OF POSSIBILITY David Levithan USA 2004
In a series of linked poems, twenty students reveal relationships, situations and emotions. Mary struggles with anorexia. Cara thinks only of herself. Daniel and Jed are happy in their steady relationship.

WHAT MY MOTHER DOESN'T KNOW Sonya Sones USA 2001
This ordinary fifteen-year-old's life seems less than ordinary to her. Her body, boys and parents just seem too hard to fathom and manage. Sad and funny.

FRENCHTOWN SUMMER Robert Cormier USA 1999
One of the last books of this late, great writer, in a much mellower mood than in his many gritty novels. With glowing words, Cormier paints pictures of his twelfth summer in 1938: a distant father, his first love, poverty, important friendships and the suicide of his uncle.

See also Poets Raiding the Novelists' Shelves, page 22.

Jinx ➤ MARGARET WILD

Do not get to know me.
Do not ask me out.
Do not love me.
Be warned!
I am Jinx.

She is Jen.
Not yet
Jinx.

The short, easy-to-read fragments of blank verse allow Margaret Wild to present with humour and compassion many voices, moods and situations. Angry, confused and uncertain, as her personal and family lives start to unravel, Jen becomes Jinx – unpredictable, fierce and increasingly unlike the 'good girl' Jen used to be.

Jen's parents have split up. Her boyfriend disappears. Friends become treacherous. Her sister Grace is all too quick to accept the relationship between their father (the rat) and his new lady, Stella.

Jinx's relationship with Hal stops and starts, and we get acute insights into the tensions and dramas of friendships and being a teenager. A special feature is Jen's unusually warm relationship with Mum. This is also a lovely story about mothers and daughters and family life today. *Jinx* is a welcome change in style for one of our best picture book creators. Read also Wild's equally engaging second verse novel, **ONE NIGHT** (2003).

LIFE, LOVE & LOSS   122

The Life and Times of Gracie Faltrain

> ## CATH CROWLEY

YA AUSTRALIA 2004

It wasn't my fault that the only soccer team in school was all boys. I had to play. Waiting until Year 8 would have been torture, so I started turning up at training. Without an invite.

Gracie loves playing soccer and is happy to be the only girl in the soccer team. Life seems perfect. But Gracie is growing up and finding that things can change in sudden and frightening ways. First, her best friend, Jane, leaves Australia. Then she makes a fool of herself with a boy and becomes a laughing-stock. (There's an incident with an ear and a tongue.) When the boys decide they don't want a girl, particularly an opinionated one, in their team, Gracie is devastated. Gracie's mother understands. She says of Gracie, 'She has no idea how to fail.' Gracie looks to her family for support and sympathy, but all is not well there either.

In an impressive debut, Cath Crowley lets her characters speak for themselves in short bursts, providing intriguing glimpses and different points of view. Gradually the fragments of Gracie's life come together again. This is the first in a lively series about varied aspects of teenage life, including romance, friendship, ageing grandparents, the importance of music, the desire to escape small town life, and, of course, soccer. Followed by **GRACIE FALTRAIN TAKES CONTROL** (2006).

Little Wing ➤ JOANNE HORNIMAN

YA/A AUSTRALIA 2006

Emily thought that if she could just push herself forward and pretend that she was operating okay, one day her engine would start up again.

If you've read **MAHALIA,** you'll know that Emily left soon after giving birth to Mahalia, leaving Matt to care for the baby. Matt was a terrific dad and looking after his child gave purpose and direction to his life. But why did Emily leave after so looking forward to the baby and clearly loving Matt?

With her usual delicate touch, Horniman shows a young girl – depressed, frightened and adrift to the point of self-harm. Emily is not ready for motherhood. She leaves the hippyish life in Lismore to stay with her godmother in the Blue Mountains. She is loved and cared for and given space. She sleeps and drifts and then meets Martin and begins to take part in his life as a stay-at-home dad (another great dad!). Martin welcomes Emily and asks few questions. He even manages to allay his wife's unease at allowing Emily to be with their little boy, Pete. This unlikely, undemanding friendship is a typical Horniman touch. Very gradually, Emily gets better and eventually returns to Lismore and re-establishes contact with Mahalia. Horniman has a sure touch with the nuances of relationships. When Emily thinks she might take Mahalia away from Matt, it becomes clear that to heal and mature she must understand Matt's strength and determination, and that the best she can hope for is to share the little girl.

Lonesome Howl ➤ STEVEN HERRICK

YA AUSTRALIA 2006

I don't really know

where the wild dog lives.

I've decided I'm getting away from this farm.

So I tell Jake about the rock on Sheldon Mountain.

It's the sort of place a wolf would stand

looking over the whole valley,

looking for a mate,

looking for food.

If I was the queen of this Valley

it's where I'd live.

This is Lucy's clear voice. Her life couldn't be more different from Jake's. He lives in a loving family and has a close bond with his father. For years, Lucy has endured her father's bitterness and anger, which often result in beatings. Her mother lives in fear, too, and seems defeated. Only her younger brother, Peter, keeps making excuses for his dad. The wolf, or other creature, that has been prowling for years inhabits everyone's consciousness, and Jake is determined to find it. Lucy and Jake are drawn to each other, and in spite of her father's inevitable disapproval and fury, Lucy decides to hike up Sheldon Mountain with Jake. Lucy is searching for more than the wolf. When Jake twists his ankle the two are forced to spend a cold night in a cave. Everything changes for Lucy and also for Jake.

By becoming close to Jake, Lucy also comes to understand the true possibilities of a home and a family. By making a stand, Lucy also empowers her mother.

Herrick's beautiful, spare verse novels just keep getting better. Here, as in **BY THE RIVER** (2004), he moves from his more light-hearted earlier works to creations of great depth and beauty.

Lost Property ➤ JAMES MOLONEY

YA AUSTRALIA 2005

Why doesn't my brother have anything to do with us? The reasons seemed obvious enough when I left Sydney. Back then I carried an image of Michael in my head, of an angry guy with a restless heart running away from a world that had become too hard for him.

Lost Property is all about change: physical change as teenagers get older; changes in family dynamics; changes in how one sees one's family; changes in loyalties and relationships; changes in perception. Ask Josh's brash, successful car salesman dad and he'll tell you his older son Michael, who has taken off, is 'lost property'. But at sixteen, younger brother Josh is also lost, as all his certainties about himself, his brother and what is important are shaken. A holiday job at the Lost Property Office in the bowels of inner Sydney forces Josh to see the details of people's lives and what matters to them in different ways. So Josh goes in search of Michael. He has some good, but also some frightening and bruising (literally), experiences on the way. And when he finally tracks down his brother, everything he had been told about Michael is also deeply challenged. A solid, thoroughly engaging story of young people moving into adulthood, what they find and what they have to leave behind to be true to themselves.

Love Lessons ➤ JACQUELINE WILSON

Y/YA UK 2005

Grace isn't three or four, as you might expect. She is eleven years old and very weird.

I know I am weird too. I can't seem to help it. I don't know how to be a proper teenager.

Grace and Prudence, fifteen, are virtual prisoners. Home-schooled by an old-fashioned, eccentric father, they have little contact with the real world. Father runs a musty bookshop but refuses to pay bills, have TV, or be realistic about his daughters' education. He dominates their kindly, dithering mother, too. When Father has a stroke, the girls are forced to go to the local comprehensive school. Father rules even from his hospital bed – for a while anyway. Money is scarce and the girls are ridiculed for their unfashionable, homemade, girly clothes. Grace soon makes friends, but Prudence is too weird. She can't and won't do maths but reads voraciously and is talented at drawing. Prudence quickly becomes attracted to her rather frustrated art teacher, and this situation soon escalates. Teacher–pupil relationships are a touchy subject, and topical in Australia, too.

Jacqueline Wilson knows how to get readers in. She creates an over-the-top, almost hysterical story that matches the out-of-control behaviour of poor, lost Prudence. Mother does take control in the end, and there is an almost fairytale solution to the family's financial woes.

An easy-to-read story that deals with serious matters in light, but never trivial, ways.

Monica Bloom ➤ NICK EARLS

YA/A AUSTRALIA 2006

It was my last year at school, our last year that began in the house on the hill in Hamilton, and it did not become the year any of us had expected. It started well enough when on the final day of the holidays, a new voice made its way over the fence from the neighbours' pool. It was the twins' cousin, Monica Bloom, arrived that day from Dublin.

Can anyone write a gentle, subtle, engaging love story in which the two people meet only five times and barely exchange a few words before ending up in different hemispheres? Nick Earls can.

Matt's life is different from that of the wealthy Hartnetts next door. They have lived on the hill for two generations, while Matt's family has moved around to follow his father's engineering work. Starting his last year of school, Matt is uncertain about his future and his place in the world. He relies on the Hartnett girls for company and direction, and he becomes enthralled with Monica, though he has only sporadic contact with her. She has been sent to finish school with her cousins, and, like Matt, we only glean snippets of her troubled life in Ireland and then in Queensland. Turmoil erupts in Matt's family when his father is caught up in an embezzlement scandal perpetrated by one of his staff. It happened on 'his watch' and costs him his job.

Earls paints the financial, social and emotional costs with a light touch. Matt helps where he can but is absorbed by Monica, and, in subtle ways, this shields him and gets him through. The long, hot, Brisbane summer diffuses tensions and slows reactions; Earls uses the location and weather to great effect. (See page 318 for Nick Earls in a more humorous mood.)

One Whole and Perfect Day ➤ JUDITH CLARKE

YA AUSTRALIA 2006

Freakish, thought Lily; that was the word which perhaps best described her family. Not Freaks exactly, but – getting there. They were a family that somehow didn't fit, at least, not into the orderly suburb where they lived . . .

Lily is fed up with being the sensible one in the family, sick of thinking of shopping and the next meal rather than focusing on her schoolwork. Dad took off to America long ago. Social worker Mum does her best, but frets about Lily's older brother, Lonnie, who keeps dropping out of courses and is living in a boarding house to escape Pop's hassling.

Those who know Clarke's Al Capsella books will remember her eye for detail, her gently satirical humour and her empathy for those who don't fit. Here, everything seems to be falling apart, but when Nan decides to have an eightieth birthday party for grumpy Pop, Clarke pulls together all the players, even those with bit parts (including Nan's apparently imaginary friend), for a grand finale that celebrates family and friendship. Clarke has created a delicious fairy story, yet the characters, emotions and situations are sharply observed and very contemporary.

Rose By Any Other Name ➤ MAUREEN McCARTHY

YA/A AUSTRALIA 2006

I never expected LOVE to come when it did. Nor the way it came. Nor the complete mess it made of my life. I wasn't hanging out for it either like some people . . .

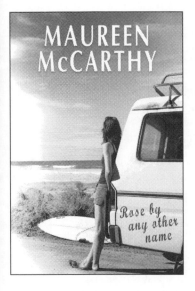

This is a big, busy roller-coaster of a story. Bands, music and surfing are important. Maureen McCarthy is again writing with verve and colour about family and friends, and cleverly slipping in pointed social comment. Rose O'Neil is the youngest of four girls in a well-to-do family. She has just finished school and expects to follow her QC father into law. She meets an appealing young man and all seems set for an easy ride. One thread pulling the story along is a journey in an old van, as Rose and her mother head to Port Fairy on Victoria's south-west coast, where Rose's paternal grandmother (a wonderfully cranky, feisty old woman) is dying. The story takes an entertaining and revealing detour when Mum insists they pick up a hitchhiker. The perfect family is split asunder when Dad suddenly moves out with a younger woman. McCarthy presents a gritty picture of a woman falling apart, but also shows her daughters pulling together to keep her going. We later see that life is tough for Dad, too. The four sisters' often fraught lives and tense relationships are vividly presented with touches of wild humour. In all this turmoil, Rose falls in love with the wrong, much older man. We come to see the parallels between the complex emotions of father and daughter, and their longing for beauty, pleasure and intensity.

grand love stories

ROMEO AND JULIET William Shakespeare A/YA UK 1597
The ultimate tragic story of warring families trying to forbid
young lovers from being together. Immortalised in many films
including one made in 1968 by Florentine director Franco
Zeffirelli, and one by Australian Baz Luhrmann in 1996.

ANNA KARENINA Leo Tolstoy A/YA RUSSIA 1873–1877
Originally written in instalments, this novel follows the
illicit liaison in St Petersburg between fashionable married
woman Anna Karenina and handsome Count Vronsky.
It ends tragically with one of the most famous suicides in
literary history.

COONARDOO Katharine Susannah Prichard A/YA AUSTRALIA 1929
A forgotten classic about the difficult, unexpressed love
between an Aboriginal woman, Coonardoo, and the
owner of a remote desert station where she works as a
housekeeper. Bold and shocking at the time, it still raises
important questions about contact between black and
white Australians.

GONE WITH THE WIND Margaret Mitchell A/YA USA 1939
Mitchell's only novel continues to be as popular as the
equally famous film. The epic romantic story follows Scarlett
O'Hara's tumultuous love affair with Rhett Butler, and
provides a fascinating picture of the American South, as well
as exploring attitudes to women, slavery and black people.

DR ZHIVAGO Boris Pasternak A/YA RUSSIA 1957
Extreme weather and extreme distances seem to create
extreme behaviour. During the chaos and violence of
the Russian Revolution, lovers Dr Zhivago and Lara are
separated and never find each other again. Banned in the
Soviet Union, the manuscript was smuggled into Europe
and became a bestseller. A grand film, too. (See Anne Fine's
THE ROAD OF BONES, page 277.)

A Swift Pure Cry ➤ SIOBHAN DOWD

YA/A IRELAND 2006

Shell . . . had no time for church: not since Mam's death, over a year back . . . Mam had liked the priests, the candles, the rosaries. Most of all she loved the Virgin Mary. She'd said 'Sweet Mary this and that' all day long. Sweet Mary *if the potatoes boiled over; if the dog caught a crow.* Sweet Mary *if the scones came out good and soft.*

Then she died.

After Mam's death, Shell Talent's father falls apart. He stops working, drinks even more, and takes to rattling tins – supposedly collecting for the church. It is left to Shell to care for her younger siblings, Trixie and Jimmy. She does well with very little, but is unloved and lonely, desperately missing her cheery mother and often frightened of her unpredictable father. She stops going to school. It is no wonder she finds some solace in the arms of the charming but two-timing Declan.

For a long time, Shell blocks out the signs of her pregnancy. But catastrophe is inevitable as the story of deaths, secrets and bumbling police becomes increasingly complex and dramatic, unfolding like a thriller. Shell is only supported by her extraordinarily astute and compassionate younger siblings.

It is hard to believe that this heartbreaking but totally gripping story is set as recently as 1984. Irish village life, dominated by priests and religion, seems not to have changed for decades. Poverty, ignorance, gossip, Catholic guilt – but also pockets of kindness in the community – together with Shell's growing courage and determination, make this an unforgettable story that richly deserves the acclaim it has received.

if you want to **cry** ...

THE BOOK OF EVERYTHING Guus Kuijer
Translated by John Nieuwenhuizen Y/YA HOLLAND 2005
A tiny heart-wrenching gem about war, anger, an abusive father
and his unyielding religious beliefs. But the local women, his
sister, his imagination, some helpful chats with Jesus, and a love
of books allow Thomas, nine, to achieve his aim of being happy.
(See page 204)

CLAIMING GEORGIA TATE Gigi Amateau YA USA 2005
When grandmother dies, Granddaddy decides Georgia's place
is with her father – but her father is a drunk who wants more
than her housekeeping skills. Will Granddaddy save Georgia?

DEAR NOBODY Berlie Doherty YA UK 1991
Helen, seventeen, gets pregnant. People's responses vary
wildly. Frightened and confused, yet determined, Helen writes
heartbreaking letters to 'Dear Nobody', her unborn baby.
Will she eventually let the loving Chris back into her life and
that of his child? A multi-award-winning book.

GOODNIGHT MR TOM Michelle Magorian Y/YA UK 1986
As World War II looms, neglected, deprived little Willie is
evacuated to the country, where he lives with surly, gruff
Mr Tom. Just as an unlikely bond begins to develop, Willie's
mother summons him back to London. A sad, affecting journey
for characters and readers alike, and an enduring classic.

HANA'S SUITCASE Karen Levine Y CANADA 2003
The unforgettable retelling of how a small battered suitcase in the
Tokyo Holocaust Education Resource Center leads to the story
of its owner, a little girl who died in Auschwitz. (See page 273)

THIRD DEGREE Tania Roxborough YA NZ 2005
Ruth begins to confront the anguish of feeling abandoned in
hospital, of seeing other terribly ill children and of suffering
horrific burns nine years ago.

The Tiggie Tompson Show ➤ TESSA DUDER

YA NEW ZEALAND 1999

You know, no one chooses to get pneumonia. I didn't say to myself, right, now what's the best revenge on classmates who swiped all my clothes out of the shower and made me walk down a bush track stark naked and freezing my tits off in the middle of winter. Hey, let's get pneumon-ia! Stand clear – Girl Power at work!

Tiggie's authentic, argumentative and feisty voice powers this book. Already in the shadow of a glamorous TV celebrity mother, uncertain about herself, and larger than the regulation size ten, Tiggie is pushed to an all-time low by the incident in the quote above. However, it also precipitates a big change. Tiggie insists on changing schools, hoping to lose herself in a large, less exclusive, city school. Almost despite herself, she becomes involved in acting and lands an ongoing role in a TV soap, then a major drama. She generally gets a life, and fights the obsessive attention to body image that plagues the life of her actor friend, the closet anorexic Vita.

The first of a trilogy, *The Tiggie Tompson Show* was a major New Zealand award winner. Drawing on Duder's own experience in theatre and in a New Zealand soap opera (*Shortland Street*), the Tiggie books reveal the inner lives of teenagers on the cusp of adulthood. The stories are warm, lively and easy to get lost in. The characters sound real and are easy to identify with. Read also **TIGGIE TOMPSON ALL AT SEA** (2001) and **TIGGIE TOMPSON'S LONGEST JOURNEY** (2003). Duder also wrote the hugely popular and enduring Alex quartet.

Walking Naked ➤ ALYSSA BRUGMAN

YA AUSTRALIA 2005

How unfortunate for her to have a name that was hard to say –
Purdeetah Wigweegan – on top of being the most despised creature
in the whole school.

Does popularity and being a part of the 'in' crowd bring true friendship and happiness? Should teenagers give in to peer pressure? Teenage girls will be all too familiar with this dilemma. It can be a tough, cruel world in the zoo that is school.

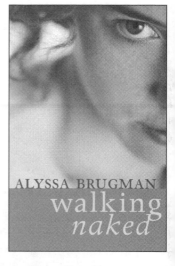

Megan has always felt secure among her group. One day she is sent to detention and finds herself with Perdita, tagged 'The Freak' by most. Every school has one! Despite herself, Meg begins to see the real Perdita, an intelligent, articulate, intellectually sophisticated girl. Brugman realistically portrays the emotional turmoil and difficult choices Meg faces. There is a lot at stake for Meg: will she lose her friends and her place in a safe universe? Ultimately, the choices she makes have terrible consequences.

Walking Naked is the first of Brugman's books to be published in the US and was described by one reviewer as 'an extremely powerful piece of literature'. The book is given further emotional power by well-placed pieces of poetry. Brugman seems to have a direct line to the inner world and social behaviour of teenage girls, and she does not cast any of the characters or their actions in a rosy light.

Brugman's latest book, **SOLO** (2007), is a psychological thriller that shows her range.

more girls' stuff ➤➤➤

girls' stuff

FIFTEEN LOVE Robert Corbet YA AUSTRALIA 2003
Rashelle, thirteen, wrote about *Fifteen Love*: 'Will is captivated by
Mia's beauty, but isn't confident enough to talk to her. Mia thinks boys
are immature and only think about themselves . . . This story grabs any
teenager . . . who falls in love or wants to know how it feels.'

THE GETTING OF WISDOM Henry Handel Richardson A/YA AUSTRALIA 1910
A turn-of-the-20th century Australian classic. An unconventional
country girl struggles to fit into boarding school life. The nastiness
of other girls, the death of her father, and her musical talents
complicate life.

LEAVING JETTY ROAD Rebecca Burton YA AUSTRALIA 2004
A year when everything changes for three best friends. Nat gets a job
and meets Josh, solitary Lise takes control of her life and her weight,
and popular Sofia falls in love and gets a nose ring!

LITTLE WOMEN Louisa May Alcott YA/A USA 1868
Alcott's charming story of Meg, Jo, Beth and Amy was unusual when
it was published because of its portrayal of the headstrong, boyish
Jo, determined to be true to herself. We can now also read Geraldine
Brooks's 2006 Pulitzer Prize–winning, **MARCH**, which boldly imagines
the life of John March, the absent father from *Little Women*.

SURVIVING AMBER Charlotte Calder YA AUSTRALIA 2005
When cool, self-absorbed, city girl Amber and her mother and sister,
join Amber's cousins on a remote farm, trouble is inevitable . . . until
a disaster turns the girls to each other.

PIRATES Celia Rees Y/YA UK 2003
A swashbuckling tale full of sword fights, murder, true love and more.
Set around the Caribbean during the 18th century, the heroic pirates
are girls! Rees also weaves in the plight of slaves – and women.

WITH LOTS OF LOVE FROM GEORGIA Brigid Lowry YA AUSTRALIA 2005
Georgia writes endless lists and negotiates friendships, life with her
mum, shopping, photography and finding a job. Will she find that
boy? And is her bum too big?

Will ➤ MARIA BOYD

YA AUSTRALIA 2006

Me, I was a soccer-playing skip, an honorary wog, though I'd pulled out this season. I just wasn't interested. Something else Danielli had given me a hard time about. I thought about what he said about me being different from last year. I didn't know what to think about that. Danielli and the others reckoned I was going through a difficult time. No doubt they'd collect the moon incident as further evidence to support this finding.

Seventeen-year-old Will is having a hard time. This has something to do with his absent father, but Will is reluctant even to mention his father, so it's a while before we find out the truth. In the meantime, Will keeps doing crazy, if harmless, things – like mooning the girls in the local Catholic girls' school bus. So, of course, he keeps getting into trouble. But he gets on well with, and really cares for, his mother.

Part of the charm of this debut novel is the portrait of a gentle, sophisticated, but quite ordinary lad with a self-deprecating line in humour and some sharply observed comments on what happens around him. There is nothing really heavy, but lots of difficult stuff that Will can't come to grips with, as we see from the extract above. People care about Will, but when his English teacher, Mr Andrew, comes up with a novel punishment for the mooning effort, Will just wants to disappear. Only nerds and geeks participate in the school musical. What will it do to his 'cool' reputation?

As well as playing in the muscical band, Will is expected to be a general dogsbody. Soon, Will has to cope with the adulation of Zac, the 'Freak', an eccentric Year 7 boy, who inadvertently teaches Will a lot about stereotypes and acceptance – the themes of the book. Then lead singer, Mark, who is also 'different', confides in Will. Will is surprised that Mark seems happy to sing and is comfortable with his sexuality. But the biggest event in Will's startling new life is the female lead, the gorgeous Elizabeth. Mr Andrew's clever 'punishment' turns everything around for Will.

in praise of pink books

by Lili Wilkinson

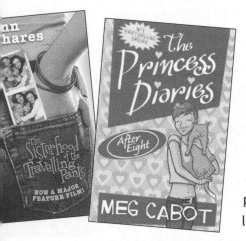

To say (as many have) that Pink Books are vapid trash is like saying that pink is for girls. Pink *is* for girls. But pink is also for Pink Floyd, pink elephants and Mr Pink from **Reservoir Dogs**. And while some Pink Books *are* trash, others explore family, ecology, politics, showbiz, sex, sexuality, love and friendship.

A Pink Book doesn't necessarily have a pink cover. **Emma** and **Jane Eyre** are Pink Books. A Pink Book has a female protagonist. It's realistic and contemporary, and is wryly funny. The focus is on personal relationships.

At the wholemeal-bread end of the Pink Book scale is **The Sisterhood of the Travelling Pants** by Ann Brashares. It brims over with messages like Nice Boys Wait and A Girl's Best Friend is her Best Friend. Sarra Manning's **Guitar Girl** is more grungy than girly, looking at the highs and lows of superstardom. Louise Rennison's **Angus, Thongs and Full-Frontal Snogging** is about Georgia Nicolson's struggles in love while she tries to keep control of her boy-entrancers and her nunga-nungas.

My all-time favourite Pink Book is **Ready or Not** (see page 288). It's the sequel to Meg Cabot's **All American Girl**. In Book One, Samantha Madison becomes famous for accidentally saving the President's life, and ends up dating his son, David. In **Ready or Not**, Sam has much bigger things on her mind. Is she ready to sleep with David? Sex, contraception and masturbation are all explored humorously and honestly. If Melvin Burgess had written this book, it would be banned. But because it's got a pink cover and it's by that nice lady who wrote **The Princess Diaries**, it slips under the radar.

Cecily von Ziegesar's **Gossip Girl**, on the other hand, sets off smoke-detectors, makes alarm bells ring and forces everyone to evacuate the building. It's about a bunch of bright young things living in New York. They drink, take drugs, have sex, and are obsessed with designer brands and labels. Feminist Naomi Wolf's reaction to the series has been particularly vitriolic: 'Sex and shopping take their places on a barren stage, as though, even for teenagers, these are the only dramas left.'

Naomi's missing the point. Pink Books critique banality and consumerism. The whole point of **Gossip Girl** is that although these girls have money and clothes and status, they are not happy. And that isn't subtext, it's just plain old text: 'Serena sighed . . . If only true love was something you could buy.'

Certainly some characters in Pink Books are awful. But that doesn't mean they're going to corrupt our children. Think of Evelyn Waugh's **Vile Bodies**, Brett Easton Ellis's **American Psycho** or Peter Carey's **Bliss**. Do we really think that the media-savvy teenagers of today are unable to recognise the delicious satire of Cynthia D Grant's **Cannibals**?

These books aren't corrupting anyone's moral fibre. They tell us that no matter how much money you have, or where you live, the problems facing teenagers are the same. Bring on the Pink.

my place in the world

Why are so many people desperate to find a safe place? People the world over have faced war, poverty, religious persecution, class or gender inequality, diseases, epidemics such as AIDS, scarcity of drugs and medical aid, and poverty and lack of educational and employment opportunities. Many people, including hundreds of thousands of young people, have lost families, been made homeless and spent years in refugee camps and detention centres. They all hope to find homes, work, education and peace.

Even when people have been in a country for generations there may be racial tension between groups, such as those of Asian and Caribbean origin in the UK, and blacks and whites in South Africa or the USA. In affluent Australia, many Aboriginal people still live in appalling conditions. Hostility towards groups (such as Lebanese Australians) who have lived here for generations can flare, and asylum seekers have increasingly met a less-than-friendly welcome. Economic and social hardship, a sense of alienation, and political and social attitudes may lead to many young people struggling to find acceptance and their place in the world. Such dramatic and tragic situations can fire the imagination of writers, generate absorbing stories and provide readers with ways of walking in the shoes of others.

Aliki Says ➤ IRINI SAVVIDES

YA AUSTRALIA 2006

They headed off. Liza looking for a yiayia she had not wanted in her house in the first place. Pavlos looking for a mother he had not talked to in ten years, and Maria looking for the woman who had changed her life more in the past few weeks than ever before . . .

If I find her, I'll kill her, thought Aliki. Fair go. Hasn't she caused enough trouble? Where on earth was she wandering to? And where am I going, anyway?

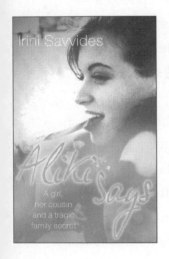

Liza and Aliki are cousins and best friends heading into their final school year. Both are bright. Aliki is gifted in literature, writes poetry and loves to argue. When their Yiayia (grandmother) arrives from Greece, suffering from Alzheimer's disease, the past comes with her.

Aliki's confusion and anger are fuelled by her need to know how her mother died on a trip to Greece, and Yiayia's role in this. She craves her father's attention and is hostile to her stepmother and to life in their opulent 'marble mausoleum' decorated in 'Napkin White'. But when Yiayia goes missing, Aliki's plan to escape founders, and the family is forced to pull together and face the secrets of the past.

Savvides uses the preparation for a performance of *King Lear* as a running commentary on the complexities of dealing with ageing, mental deterioration and family tensions. She weaves poetry and her own passion for teaching, writing and literature into an emotion-filled roller-coaster of a story.

The Birthmark ➤ BETH MONTGOMERY

YA AUSTRALIA 2006

Like many Gilbertese, Tepu's family had come to Tevua to gain work mining for phosphate. He'd forgotten almost everything of his life in the Gilberts, everything except the gifts from his grandfather: the black stone and a few words about magic.

A dramatic story of how the past can haunt the present. Alternating between 1942 and 2004, Montgomery's first novel is rare in its portrayal of the lives of people who have lived for a long time on islands just north of Australia. The fictionalised Tevua could well be Nauru, exploited by the British and Australians – and by the Japanese during World War II – for its rich deposits of phosphate. Montgomery's focus is the resilience and loyalty of the Tevuans and the Gilbertese (who coexist on Tevua) in the face of suffering and treachery under the Japanese. Gradually, the 2004 story of Hector and his wise Ibu (grandfather) are linked back to the terrible betrayal by the Japanese of young Tepu and his beloved Edouwe, living on a leper colony. The impact of strong cultural beliefs, magic and powerful talismans is interwoven with the contemporary sense of alienation and abandonment experienced by many indigenous communities. Also intertwined is the story of teenage Lily, who grapples with problems so often present in stories about contemporary Pacific Island or Aboriginal existence: boys, alcohol, drugs, boredom, and parents rendered ineffective by these elements. Lily's story and the involvement of Christina, a sympathetic Australian girl, make it possible to unravel the grim saga of the past and its connection to the present, and to create a story of and for today.

Dark Dreams: Australian refugee stories by young writers aged 11–20 years

➤ SONJA DECHIAN, HEATHER MILLAR AND EVA SALLIS (eds)

YA/A AUSTRALIA 2004

Since I opened my eyes into this world I heard the sound of rockets, missiles and all kinds of artillery firing around my house . . .

I don't have any good memories of my childhood. One of my memories is that of losing my playmates. One day my friend named Maryam . . . was suddenly blown in the air by an explosion from a Soviet Union bomb. Her body was never found. (Nooria Wazefadost, fifteen.)

This valuable book for our confused times is the result of a national competition titled 'Australia **is** Refugees'. Young people aged eleven to twenty were asked to listen to and then write down the story of someone who came to Australia as a refugee, and many of them heard stories that amazed, dismayed and moved them. Even family members heard tales of escape and hardship (for example, from Vietnam) that had been kept secret. There are personal stories, friends' stories and stories from people who are still in detention centres. The collection is often grim and reflects poorly on Australia, ostensibly a compassionate and egalitarian country that upholds the right to a fair go. However, the stories are also testimony to the resilience and spirit of young people and their families.

An equally powerful and impressive second volume of stories, **NO PLACE LIKE HOME,** was published in November 2005. The *No Place Like Home* competition invited young writers to tell stories of refugees or indigenous Australians who had been displaced. Writers were encouraged to focus on what it means to be exiled or forced to leave home, and how people cope and rebuild their lives.

three **different** ways
of reading about **refugees**

AUSTRALIA AND THE REFUGEE/ASYLUM SEEKER ISSUE
John Kilner YA AUSTRALIA 2004

An excellent resource for middle and upper secondary students
that provides background and context to some of the rich
fiction available on this subject. This comprehensive overview
addresses key questions such as: Who are refugees and where
do they come from? Why does Australia take immigrants and
refugees and how many should we or can we take? Should
asylum seekers be kept in detention centres here and/or
offshore? It also examines major events such as the Tampa
incident and the 'children overboard' affair. John Kilner is the
manager of *The Age* Education Unit, and his focus is partly
on examining the role and responsibilities of the media in
presenting these issues

REFUGEES David Miller Y/YA AUSTRALIA 2004

A beautiful, compelling, award-winning picture book for all
ages about the plight of two displaced ducks looking for refuge.
Miller writes, 'In the current global political environment . . .
I wanted [to] show that the displaced are real and with genuine
needs.' The few telling words accompany the rich colours and
skilful assembly of Miller's distinctive collages.

THE ARRIVAL Shaun Tan Y/YA/A AUSTRALIA 2006

A stunning graphic novel illuminating the plight of displaced
people everywhere (see page 198).

Falling ➤ ANNE PROVOOST Translated by John Nieuwenhuizen

YA/A BELGIUM 1997

Benoît: *'And, please, don't tell me I hate foreigners. Other cultures fascinate me. I have tremendous respect for them. But their different character cannot be fully developed here. Can you imagine: Africans in jeans, Indians in runners? That can't be what we intend? We must protect them from Western influences and send them back to the land of their birth.'*

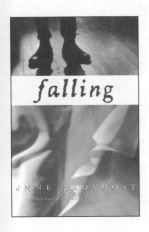

It's a hot summer in a small hilltop village in Belgium. Lucas's grandfather has just died, and Lucas gradually realises he knew little about the old man. Lucas is soon forced to confront his grandfather's role in the betrayal of some Jewish children to the Nazis.

The book starts with the consequences of a horrific accident that requires Lucas to make a terrible decision about the young visiting dancer, Caitlin, to whom he is attracted. Caitlin is staying in the convent next door, the same convent where the Jewish children were hidden during the war. Now, it is proposed that some refugees be housed there. Will they also be betrayed and the past repeated?

Benoît, a clever, plausible extremist, wants action, but also wants to keep his own hands clean. Lucas becomes a handy agent. Bored and confused about life, he becomes easy prey for those, like Benoît, who are stirring up racist violence and offering simplistic answers to complex questions about the past, and the situation of refugees and the unemployed today.

Falling asks us to think hard about intentions and consequences, about the seductive power of extremist politics, and about the importance of understanding history and taking responsibility for one's actions. Why are refugees increasingly unwelcome in many countries, including Australia? Why did the Cronulla and Redfern riots occur? Provoost's complex, multi-award-winning book is provocative, deeply political and entirely relevant to today's Australia.

The Glory Garage ➤ NADIA JAMAL AND TAGHRED CHANDAB

YA AUSTRALIA 2005

From the authors: '*We have quite a few nevers to our names. We never went on a school camp, we never wore a swimming costume and we never slept over at a friend's place . . . Strictly speaking, none of this was about our religion, but our families' version of the Lebanese Muslim culture in Australia.*'

It's time young Muslim people see themselves in books, and tell their diverse stories. *The Glory Garage* is subtitled: *Growing up Lebanese Muslim in Australia.* These snapshots, by two feisty young journalists, personalise aspects of their experience: differing family values and expectations, the spectre of arranged marriages, the conflicting demands of being Muslim and living in a secular society. Yet the girls share laughs, study, friendship, shopping (one has sixteen dinner sets in her 'glory garage'). While not as tough as the writing of Malorie Blackman or Bali Rai, or as detailed and personal as Randa Abdel-Fattah's books, Jamal and Chandab's stories are engaging and important, and remind us how little of Australia's rich non–Anglo Saxon multicultural life is explored in books, especially for and by young people.

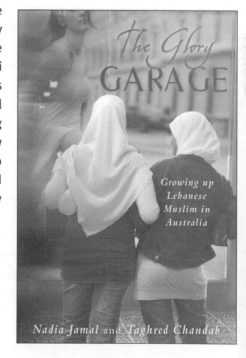

Just Like Tomorrow

➤ **FAÏZA GUÈNE Translated by Sarah Adams**

A/YA FRANCE 2006

The teachers, when they weren't on strike . . . decided I was shut down or depressed or something . . . I guess I've been like this since my dad left. He went far away. Back to Morocco, to marry another woman who's younger and more fertile than my mum . . . Dad wanted a son. For his pride, his reputation, the family honour . . . It's been over six months.

Sharp, sassy and hurt, Doria tells the short, angry story of her life with her struggling mother in a highrise north of Paris. The first work of Guène, a nineteen-year-old writer of Algerian parentage, this has been a surprise bestseller in France. Full of grim humour and sly observations about growing up Muslim and poor in France, *Just Like Tomorrow* presents life as it is lived by others, too: shopkeepers, drug addicts, petty criminals and families trying to cope with

bureaucracy and language problems. Some take advantage, but some friends – and even social workers – actually help. Things change. Despite her failure at school, Doria is bright enough to take advantage of the hairdressing course she reluctantly takes up. She is also proud and delighted to see her mother learning to read, fighting exploitation and taking steps towards independence. Doria concludes, 'I shouldn't spend so much time with Nabil. I'm getting way too political . . .' We understand that she is finding her way and her voice, and we cheer for her!

The Last Taboo ➤ BALI RAI

YA UK 2006

Everyone who had seen the fight had to give statements . . . It turned out that Mr Brown had been stabbed and was seriously injured. Two lads from our school also had stab wounds, and six from the other school had serious injuries too. And one of the residents, who had tried to stop the fighting, had collapsed from a heart attack.

The violence goes on and on. Much of it stems from a clearly misguided belief in racial and family solidarity; in keeping to – and looking after – one's own. Sports matches between schools are breeding grounds for racial tension that often spills over into street life. In this climate, some think that Simran, of Punjabi Indian origin, is asking for trouble when she becomes increasingly involved with the handsome, black Tyrone. This is the 'last taboo', despite the fact that Simran's parents both escaped arranged marriages, have black friends and reject racial stereotyping. Family members meddle, jealousies flare and the local lads run amok as they try to enforce their notion of how to protect 'their' girls' honour.

Another rough, tough, uncompromising story from a writer who uses the language of the streets to boldly portray, and challenge, the norms of life in the grittier suburbs of the UK. A follow up to **RANI AND SUKH** (2004).

more bali rai ➤➤➤

bali rai

(UN)ARRANGED MARRIAGE 2001
This story, set partly in England and partly in the Punjab, is of a Punjabi boy, Manny, who is resisting the marriage that his father has arranged for him.

THE CREW 2003
Meet Billy, Jas, Della, Will and Ellie – the 'Crew'. In the concrete jungle, the big city where they live, they need each other for support, especially when they find a very large bundle of bank notes. They warn, 'Mess with one of us – then you have to deal with us all . . .'

RANI AND SUKH 2004
Rani is a Sandhu, and Sukh is a Bains, so going out together is asking for trouble. The story swings from modern-day Britain to the Punjab of the 1960s and back again in a ceaseless cycle of tragedy, blood feuds and conflict.

THE WHISPER 2005
About the same 'crew' as above. In the ghetto, things are getting tough again during 'Operation Cleanup'. Someone is pointing the finger at Crew members for naming drug dealers. Ellie is picked on at school; Billy is mugged and his house is targeted. Before someone gets seriously hurt, the real culprit must be found.

A Little Piece of Ground ➤ ELIZABETH LAIRD

YA UK 2003

*Karim had just scored a peach of a goal and was enjoying his triumph
with crows of delight when the caretaker came running around the side of
the building. His red and white checked 'keffiyeh' headdress was flapping
round his shoulders and he was waving his arms urgently.*

*'Out! You've all got to get out now!' he shouted. 'I'm shutting up the
compound! I've got to get home before the tanks come back'.*

*Karim felt a thump of anger and savagely kicked at the ground.
The precious two hours of normal life were over. There was no telling when
the next time would be.*

A timely, penetrating look at life in one of the world's hot spots:
Ramallah, in Palestine. The lives of Karim and his family are circumscribed by the curfews, tanks, shooting and shortages caused by
the Israeli presence. The minute the curfew lifts, members of the
family dash in different directions: father to see how his electrical
goods store is surviving and if there are any customers, mother to
stock up on food and urgent antibiotics for the baby, older brother to
attend to secret (political?) business, and Karim to find friends and
snatch a game of soccer at school or on a disused piece of land. Life
is constantly dangerous, but play, courage – and
defiance – keep people going.

Laird has lived and worked in the Middle
East and Africa and has a sharp understanding
of, as well as sympathy for, the lives of children
and young people caught in conflict and poverty.
Read also her moving book **THE GARBAGE KING**
(2003), about children and even babies trying to
survive on the streets of Ethiopia.

The Other Side of Truth ➤ BEVERLEY NAIDOO

Y/YA UK 2000

Sade is slipping her English book into her schoolbag when Mama screams. Two sharp cracks splinter the air. She hears her father's fierce cry, rising, falling.

'No! No!'

The revving of a car and skidding of tyres smother his voice . . .

Papa is kneeling in the driveway, Mama partly curled against him . . . His strong hands grip her, trying to halt the growing scarlet monster. But it has already spread down her bright white nurse's uniform. It stains the earth around them.

The children of a Nigerian activist and journalist are smuggled out of their country when their mother is gunned down by members of the corrupt military government. The bullets were clearly meant for Sade and little Femi's father. But treachery awaits the children in London. The woman who was supposed to look after them disappears and they find themselves abandoned and lost in the huge, cold city. The uncle they were meant to stay with is also nowhere to be found. Despite having no money, the children know they can't ask for help as they are in the country illegally. What will happen to them, and how welcoming will this democratic country be?

The book won the Carnegie Medal but is controversial for its toughness and its author's determination not to sugar-coat the situation for younger readers. Naidoo was born in South Africa, and her writing reflects a strong interest in cross-cultural issues. She has set several books in South Africa and edited the notable collection **OUT OF BOUNDS: SEVEN STORIES OF CONFLICT AND HOPE** (2003), in which each story is set in a different decade.

Red Moon ➤ RACHEL ANDERSON

YA UK 2006

*'Such desolation,' said Anne-Marie. 'Too much of desolation. This is
a too sad destination for them, whoever they are. They must be expecting
a welcome so much better.'*

Hamish said, 'Are those Turks then?'

*Anne-Marie said sharply, 'The Turks? How should I know? But whoever
they are the sight of them is depressing.'*

Anne-Marie is French, hence the stilted English. She and Hamish are
driving to France after Hamish's father has been killed in a random
stabbing. (The randomness of what happens to people is one of the
themes of this book.) In the beautiful seaside town in the south of
France, the local people and dignitaries welcome Anne-Marie and
Hamish. But they are much less welcoming to North African asylum
seekers such as Ahmed. Washed up on the shore almost below
Hamish's window, Amhed is the only survivor of the machinations
of people smugglers. He comes from an unspecified North African
country, made dysfunctional through violence and poverty. He's one
of the thousands who head for France, full of false expectations and
with no idea of where they are going. Inevitably, the two boys are
thrown together and Hamish must take a stand. These experiences
shape the rest of his life.

An easy-to-read story about a difficult subject, this book feels
particularly relevant at a time when many governments and people,
including in Australia, are increasingly hostile to so called 'queue
jumpers' and 'illegals'.

Refugee Boy ➤ BENJAMIN ZEPHANIAH

YA UK 2001

Ethiopia: *As the family lay sleeping, soldiers kicked down the door of the house and entered, waving their rifles around erratically and shouting at the top of their voices. Alem ran into the room where his parents were, to find that they had been dragged out of bed dressed only in their nightclothes, and forced to stand facing the wall.*

When bloody war breaks out between Ethiopia and Eritrea, the implications for Alem's family are horrific. His father is Ethiopian, his mother Eritrean. Alem's father takes him on a short holiday to London and, in a desperate attempt to save him, leaves Alem behind in a boarding house, hoping he will be granted asylum. Alem is well looked after at first and attends a local high school, where he proves to be an excellent and popular student. Then the British immigration bureaucracy grinds into action and it looks as though Alem must leave. But local students, together with teachers and the community, become involved, and lively, well-planned grassroots action provides Alem with the support and home he needs and deserves.

Saving Francesca ➤ MELINA MARCHETTA

YA AUSTRALIA 2003

*This morning my mother didn't get out of bed . . . this morning there is
no song. There is no advice on how to make friends with the bold and
the interesting. No twelve point plan on the best way to make a name for
myself in a hostile environment. No motivational messages stuck on my
mirror urging me to do something that scares me everyday.*

There's just silence.

Everything changes for Francesca on the day her mother, Mia,
fails to get out of bed. How can the family function without her?
Francesca attends St Sebastian's, 'a predominantly all-boys school
that has opened its doors to girls in Year Eleven for the first time'.
She says, 'There are thirty of us girls at St Sebastian's and I want so
much not to do the teenage angst thing, but I have to tell you that I
hate the life that, according to my mother, I'm not actually having.'
Marchetta is very good at doing 'the teenage girl thing' and also
has an unerring ear for teenage dialogue. It is soon obvious that
Francesca *is* angst-ridden and that her mother's sudden descent
into deep depression makes her life even more difficult. Apart from
needing her mother and negotiating school and friends, she also has
to pay attention to her younger brother, her father and the demands
of her extended Italian family. There is a lot of living happening, a lot
of tears, laughter and unexpectedly loyal friends – and eventually
answers to questions about what *has* happened to Mia.

Marchetta's interests are school life, teenagers living between
cultures and the strengths and stresses of family life. Here, more
than ten years after the bestselling **LOOKING FOR ALIBRANDI**
(1992), she again successfully melds these three elements into a
strong, engaging story. In her next book, **ON THE JELLICOE ROAD**
(2006), Marchetta pursues similar themes, but with an intriguing
departure in style.

The Spare Room ➤ KATHRYN LOMER

YA AUSTRALIA 2004

Ours is a bit of a complicated relationship, I suppose, which is not surprising given its beginning. And I decided that one way to sort out how I feel would be to go over it all – my time in Australia, the things that happened between Angie and me. And the rest of the family for that matter. I thought that writing it all down might help me get it straight. I thought it might be like ringing and talking to you. So that's why I've started Satoshi, and why I'm writing to you.

A quiet, delicate first novel that showcases the author's artistry and poetic flair. Akira, twenty, goes from Japan to Tasmania to learn English. His host family, the Moffats, are welcoming, but Akira soon realises that the silences and tensions within the family are not due to his inability to understand English. Why is everyone so sad? Why does the mother hate motorbikes? And why does Angie seem so resentful of Akira? What is the secret everyone avoids confronting? We see the complexities of understanding a new language and trying to read the unspoken signs of a very foreign culture. As Akira gains confidence and takes on some of the more outgoing traits of the Australians around him, some of these mysteries are solved and Akira too can lay the past to rest. In the meantime, Akira also discovers a love of cooking, a talent he would never have been able to pursue in Japan, where it was simply assumed he would enter his father's company.

A Step from Heaven ➤ AN NA

YA KOREA/USA 2001

Apa is not happy.

Uhmma is not happy.

Halmoni, who is old and has a sleepy blanket face, says that a long time ago Apa was young like me and she could boss him round.
But not anymore.

Now, Halmoni can only shake her head when Apa comes home late stinking like the insides of the bottles that get left on the street. Her lips pinch tight, then she hides with Ummah and me. Because when Apa is too quiet with the squinty eye, it is better to hide until he falls asleep or else there will be breaking everywhere.

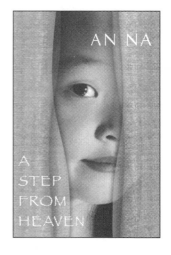

At four, Young Ju leaves her fishing village in Korea believing she will be flying to heaven. Real life in Mi Gook (America) proves very unlike paradise. We follow Young Ju's difficult existence until she is a teenager. Very poor, struggling to deal with her father's disappointment and anger, trying to learn English and fit in, caught between two cultures, Young Ju is wretched. Trying to hide her 'Korean life' from her school mates and her 'American life' from her parents is complicated and exhausting and makes Young Ju very lonely. She also fears for her mother's safety as her father's drinking gets increasingly out of control.

Korean culture says a family must cope with its own problems. But it is only when Young Ju decides to break with this tradition that she begins to find an identity. The power of this story is in its spare, flowing, poetic writing, rather than in the sad situation it portrays. It will make you cry, but also rejoice in Young Ju's courage and the beauty she still manages to find everywhere.

Ten things I hate about me ➤ RANDA ABDEL-FATTAH

YA/A AUSTRALIA 2006

Unlike Danielle and Ahmed, I don't have the courage to be upfront about who I am. I'd rather not deal with people wondering if I keep a picture of Osama Bin Laden in the shape of a love heart under my pillow . . . So I've Anglicised my name. And dyed my hair blonde. And I sometimes wear blue contact lenses.

Jamie is exhausted from concealing the fact that she is really Jamilah, and that she is bilingual and a budding musician. Since her mother died (when Jamie was nine), her father has become increasingly protective. Jamie has a 'Charter of Curfew Rights' on her fridge. Father seems constantly focused on what others in the Lebanese Australian community might think. He means well, but is bereft and lonely, working long hours as a taxi driver though he is university educated. Jamie's older sister is a feminist and political activist. Father can no longer control her, or their brother, who, of course, has much more freedom. But it is at school that Jamie suffers most, especially from arrogant, bigoted Peter and his mates and female groupies. Jamie is desperate to gain their approval and attend the Year 10 formal. Why can't she be more like the appealing new boy, Tim, who ignores taunts and goes his own way? Jamie's only solace comes from the understanding 'John' she meets in an online chat room. But who is John?

As in her first, strong book, **DOES MY HEAD LOOK BIG IN THIS?** (2005), Abdel-Fattah presents a compelling insider's account of feeling trapped between two cultures. Why do some girls struggle to be themselves? And do our leaders and schools truly foster tolerance and a respect for difference?

growing up **between cultures** in australia

ALIEN SON Judah Waten A/YA 1952
Exploring the immigrant experience, this powerful
collection of stories has been described as one of the
'greatest of all Australian books'. Having arrived in
1949 and suffering for my 'funny name' and my exotic
salami-on-rye bread lunches, I found recognition and
insights in these stories.

LOOKING FOR ALIBRANDI Melina Marchetta YA/A 1992
Considered the first Italian–Australian young adult novel.
A lively, hugely popular bestseller about growing up
between two cultures. A stirring movie, too.

A PROMISED LAND? Alan Collins YA 2001
In this compilation of **THE BOYS FROM BONDI** (1987),
GOING HOME (1993) and **JOSHUA** (1995), Collins tracks
the lives of Jewish Australians from Depression-era
Australia to a greater understanding of the Holocaust
and the ongoing tensions between Jews and Arabs.

WILLOW TREE AND OLIVE Irini Savvides YA 2001
A Greek *Looking for Alibrandi*, but more sombre, as
there are secrets and pain in Olive's life. Poetry, myths,
the Greek people, their warm sun and olive groves help
her to heal.

Under the Persimmon Tree

➤ SUZANNE FISHER STAPLES

Y/YA USA 2005

'Why won't you go back to Kunduz with your uncle?' asks Nusrat.
'He will take me back and force me to marry someone. He will send me
away and he will take my father's land. My father did not want him to
have our farm any more than he wanted the Taliban to have it.'
Najmah speaks bitterly.

A long, dangerous journey from an Afghani village brings Najmah and Nusrat together. Both love learning and are fascinated by stars. Both have to make difficult decisions about the future. In Peshawar, Pakistan, Najmah is a refugee. Her father and brother were taken by the Taliban, and her mother and newborn brother were killed by American bombs. Nusrat is an American teacher who has married and become a devout Muslim. Like her, we learn that most Muslims are not fundamentalists and that, when practised truly, most religions are similar. Nusrat's husband, a doctor working with the wounded, has gone missing and she has set up a small school for refugee children under the persimmon tree in her garden. She is generous and wise but desperately sad and lonely. Danger lurks everywhere, especially for women and girls. Under the Taliban, having the coloured hem of a dress showing beneath a burka can cost you your life. Even when the Taliban is ousted, life is tough.

Staples's book, like Deborah Ellis's Parvana series (see page 162) shows what Afghani refugees who have made their way to Australia (and other countries) have had to endure. Yet Staples also shows that amid the hardship and violence there is warmth, friendship and a desire to improve people's lives, especially those of children. She always eschews stereotypes and generalisations. As in her much-loved books **DAUGHTER OF THE WIND** (1989) and the sequel, **HAVELI** (1993), Staples reveals her fascination, respect and compassion for those from other cultures.

the tragedy of afghanistan

BOY OVERBOARD 2003 and **GIRL UNDERGROUND** 2005
Morris Gleitzman Y AUSTRALIA
Gleitzman has had the distinction of being criticised by the
Minster for Immigration for bringing the plight of refugees to the
attention of younger readers, who, the Minister believed, should
be shielded from such tough issues. These moving, accessible tales
for younger readers, using the 'hook' of children's love of soccer,
put a human face to the situation of asylum seekers and to the
notorious Tampa and 'children overboard' sagas. Informed by
real-life examples, the books expose disturbing attitudes toward
those seeking asylum in Australia.

THE KITE RUNNER Khaled Hosseini A/YA AFGHANISTAN/USA 2004
A first novel and runaway bestseller, this book manages to meld
the personal and political. Amir, son of a wealthy businessman,
and Hassan, their servant's son, are inseparable. However, in one
annual kite-running competition, Amir betrays Hassan. Many
years later, Amir's guilt forces him from the safety and comfort of
the USA back to Afghanistan under the Taliban. Many twists and
secrets are revealed in this haunting story.

MY FORBIDDEN FACE Latifa Translated by Lisa Appignanesi
A/YA AFGHANISTAN/FRANCE 2002
An account, written under a pseudonym, of the privations and
pains of growing up under the Taliban (see page 180).

OUR WOMAN IN KABUL Irris Makler A/YA AUSTRALIA 2003
Australian journalist Irris Makler was one of the first to get into
Afghanistan once the Taliban took over. Documenting the US
invasion and the defeat of the Taliban in this harsh country, with
its proud but despairing people, she reveals what it was like to
be a female correspondent in this environment. She explains the
background to the rise of the Taliban and Osama Bin Laden.

▶▶▶

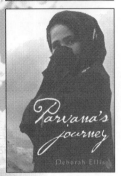

PARVANA 2001, **PARVANA'S JOURNEY** 2002 and **SHAUZIA** 2003 Deborah Ellis Y/YA CANADA
A bestselling trilogy about the plight of a middle-class girl caught under the Taliban in Afghanistan, and about the dangers faced, and heroism shown, by Parvana and many others she encounters. Engaging and very popular with younger readers.

THE SEWING CIRCLES OF HERAT Christina Lamb A/YA UK 2004
A noted writer and foreign correspondent, Lamb gained unique insight by covering Afghanistan during the end of the war with the Soviet Union. Access to many high-level insiders has given her account depth. Like Deborah Ellis and Latifa, Lamb shows the courage of women and girls who continued to attend and run secret schools. She also explains that much of what happened under the Taliban was a perversion of what the Koran decrees.

SORAYA THE STORYTELLER Rosanne Hawke Y/YA AUSTRALIA 2004
This book covers the same territory as **WALK IN MY SHOES** (see page 163), but for a younger audience, focusing on the uncertainties of life under a Temporary Protection Visa. This lovely, sad, gentle tale is enriched by stories from **A THOUSAND AND ONE NIGHTS** and by stories written by Soraya that recall the terrors of her family's life in Afghanistan under the Taliban.

THE SWALLOWS OF KABUL Yasmina Khadra A/YA FRANCE/ALGERIA 2004
In this short, harrowing novel of life in Afghanistan under Taliban rule, Khadra shows the effects of repression on two Kabul couples. Yasmina Khadra is the pseudonym of former Algerian army officer Mohamed Moulessehoul, who took the feminine pseudonym to avoid scrutiny by military censors while he was still in the Algerian army. He went into exile in France in 2000. He has also written controversial books about the civil war in Algeria.

Walk in My Shoes ➤ ALWYN EVANS

YA AUSTRALIA 2004

As I waited I wondered, as I often did, if ever we got out of this dot on the empty, wide red land, where we would live. Is it all the same as this? How would we earn money to live on? The land looked so barren. So dry. But I wanted to leave the Camp so desperately.

Having lost father and siblings in Afghanistan, those left in Gulnessa's family expect Australia to be a place of shelter and a place to call home. Instead they face years in the hot and hostile environment of a detention centre. Some make it, but many don't. If they do get out, there is another gruelling struggle to gain shelter, work and, above all, permanent resident status. However, Gulnessa, her family and her young man, Abdul, do meet compassionate Australians in and out of the detention centre.

Evans is a West Australian writer and activist who has worked with asylum seekers and so can accurately describe the life behind razor wire experienced by many who came here in the hope of freedom and security. She writes from outrage and a desire to show that fiction can inform, and perhaps change, attitudes and lives. Her story tells of difficult experiences in a straightforward but engaging way. Many young readers say they have been shocked, but also inspired, by Gulnessa's journey.

White Ghost Girls ➤ ALICE GREENWAY

YA/A UK 2006

Secret sisters. Shipwrecked sisters. Viet Cong sisters we call ourselves.

There's a story in the paper about a bomb in Wanchai blowing off a policeman's hand: 'A homemade bomb made from firecrackers stuffed in a biscuit tin.' Dozens of bombs have exploded in Hong Kong since the beginning of July . . .

Maybe it's unfair the way I remember it. Maybe I'm too hard on my father. Maybe my memory exaggerates. Maybe he knew everything. He just couldn't help us. Like we couldn't help him. He hides in tunnels, behind his camera lenses, like I hide in the dark from Frankie, don't answer questions, pretend to be asleep . . .

Hong Kong is to be handed back to Communist China. Red Guards and danger lurk. It is the sixties. The Vietnam War is raging. Kate is twelve, Frankie a little older. Their lively, beloved father is seldom home, being more and more consumed by photographing the war in Vietnam for *Time* magazine. Mother retreats into painting genteel landscapes. The girls are mostly cared for by their Amah, Ah Bing: testy, often foul-mouthed but wise, caring and with an acute sense of what is going wrong for the girls. She also tells them wonderful stories and provides them with a sense of place and history. Frankie grows daily more voluptuous, flaunts herself, flirts with men, takes more and more risks and behaves outrageously. Kate tries desperately to keep her sister safe but feels it shouldn't be her task. Both need the attention of their parents. On a trip with Ah Bing to nearby Lantau Island, Frankie rashly, but unintentionally, drags Kate into a situation that causes several deaths. Life for the girls and their family spirals into tragedy. The sea and the shimmering heat increase the hallucinatory effect of this beautifully written, haunting first novel about a period in history during the death throes of colonialism, when many lives were seriously dislocated.

The Year the Gypsies Came ➤ LINZI GLASS

YA/A USA 2006

In those vibrant years of the sixties my parents used a powerful formula that kept our family together. As soon as the tension between them became unbearable, they would invite a house guest to come and stay with us.

Linzi Glass says, 'The idea of writing about a dysfunctional family in a dysfunctional society and how love in all its many forms would be the glue to mend such a fractured family and country was the inspiration for my story.'

Emily tells of the complex, unhappy life in an affluent household on the outskirts of Johannesburg, South Africa, in the mid 1960s. Father imports fine Belgian chocolates. Mother is bored, frustrated and obsessed with her looks and fashion. She becomes increasingly reckless in her relationship with husband-of-a-friend Dennis, and she neglects her daughters, Emily and Sarah. The sisters are cared for by their black servant, Lettie, and the old Zulu doorman, Buza, who has a store of spell-binding fables that illuminate aspects of the girls' lives. Then the 'gypsies', a wandering, equally dysfunctional Australian family, turn up. Jock is a passionate but embittered nature photographer. (Unfortunately he talks like an American cowboy.) Sarah naively befriends the dangerous, lumbering Otis. Emily gets real friendship from the younger Streak. But there are too many secrets, too many tensions, too much anger, so what should be some much-needed distraction flares into violence and tragedy.

Born in South Africa, Glass still feels strongly about the corrosive impact of apartheid on both blacks and whites. This is an assured and ambitious first novel that demands attentive reading to reveal the links between the public and private horrors of the times.

lost without translation

by John Nieuwenhuizen

A memory from when I was twelve or fourteen. There was great excitement at my grandparents' home. My youngest uncle had just received the first paperback volume of what was going to be the complete novels of Charles Dickens – he had subscribed to the whole series. This was not too long after World War II, and such a publishing enterprise was a totally new experience. Paperback publication was new. But what's wrong with this story? – None of my uncles could read English! What's right with this story? The complete works of Dickens was being published in TRANSLATION!

You probably have fond (or scary!) childhood memories of hearing or reading fairy tales. Chances are, most of them were TRANSLATIONS. (Unless you were already fluent in Danish, German, French and Latin.)

And did you, too, graduate to Tintin and Asterix not too much later? Unless you were a very precocious French reader, you must have read them in TRANSLATION.

I don't know if you are religious or not, but you have probably read at least parts of the Bible. In TRANSLATION, of course: like most Anglophone people, your Aramaic and Ancient Hebrew and Greek aren't really up to it.

And as you grew up, you must have come across some quixotic person tilting at windmills! If you find this paragraph sounding a bit foreign, you're right: Don Quixote de la Mancha, the sad knight who fought windmills thinking they were dangerous giants, is the hero of one of the greatest novels of all time, written in Spanish by Cervantes, and accessible to most of us only in TRANSLATION.

And did you ever come across someone with a gargantuan appetite, given to telling Rabelaisian stories? The story of Gargantua and his son Pantagruel, which gave us those words, was written in French by François Rabelais, and we only know about it through TRANSLATIONS.

And what a wonderful ambition it is to travel around the world. In eighty days, of course. Did you get this idea from **Around the World in Eighty Days** by Jules Verne? Most unobligingly, he wrote this in French . . .

But enough of this frivolity. You are probably a serious and scientifically minded person. As such, you have of course heard about Einstein's theory of relativity. And although Einstein later lived in the US and wrote in English, the original paper on relativity was in German and had to be TRANSLATED for us.

And why did I become a TRANSLATOR from Dutch to English or at all? I realised one day that my own children (who only speak English, alas) had no access to most of the books that shaped my consciousness and helped form my values – their cultural heritage.

In short, TRANSLATION enriches our lives (and our language) and gives us access to the rich variety of cultures which are just that interesting bit different from ours. How much poorer we would be without **The Shadow of the Wind**, **War and Peace**, **The Diary of Anne Frank**, **Anna Karenina**, **Pippi Longstocking**, **Madame Bovary**, **Mimus**, **Emil and Karl**, **Crime and Punishment** and assorted Nobel Prize winners!

And for an hilarious thriller, try **The Fairy Gunmother** or **The Scapegoat** by French writer Daniel Pennac. (In TRANSLATION, of course!)

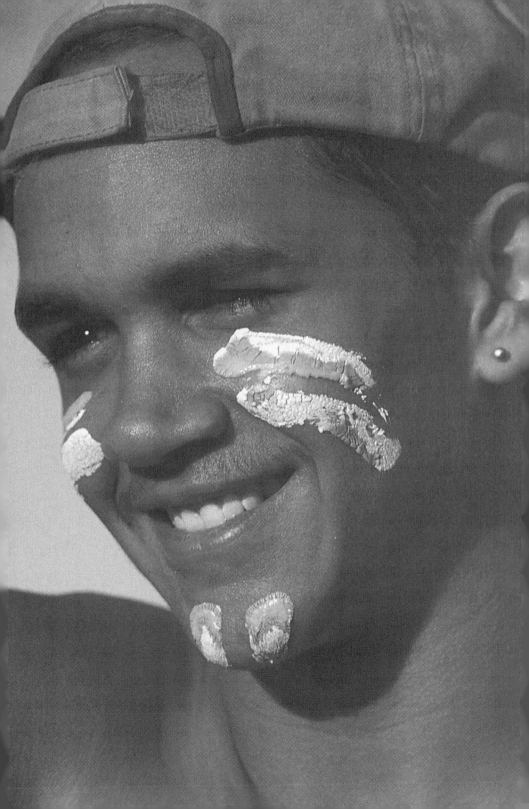

not such ordinary lives

Do you enjoy reading about exciting, fascinating or terrible experiences? Stories about extraordinary lives can be found in novels or in biographies, autobiographies or memoirs. There are intense personal experiences, stories of daring adventures and of growing up in difficult or unusual situations. There are tales of poverty and of coping with a disability or illness; of living in a war-torn country and of devotion to family or a cause. Some are sad and some scary. Some are full of adventure, daring and courage, and others mix all these qualities.

The Black Dress: Mary MacKillop's Early Years > PAMELA FREEMAN

Y/YA AUSTRALIA 2005

'Can I have a new dress, now?' Maggie asked . . .

'Yes!' said Mamma, smiling. 'What about you, Mary, what would you like?'

'Oh, Mary would like a new Bible, wouldn't you?' Annie teased.

'No, not a Bible, a new missal,' said Lexie. 'She's almost worn out the old one.'

'She doesn't need a missal,' Annie replied. 'She's memorised the Mass already.'

On the Read Alert blog, author Cassandra Golds wrote, 'My favourite book of 2005 was *The Black Dress* by Pamela Freeman. I thought that, in a marvellously unaffected and matter-of-fact kind of way, it was entirely successful in turning a stained glass window into a living, breathing woman.'

Mary MacKillop muses about her life, from her death bed in 1909. She is 67. This is a fictionalised first-person biography of the unconventional, devout – but never bigoted – Scottish Catholic girl who started the Institute of St Joseph in Penola, SA. Her mission was to provide free education to poor children, and, even more controversially, Aboriginal children, if they chose to attend.

The focus is on Mary's childhood with a warm, long-suffering mother and charming, intelligent, educated father. Loved passionately by his wife and children, Mary's father was, nevertheless, feckless, rash and outspoken to the point where he became unemployable. Mary had to work to help pay for food and rent. This is a strongly presented portrait of life in Australia in the second half of the 19th century. We see the generous support offered by large extended families but also the petty jealousies and hardships in families and within the church at a time when the expectations of the church pervaded every aspect of life. Mary MacKillop was beatified by the Pope in 1995 and is likely to become Australia's first saint.

Follow the Rabbit-Proof Fence

> ➤ DORIS PILKINGTON

Y/YA/A AUSTRALIA 1996

The fence cut through the country from south to north. It was a typical response by the white people to a problem of their own making.

For the three runaways, the fence was a symbol of love, home and security.

'We're nearly home,' said Molly without realising that they had merely reached the halfway mark, they had almost eight hundred kilometres to go.

'We found the fence now. It's gunna be easy,' she told her younger sisters. They were glad to hear that because each morning when they awoke they were never sure whether they would survive another day.

Doris Pilkington/Nugi Garimara tells the story of her mother, Molly, who, with her younger sister and cousin, was taken from her Aboriginal family in Western Australia in the 1930s. Fourteen-year-old Molly led the younger girls on an extraordinary 1600-kilometre walk home. Despite being tracked by native police and search planes, the girls survived by using their bush knowledge and following from south to north the rabbit-proof fence (supposedly built to keep rabbits from the east out of farms in the west). A powerful account of indomitable spirit, determination and survival in the face of a cruel, senseless policy to separate children from their families in the name of education and a misguided government view.

Ten years after the period in this account, Pilkington herself was removed from her home station and her mother and baby sister and committed to Moore River Native Settlement. At eighteen, Doris left the mission system and trained as a nursing aide. Later, she studied journalism. Her first book was **CAPRICE: A STOCKMAN'S DAUGHTER** (1991). In 2002, Australian director Phillip Noyce brought this dramatic story to the screen in the popular and much-praised film *Rabbit-Proof Fence*.

Great Australian Girls and the remarkable women they became ➤ SUSAN GEASON

A/YA AUSTRALIA 1999

Susan Geason writes in the introduction: '*What could a convict girl transported for horse theft have in common with a champion tennis player or a trapeze artist? How could a pioneer aviator be compared with a musical prodigy? . . . they all shared two unshakeable convictions – one was a strong belief in themselves; the other was the belief that girls can do anything.*'

The twenty-three revealing and fascinating stories of women, who began to make their mark as girls, include writer Sonya Hartnett (see pages 74, 75 and 219), whose first book, **TROUBLE ALL THE WAY,** was published when she was fifteen; and Mary MacKillop, whose story is told by Pamela Freeman (see page 70). Others whose lives are explored are swimmer Dawn Fraser; wheelchair racer Louise Sauvage; May Gibbs, creator of the children's classic **SNUGGLEPOT AND CUDDLEPIE;** and Monique Truong for 'Outwitting Kidnappers'. In 2001, Geason followed this volume with **AUSTRALIAN HEROINES: STORIES OF COURAGE AND SURVIVAL,** illuminating the lives of ten women who showed great determination to succeed or to survive or make a difference. One is Tasmanian Aboriginal woman Truganini, who died in 1876. She has become the symbol of the struggle and survival of Tasmanian Aboriginal people. Another is a holocaust survivor, and yet another is Susie Moroney, the famous marathon swimmer. Another, Mary Bryant, convict woman, sailed a small boat from Botany Bay to Timor in 1791 in her bid for freedom. All these girls and women, some from poor or disadvantaged backgrounds, showed that they could have lives less than ordinary.

uniquely australian lives

ANNIE'S COMING OUT Rosemary Crossley & Anne McDonald
A/YA 1980

Anne McDonald suffered from cerebral palsy and existed for many years in a facility in inner-city Melbourne. Then Rosemary Crossley decided that Annie was intellectually capable but unable to communicate. Crossley, with Annie's full cooperation, embarked on a mission, ending in the courts, to get Annie out of the institution. She used the controversial method of 'facilitated communication' to demonstrate Annie's capabilities. The story documents the two women's determination, courage and ultimate triumph. It was made into a notable movie in 1984. With Crossley's continuing support, Annie began a life full of travel, activity and activism on behalf of others like her.

A FORTUNATE LIFE AB Facey A/YA 1981

Published when Facey was eighty-seven, this memoir became an instant bestseller, perhaps because it is a straightforward, unassuming account of the extraordinary life of an ordinary man. Albert Facey started work at eight in rural Western Australia. Despite much struggle, loss and suffering – doing whatever jobs he could get, the horrors of Gallipoli, the loss of his farm in the Depression, the death of his son in World War II and of his beloved wife of sixty years – looking back, Facey felt that his life was fortunate.

I CAN JUMP PUDDLES Alan Marshall Y/YA/A 1955

Alan Marshall, a much-loved and respected writer, was born in country Victoria in 1902. He contracted polio at the age of six, spent eighteen months in hospital and eventually lost his right leg. He spent his life in a wheelchair but did not allow this to deter him from riding a horse, travelling the world, having many adventures and encouraging others with disabilities to do whatever they wanted. Marshall recounts his childhood in his lively yet simple memoir, now considered a classic. The book was

▶▶▶

made into an Australian TV miniseries. Marshall wrote many books and short stories. He loved the bush, animals and tall stories, and was a noted teller of stories himself.

KIMBERLEY WARRIOR: THE STORY OF JANDAMARRA
John Nicholson Y/YA 1997

Set in the rugged Kimberley ranges of Western Australia about a hundred years ago, *Kimberley Warrior* tells the story of Jandamarra, who led his people against the white occupation of the Bunuba lands. Caught between two worlds, he was a hero to his people and considered a villain by white people. Jandamarra was dead by twenty-four. This retelling of Jandamarra's story was authorised by the Bunuba people. Nicholson, an artist and writer, is the creator of many award-winning non-fiction books for young people.

MY PLACE Sally Morgan A/YA 1987

Sally Morgan is a renowned artist as well as a writer. The eldest of five children, Morgan was fifteen before she found out that she and a sister were descendants of the Palku people of the Pilbara. Her book recounts her life in Perth in the 1950s and 1960s, and traces her quest for truth and identity as she gradually picks up hints about her background. When asked what she considered her most important works, Morgan replied, 'My Place – because it tells the story of family, and **WANAMURRAGANYA**, my grandfather's story, because it further extends that history. I think both books have also encouraged other people to tell the stories of their families.' A landmark book, *My Place* has sold more than half a million copies and been widely translated.

YUMBA DAYS Herb Wharton Y/YA 1999

Herb Wharton was an Aboriginal stockman and a gifted storyteller. Providing an engaging insight into the life of a close Aboriginal family living on the edges of a small Queensland town in the 1930s, this is an adaptation for younger readers of Wharton's first book, **UNBRANDED** (1992).

Joan of Arc   ➤   LILI WILKINSON

Y/YA AUSTRALIA 2006

Before Joan met the dauphin, she had never owned a horse. Perhaps she had
never even ridden one. She was so short that she needed a block of wood to
be able to mount her horse. Before she arrived in Chinon, Joan had never
worn armour, or held a sword. And now she was leading an army –
with no military training at all.

How does a peasant girl born in a tiny village in the north of France in 1412 become a hero and a legend for leading an army, fighting in battles and then being burnt at the stake at the ripe old age of nineteen? These questions are tackled through a lively mixture of fact and fiction in Lili Wilkinson's assured first book.

Joan of Arc, actually Jeanne d'Arc, stepped out of her ordinary life at thirteen when she began to hear voices and have visions. The first apparition, Saint Michael, told her to be good and that she had 'a great mission to fulfil'. There has long been speculation about Joan's visions and voices. Was she epileptic or schizophrenic, did she accidentally take poison, or was she merely inventive? Whatever the truth, Joan believed the voices were from God and they led her to run away from home to the Dauphin (the eldest son of the king), with the mission to help him become King of France. It was thus Joan came to lead an army of, perhaps, 3000 to 5000 men at a time when women had no power and were forbidden even to wear men's clothes.

Joan's story is one of courage, daring, battles, adventure and utter determination. Like all the books in The Drum series, here detailed research is woven into a carefully assembled and coherent patchwork. Here this is made up of eyewitness accounts, invented snippets, recounted historical information and linking pieces of information about clothes, food, armies, religion, battle tactics and court proceeding. This beguiling book makes us even more curious about the strange girl who carried out extraordinary deeds and died for her beliefs. Keep an eye out for Wilkinson's next book **SCATTERHEART** (2007).

Keep Your Hair On! ➤ ELIZABETH VERCOE

YA AUSTRALIA 2003

Jess had never felt more alone in her life. It wasn't so much that her hair had fallen out . . . The worst bit was the whispering. The glances across the courtyard, the stares that she could feel from other students and teachers. One year seven kid had even asked her if she was contagious.

Jess has cancer. She is determined to keep it secret, particularly from her twelve-year-old brother, Spud. After her first course of chemotherapy, she sees handfuls of hair swirling in the shower. Her schoolmates are uncomfortable around her and some find it hard to visit. Her mother seems overprotective. While all this upsets and puzzles Jess as she tries to manage her nausea and other unpleasant symptoms, she is most upset and frightened about what she might miss. She is only sixteen and there should be a lot of fun to be had and life to be lived and boys to be kissed. A particular strength of this brave and honest book is the way Jess comes to understand that hiding the truth from those who care about her is, in fact, hurtful to them.

Vercoe herself 'got cancer' at twenty-five. She writes, 'It is now almost ten years since my dalliance with cancer. I don't like calling it a battle because I was not really at war with myself.' Vercoe's own story, buoyant optimism and continuing struggle with after-effects are worth sharing, but the book, its characters and their strong voices stand on their own. And there are even welcome flashes of humour at most unexpected moments.

Mao's Last Dancer ➤ LI CUNXIN

A/YA/Y AUSTRALIA 2004

I was nearly eleven years old when . . . the headmaster came in with four dignified-looking people . . . They were here to select talented students to study ballet and to serve in Chairman Mao's revolution . . . just as they were walking out of our classroom, teacher Song . . . pointed at me. 'What about that one?' she said.

The gentleman from Beijing glanced in my direction. 'Okay, he can come too . . .'

A runaway bestseller, *Mao's Last Dancer* is an exhilarating, heart-wrenching evocation of the way a young person can create a new life against all odds. Living in a poverty-stricken Chinese village during Chairman Mao's Cultural Revolution, the small boy Li (actually his family name), is chosen at random by his teacher to train in faraway Beijing as a ballet dancer in Madam Mao's ballet school. He has no training or apparent aptitude and is frightened and homesick. But he has extraordinary stamina and determination and gains a couple of mentors. After years of gruelling training and intensely hard work, Li wins a scholarship to the Houston Ballet in the USA, where he defects. (The details of this defection make another dramatic story.) Li needs to learn English and to function in a very different society. He marries, his fame grows and he meets the Australian dancer who becomes his second wife. Li becomes a star in the Australian Ballet, but as he gets older and considers the needs of his growing family, he starts a new life as a stockbroker – and a writer.

Mao's Last Dancer is fascinating on several levels: for its depiction of life in China during a period of intense turmoil and hardship, for its insight into what it takes to become an internationally renowned dancer, but above all for its portrait of a uniquely talented, steely – yet modest and approachable – dancer, husband, father, devoted son, and communicator. This book, and a version for younger readers, has also made Li a sought-after inspirational speaker.

more about the cultural revolution ➤➤➤

girls and women in the cultural revolution

RED AZALEA Anchee Min A/YA CHINA/USA 1994
A heartfelt account of a woman's rise and fall in the Red Army.

RED SCARF GIRL: A MEMOIR OF THE CULTURAL REVOLUTION
Ji-li Jiang Y/YA CHINA/USA 1998
A charming, affecting story for younger readers that successfully
makes real and comprehensible the intentions, excitement,
methods and ultimate horror and brutality of the Cultural
Revolution in China. Set in Shanghai, Ji-li's story starts in 1966
when Mao enlists children and teenagers to rid people of any
bourgeois or capitalist sentiments. (The older of these young
people became the notorious Red Guard.) They are expected to
denounce any people not considered to be adhering to Communist
ideals and practice, including their family members and the aged.
Ji-li was even asked to testify against her father. Thousands were
sent to jail and work camps, and thousands died from ill treatment
or hunger. A story of suffering and courage.

WILD SWANS: THREE DAUGHTERS OF CHINA Jung Chang
A/YA CHINA /USA 1991
A large, sprawling book about three generations of women
living in turbulent times in 20th-century China. *Wild Swans*
took the world by storm, not least because of the author's ability
to spellbind audiences. Jung Chang is the youngest of the three
women, at first devoted to Mao but later totally disillusioned
by the cruelty and suffering accompanying his policies. Her
grandmother was a warlord's concubine. Her mother eventually
rose to a prominent position in the Communist Party and
was then, like millions of others, discredited and destroyed.
A sweeping, gripping saga for any keen reader.

Maybe Tomorrow

➤ BOORI MONTY PRYOR & MEME McDONALD

YA/A AUSTRALIA 1998

In 1982 I lost my brother . . . He was a beautiful, strong, young man . . .
Like most Aboriginal people, the pressures on Nick to conform were huge.
To get away from this pressure he had to find space somewhere. Nick could
never really find that space and so he hanged himself.

On the cover of this deeply moving landmark memoir, and behind the arresting photo of Boori Monty Pryor, are four shadowy images. All four are close relatives of Pryor and all are dead. Clearly none of them was able to find the 'space' they needed to live their lives. Yet *Maybe Tomorrow* is not sad or grim or angry or preachy. This reflects Pryor's character and attitude and the direct, passionate storytelling style enhanced by his writing partnership with Meme McDonald, another Queenslander. McDonald is also a photographer, and her photographs further enliven this book.

Pryor travelled many roads and did many things before he came to writing. His main form of employment is now storytelling and performing. He inspires and informs thousands of mostly young people, all over Australia and in other countries about his people and culture. Every student in every Australian school should read this funny, lively, informative and profound story. It introduces us to Pryor's family, his friends, his work, his philosophy and his people's long history and deep sense of place and connection. You'll laugh, but you'll also be amazed and perhaps embarrassed at some of the questions Pryor is often asked, including one of his favourites, 'When did you start being an Aborigine?' Also read the trilogy based on and inspired by Pryor's family, **MY GIRRAGUNDJI** (1998), **THE BINNA BINNA MAN** (1999) and **NJUNJUL THE SUN** (2002). (See page 221.)

My Forbidden Face: Growing up under the Taliban – A young woman's story

> ➤ LATIFA Translated by Lisa Appignanesi

A/YA AFGHANISTAN 2002

I've heard and read so much about the Taliban that I want to ignore the reports, pretend they're not true. Radio Kabul has told us they're locking up the women, preventing them from going to work or school. Women don't have lives anymore. The Taliban take away daughters, burn peasants' houses, enlist men by force. The Taliban want to destroy our country . . .

Life can't just stop like this on 27 September 1996! I'm sixteen and there's still so much to do – get through my entrance exam for a journalism course at university, for one thing.

We've read fictionalised accounts of this story in the Parvana series (see page 162) and in **UNDER THE PERSIMMON TREE** (see page 160). Latifa (not her real name), twenty-two, tells the true story of how the Taliban turned her comfortable, middle-class life upside down when she was sixteen. Girls and women faced the severest restrictions, were denied education, were virtual prisoners in their homes as it was too dangerous to be out. They were even deprived of medical care, as they were not allowed to be treated by male doctors, and women, even doctors like Latifa's mother, were not allowed to work. If they did venture out, they had to be accompanied by a close male relative and had to hide themselves under the ubiquitous burka, hence 'my forbidden face'.

Latifa would have been the last to believe that she and her mother would draw on unexpected reserves of courage to help others in the same predicament. As well as their courage, we see flashes of humour and wicked daring from the girls. In 2001, Latifa escaped to France and became a 'privileged exile'. Sadly, even in 2007, the turbulence in Afghanistan is not over and there are signs of the return of some of the dreaded Taliban's powers.

extraordinary
international lives

ANGELA'S ASHES Frank McCourt A/YA IRELAND/USA 1996

Many writers have described their harsh Irish-Catholic childhoods. Frank was the eldest of eight children (only four survived). The family's misery in Limerick was largely due to the father's love affair with alcohol, which made him virtually unemployable and ensured that the family lived in poverty. Yet Malachy, the father, was also a great storyteller and this – together with Frank's love of teaching, his memory for detail, his total lack of self-pity and his ability to see the humour in the grimmest situation and to convey it to his readers – has made *Angela's Ashes* a runaway bestseller and accessible to most readers. The US *Kirkus Review* called it 'A powerful, exquisitely written debut'.

THE DIARY OF A YOUNG GIRL Anne Frank Y/YA/A HOLLAND 1947

What has become possibly the most famous diary ever was given to Anne on her thirteenth birthday. Anne was Jewish. Today we can still hear the voice of a lively, highly intelligent teenager as she chronicled her life while hiding from the Germans in an Amsterdam attic for two years. Eventually, like many others, she was betrayed and transported to the Bergen–Belsen concentration camp, where she died of typhus in March 1945. Her father, the only survivor in the family, found the diary and had it published in Dutch and then translated. It continues to be one of the enduring testaments to the Holocaust.

▶ ▶ ▶

THE STORY OF MY LIFE Helen Keller A/YA USA 1903

Keller became blind and deaf at nineteen months as a result of scarlet fever. Her life was changed when, at seven, she met Anne Sullivan, who became her teacher, mentor and eyes and ears. Keller learned to read in several languages and devoted her life to helping others and changing attitudes to disabled people. She fought for women's rights and wrote this book while in college, very unusual for a woman in 1903. Keller's remarkable life inspired the highly regarded and popular play, and 1979 film, *The Miracle Worker*, written by William Gibson.

THIS BOY'S LIFE: A MEMOIR Tobias Wolff A/YA USA 1989

Many readers claim that this is their favourite book ever. A dazzling, inventive piece of writing, it recounts Wolff's troubled teenage years. We meet him and his divorced mother trying to outrun her violent boyfriend. Get-rich-quick plans fail, his mother marries the awful, unsuitable Dwight, and Tobias lies to forge his way into a desirable private school. Elegant, witty and irresistible.

ZLATA'S DIARY: A CHILD'S LIFE IN SARAJEVO Zlata Filipovic Y/YA CROATIA 1992

When *Zlata's Diary* appeared in 1992, it caused a storm and hit the bestseller lists. Here was a privileged, articulate ten-year-old's graphic account of a life suddenly turned upside down in her home city of Sarajevo. Caught in the escalating Bosnian conflict, Zlata is confined to her apartment with little to do except keep a diary. She documents how fast normal life can disappear: electricity and gas are cut off, food and water become scarce, and close friends and relatives are killed. Fear and disbelief are the dominant emotions. Once the diary makes it out of the war zone, it helps Zlata escape to France.

Off the Rails ➤ TIM COPE & CHRIS HATHERLY

A/YA AUSTRALIA 2003

Towards the end of 1999, we began our journey on recumbent bicycles across Russia, Siberia and Mongolia's Gobi Desert, to end in Tiananmen Square, Beijing. We were twenty at the time and spoke minimal Russian. To complicate matters, we knew very little about Russia itself, and almost everyone we spoke to said we were on a suicide mission.

Why did we persevere?

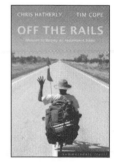

This is one of those books that makes people say, 'How on earth did they do it? And why would anyone?' Tim and Chris cover 10 000 kilometres in fourteen months on recumbent bicycles. They were, and are still, friends, but they argued all the way across Russia, Siberia, Mongolia and China. They battled bureaucracy, extreme weather conditions, frozen extremities and having to get by on less than ten dollars a day.

They are fascinated by landscape, physical challenges, people, ways of life and difference. They are also smart at raising money, and finding ways and means to survive and succeed – and they tell a fantastic tale of adventure and perseverance. Their stories of the friendship, food and encouragement they received from Russians and Mongolians, themselves struggling to survive, are heartening.

Chris returned to a less hazardous life, but Tim departed for Mongolia in 2004 for his next journey: 10 000 km from Mongolia to Hungary by horse! In more than two years in the saddle, he travelled through Crimea and southern Russia and covered about 7000 km – including a complete crossing of Kazakhstan. But before he could set off, Tim had to learn to ride a horse! Not surprisingly he was selected as Young Australian Adventurer of the Year.

more real-life adventures ➤➤➤

great **real-life adventures**

FIRST LADY Kaye Cottee A/YA AUSTRALIA 1989
Fulfilling a childhood dream, Cottee became the first
woman to sail around the world single-handed, unassisted
and non-stop. Her best-selling book details her adventure.
Following her feat, she became a national hero and Australian
of the Year, and was awarded an Order of Australia.

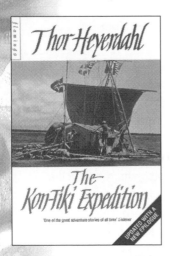

THE KON-TIKI EXPEDITION
Thor Heyerdahl A/YA NORWAY 1950
Heyerdahl, a Norwegian explorer,
ethnologist, archaeologist, philosopher,
environmentalist and author, departed
from Peru in 1947 to embark on a
6000-kilometre journey to Polynesia
aboard a tiny balsawood raft. He
wanted to prove that in the distant
past other cultures had sailed to,
and populated, the South Pacific.
Heyerdahl's project, his sailing skills
and his daring, enthralled millions
around the world. The book was made into an Oscar-winning
movie in 1951.

**THE LAST GREAT QUEST: CAPTAIN SCOTT'S ANTARCTIC
SACRIFICE** Max Jones A/YA UK 2004
There have been many accounts of Scott's heroic struggle to
reach the South Pole. Jones's recent one is considered one
of the best and most comprehensive. The 1911 tragedy cost
the lives of five explorers. After battling the intensely harsh
conditions they discovered that Amundsen, the Norwegian,

had reached the Pole a month before them. The five died on the return journey, only eleven miles from a supply camp. In 1912, a rescue party discovered their letters and diaries. Still an absorbing story of courage and determination – and one that shocked the world at the time. (For an unusual slant on Oates, one of the five explorers, see Geraldine McCaughrean's **THE WHITE DARKNESS**, page 232.)

LIONHEART Jesse Martin
A/YA AUSTRALIA 2000

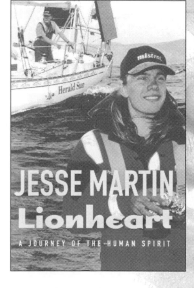

Jesse Martin was only eighteen when he became the youngest person to sail alone, non-stop and unassisted, around the world. His journey in his yacht, *Lionheart*, was enthusiastically followed by thousands through daily radio and newspaper accounts.

TRACKS Robyn Davidson
A/YA AUSTRALIA 1980

This vividly told tale of a solo 2700-kilometre trek with four camels across the great desert of Western Australia, captured the imagination of Australians and people all over the world. A mesmerising account of a young woman's physical endurance and courage and of her yearning to understand this continent, its people and herself.

Purple Hibiscus ➤ CHIMAMANDA NGOZI ADICHIE

A/YA NIGERIA/USA 2004

My form mistress, Sister Clara, had written, 'Kambili is intelligent beyond
her years, quiet and responsible.' The Principal, Mother Lucy, wrote,
'A brilliant student and a daughter to be proud of.' But I knew Papa would
not be proud. He had often told Jaya [Kambili's younger brother] and me
that he did not spend so much money on Daughters of the Immaculate
Heart and St Nicholas to have us let other children come first. I wanted to
make Papa proud ... I needed him to smile at me, in that way that lit up
his face, that warmed something inside me. But I had come second.
I was stained by failure.

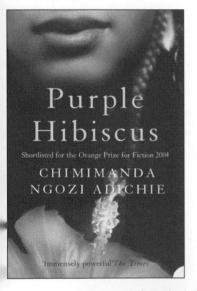

JM Coetzee, winner of the Nobel Prize for Literature and former resident of South Africa, wrote of this eloquent, deeply engaging first novel: 'A sensitive and touching story of a child exposed too early to religious intolerance and the uglier side of the Nigerian state.'

Kambili, our narrator, is fifteen. She has a younger brother, Jaya. Their father is a complex, contradictory character. Kambili is desperate for his love and approval, yet is terrified and cowed by the authoritarian man who writes daily schedules for his children that must be followed even during holidays.

Known as 'Brother Eugene', Kambili's father is a fanatical Catholic convert who rejects all links to what he calls his heathen past. Because his ancient father won't convert, the children are only allowed fifteen minutes at a time with their grandfather, and sharing his food is forbidden. Eugene beats his wife, causing two miscarriages, and even maims his children. He pours boiling water over their feet, then hugs them and sheds tears for being obliged to punish them. But Eugene is also the 'Big Man', a rich businessman, a revered philanthropist, and the owner of the *Standard*, the only Nigerian paper prepared to challenge economic and political corruption. He is up for an Amnesty Award.

The political turmoil in Nigeria, including a coup, interrogations, arbitrary violence and the politically inspired murder of the *Standard*'s brave editor, provide the context for the gradual disintegration of Eugene's authority. Jaya is the first to challenge him, one day refusing to take Communion. When Mama finally cracks, the consequences are terrible for all. Kambili is supported by her loving, liberated, academic aunt, and her three cousins. They eventually escape Nigeria for the USA. Very gradually the shy, hurt and literally tongue-tied Kambili finds her voice and some independence too.

Adichie's next book, **HALF OF A YELLOW SUN**, won the Orange Broadband Prize for Fiction. It is set in Nigeria in the 1960s, during the horrific Nigeria–Biafra war that cost the lives of millions.

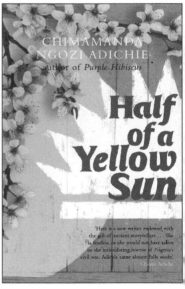

Recovered, Not Cured: a journey through schizophrenia ➤ RICHARD McLEAN

YA/A AUSTRALIA 2003

I am crouching in an alleyway. They can't see me here, so for the moment I am safe. There must be hundreds of loudspeakers projecting secret messages, and umpteen video cameras tracking every move I make.

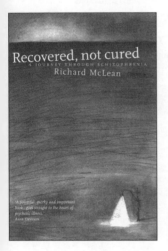

Such are the delusions and fears of a schizophrenic. McLean is an artist and worked as a graphic artist at *The Age* for some time. In this book, his artwork illuminates and enhances the story of his journey to full-blown schizophrenia at the age of twenty. He considers himself recovered rather than cured, and fortunate because he feels that his ability to express his experiences and emotions through his art helped him recover. Anne Deveson, whose book, **TELL ME I'M HERE** (1991), about her son, who eventually committed suicide, considers McLean's book important, 'because it outstrips anything else I have read about schizophrenia and for its insight into the nature of psychotic thinking and behaviour'.

McLean did not become violent and self-destructive, and managed to hide his delusional state for some time. He writes about the difficulty of getting an accurate diagnosis, finding appropriate medication and being prepared to take it. He openly points to heavy marijuana use as a likely trigger. With medication McLean is able to live a productive and creative life. Since the publication of this book he has had a number of exhibitions and has also become an advocate for people with mental illness. Young people are very interested in and responsive to McLean's story and say it provides them with insights into mental illness, which some may encounter among family and friends.

Romulus, My Father > RAIMOND GAITA

A/YA AUSTRALIA 1998

Our life at Frogmore was Spartan, but I never felt that we were poor, although I think we were judged so by others. My father had often told me of his childhood and that informed my sense of what poverty was ... I was always adequately clothed and fed, and rich in what I most enjoyed – fruit.

Raimond Gaita spent most of his childhood during the 1950s with his father, a Romanian-speaking migrant from Yugoslavia, around Maldon in country Victoria in an almost derelict farmhouse called Frogmore. Animals were important, and Gaita writes that he often slept with his dog when cold, noting that Aboriginal people are sometimes condemned for doing this. The book is full of such tiny gems of observation.

It is evident that despite their circumstances, Romulus always had his son's best interests at heart, and he ensured that Raimond gained an excellent education. This memoir evolved from Gaita's eulogy at his father's funeral. Friends there sensed the clarity of Gaita's insight into his father's life, and the strength of the bond between the largely uneducated migrant blacksmith and the boy who was to become one of our major philosophers. The early life of both his parents was engulfed by World War II. His mother, Christine, his father, and others around Raymond suffered physical and mental illnesses. As an academic, Gaita speaks out about injustices, especially to Aboriginal people, and the need for honesty at all levels of life and government. The values of the father have clearly been internalised, but Gaita never preaches or moralises, never passes judgement on his parents or others.

This elegant, simple book not only reveals the life of a decent man, but also reflects a time in Australia's history when migrants from European countries did it tough, yet rejoiced in having escaped their war-torn or totalitarian countries. *Romulus, My Father* has been made into a feature film. It has also been compared to **A FORTUNATE LIFE** (see page 173), another seminal testament to the power of the human spirit.

Unpolished Gem ➤ ALICE PUNG

A/YA AUSTRALIA 2006

*From the top floor of the Rialto building my parents see that people below
amble in a different manner, and not just because of the heat. No bomb
is ever going to fall on top of them. No one pissing on the street, except
of course in a few select suburbs. No lepers. No Khmer Rouge-type
soldiers ... Most people here have not even heard about Brother Number
One in Socialist Cambodia, and to uninitiated ears his name sounds like
an Eastern European stew: 'Would you like some Pol Pot? It's made with
100% fresh-ground suffering.'*

'Fresh-ground suffering' permeates every aspect of *Unpolished
Gem*. 'This story does not begin on a boat.' Thus Alice Pung warns
us not to make assumptions about her family, her experiences or
indeed about the experiences of any migrant. She shares her bitter,
chaotic experiences of her Chinese Cambodian Australian family,
from the age of four until she is at university, with mordant wit
and ruthless honesty. Her writing is poised and dazzling. Nothing
escapes her sharp eyes and even sharper tongue. Her father lands
a RetraVision franchise. Her mother makes gold rings and touts
them all over Melbourne, despite her lack of English. Mother strives
for ever larger 'McMansions' in Melbourne's western suburbs.
Appearance and status are everything.

Alice is expected to study hard and do law or medicine,
eventually marry someone in one of these professions, and in the
meantime look after the younger children and work part-time. Being
a girl, her freedom and activities are seriously circumscribed. Alice
learns to lie, she is exhausted and confused, she has a breakdown.
But she still gets into law. Her secret effort at a relationship with an
Australian young man flounders and fails.

This is courageous satire-as-memoir with heart and insight. A
moving strand is the Cambodian back-story and Alice's relationship
with her tough-but-loving, storytelling grandmother. 'My grandmother was very good at putting bones in her words, bones to make
the other person choke.'

When I was a Soldier ➤ VALERIE ZENATTI

Translated by Adriana Hunter

YA FRANCE 2002/2005

*In six months, at the latest, we'll be changing our jeans and T-shirts into
khaki shirts and trousers. The army for all of us.*

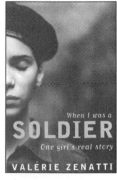

In Israel, Valérie (originally from France) and her two best
friends (of Russian origin) are about to turn eighteen. This
means they must join the armed forces for the compulsory
two years of military training, though 'girl soldiers are not
sent to combat'. The girls and most of their friends are
studying for the baccalaureate. They are sophisticated,
widely read in world literature and intensely interested in
politics and world issues, particularly the fraught issue of
Israeli/Palestinian politics.

'*What is truth?*' *Freddy asks* ... '*Well, we should
stop dominating another people, we should withdraw from Judea,
Samaria and Gaza.*'

Zenatti gives a detailed account of the two years of intensive,
even brutal, training. One of the first things she realises is that there
will be little time for reading as she gets only six hours for sleep
and twenty minutes for meals. Life is learning how to use guns,
being separated from family and friends, being selected to work in
intelligence, and being severely punished for the slightest lapse or
mistake.

Riveting in its portrayal of an entirely foreign world and existence, for its compelling and honest voice, and for how provocative
this situation could be for Australian teenagers living in an isolated,
'relaxed and comfortable' world where politics and tough physical
and mental challenges are largely unknown. Do we want ordinary
fun- and club-loving teenagers to be subjected to national service?
Are we even thinking about any of this or about the realities of life in
Israel and Palestine?

outside the square

Every now and then a book or a series comes along that is so special and such a wonderful reading experience that everyone wants to be part of the action. This may be because of the author's particularly vivid imagination or innovative use of language; it may also be the result of a unique way of perceiving and presenting the world. Such books can't easily be summarised or put neatly into categories such as 'fantasy' or 'real-life', or even targetted at a particular age group. These books often create a storm (think of the Harry Potter series). Sometimes, like *The Curious Incident of the Dog in the Night-time*, and the Philip Pullman trilogy, they create a buzz and garner just about every available award. Some of these books are snapped up and made into films; often they are widely translated so people all over the world know about them – *Harry Potter* is huge in many countries, including China. Such successes can also make their authors rich! For JK Rowling, Meg Rosoff and Jennifer Donnelly it was their first book that hit the big time. Some 'Outside the Square' books might not become bestsellers but are very special books for particular readers. Some continue to be read and looked at and loved for generations by readers of all ages. Here are a few.

A Gathering Light > JENNIFER DONNELLY

YA USA 2003

*When summer comes to the North Woods, time slows down.
And some days it stops altogether . . .*

*As I stand on the porch of Glenmore, the finest hotel on all of Big Moose
Lake, I tell myself that today – Thursday, July 12, 1906 is such a day.
Time has stopped, and the beauty and calm of this perfect afternoon
will never end . . .*

I believe these things. With all my heart. For I am good at telling myself lies.

The scene is set for a wonderful mystery and a luminous story seen
through the eyes of the young maid, Mattie. First-time novelist
Jennifer Donnelly has built her atmospheric, assured tale around a
real-life murder. The body of Grace Brown, a guest at the hotel, is
found in Big Moose Lake. The day before, Grace had given Mattie
a packet of letters tied with a blue ribbon. Grace asked Mattie to
burn them, but she hid them under her mattress. Gradually the dead
woman's and Mattie's stories intersect. As the mystery deepens,
Mattie's own story develops. She is growing up and trying to take
control of her future, not easy in 1906. She desperately wants to
get away from her limited, and limiting, rural life. Mattie's mother
is dead and Mattie has several siblings. Is it her duty to stay and
help her father run their farm? And will her adoring boyfriend, like
her family, smother her? Will she, who loves books and words, ever
become a writer?

The intricate plotting and the truth and power of Mattie's voice
combine to make this a compelling book about the dilemmas of
growing up. A reviewer in *The Times* in London wrote, 'This is surely
one of the year's best young-adult novels . . . The novel is about race,
class and wealth, about dreams and compromises, the nature of
duty and the history of women. Above all, it's a book to lose yourself
in.' The book was universally praised and won several major awards
in, among other places, the UK, the USA and the Netherlands.

Alchemy ➤ MARGARET MAHY

YA NEW ZEALAND 2002

'Anyhow, are you saying you're one of these magicians?' he demanded rather aggressively . . .

Once again their eyes met, and as they did this, Jess's eyes contracted into black slits. Narrow though they were, Roland recognised a familiar darkness beyond them. He thought he could make out a glow of distant suns. He thought he saw himself, suspended among those remote pinpricks of light.

'I'm telling you that you're one,' Jess replied.

Roland is seventeen. He is clever, good looking, and doing well at school. But for a long time he has had a nightmare about being suspended in a magician's box, of hanging in space. Suddenly he seems to be living his dream. The blurring starts when his teacher gives him a strange punishment for some petty shoplifting. (How did the teacher know about this?) He more or less blackmails Roland into spying on Jess, his reclusive classmate, in whom Roland has no interest. Soon he realises this assignment is not as simple as it seems. In Jess's house, Roland becomes trapped in an increasingly confusing and frightening world that includes Quando, the magician from his dreams, and warning voices in his head. Roland struggles to understand. Why is the teacher so interested in Jess? Why is Jess's house so silent and empty of people? And what is the significance of Jess's apparent interest in alchemy? As in many of Margaret Mahy's most challenging stories, the supernatural intersects with everyday life and becomes a metaphor for the concerns and anxieties of teenagers. Can Roland's own magical powers, together with his intelligence and willpower, overcome the dark forces of magic?

A thrilling, multi-layered read that makes you think, ask yourself questions and want to turn on the lights and close the curtains all at the same time.

more margaret mahy ➤➤➤

margaret mahy

THE HAUNTING 1982
THE CHANGEOVER 1984
THE CATALOGUE OF THE UNIVERSE 1985
THE TRICKSTERS 1986
MEMORY 1987

"Within the UK, Margaret Mahy is seen as one of the all-time greats of children's literature, studied by academics alongside Kenneth Grahame, CS Lewis, Alan Garner," says Julia Wells, editor at Faber & Faber. —Tessa Duder, *Margaret Mahy: a writer's life.*

Margaret Mahy's young adult novels sit alongside her many picture books, which can include dazzling, rollicking verse that she often performs – sometimes wearing a green wig or zany costumes. Mahy's imagination and inventiveness seem boundless. Her young adult novels frequently blend reality and the supernatural. This enthrals her readers and allows her to explore many complex emotions and situations facing teenagers and their families. The books always seem timeless as well as of their time. Having won most major awards in New Zealand and the UK, Mahy's international achievements were recognised in 2006 with the Hans Christian Andersen Award. Mahy is a much-loved and highly respected figure in New Zealand and a significant and generous supporter of other authors and programs to promote reading.

Angel Blood ➤ JOHN SINGLETON

YA/A UK 2006

Chicken Angel doesn't understand. Not like Cough Cough and I understand.
There is nothing you can do! Against trank and tox and Doctor Dearly
and primaries and lumpies and funny skin and no eyes and finger wings.
That's the Bin. That's us, spooks, four walls and leopard clawing at the door.

Lights Out has no eyes. Beautiful, ethereal Chicken Angel has the beginnings of wings on her back. Cough Cough, who reads and knows more than the others about the outside world, has more and more trouble breathing, and X-Ray has photosensitive skin. They live somewhere in Scotland in Bin Linnie Lodge.

Angel Blood is a remarkable book. It is impossible to encapsulate because of the dazzling, fragmented language that captures the ways the children see their world, and reveals to the reader how they communicate, protect each other, and express love and courage in the face of horrific mistreatment and deprivation. The book is also remarkable for its imaginative scope and its sustained vision of a world in which four children (there used to be nineteen!) born with severe disabilities are apparently used for experiments with drugs and medical procedures. How, we are asked to consider, could this happen? None of the children know about parents or family. Even their few privileges are disappearing. Food is being curtailed, sedation increased. Cough Cough realises a major medical procedure is being planned and concludes that some end-game is being played out. Cough Cough plots an escape for the children, but will he survive long enough to participate? His response to the impending showdown is heart-rending. Outside we meet the disaffected Nails (hard as), who happens on the desirable but tougher-than-he-expects Natalie.

How the lives of all these intersect makes for a heart-in-mouth finale, but also leads to a revelatory conclusion that shows the capacity for love, tenderness and change in most but not all humans. It does not do justice to *Angel Blood* to read it too literally as some, who question the realities of life in 'the Bin', apparently have.

The Arrival ➤ SHAUN TAN

Y/YA/A AUSTRALIA 2006

The Arrival is an astonishing book. Everything about it delights and amazes, from the solid weight of it (surely no picture book was ever 130 pages long before?) to the facsimile vellum-edged binding, worn with time, the browned golden ribbon bookmark and the semi-gloss 'photograph' mounted on the cover. This shows a traveller carrying a heavy suitcase, confronting a strange egg-shaped creature with a large curled tail. Which one of them is the arrival?

The production values make the reader aware that this is an artefact, a record of events bound together. The viewer is invited, as a guest who might be shown a photo album, to peruse it and create their own narrative. It has no captions, no descriptions, not a word of written text to elucidate, clarify or confuse. Working in the realm of the silent film, Tan has used the image and a range of sophisti-cated narrative techniques – montage, editing, flashbacks, lighting effects, back stories – and subtle shifts in framing and colour, to bring to life a series of stories. Long shots on double-page openings provide pauses in the action and distance and breadth, while the smaller pictures, often nine to a page, tell the story close-up and in carefully framed expositions.

These are tales of people seeking refuge from lands over-shadowed by fear of travel to a new country where everything is strange, wondrous and inexplicable. The viewer is as confused and delighted as the arrivals by the size and intricacy of this carnival world. Escher-like birds, their dart wings folded paper straight, fly in mathematically precise flocks above a city of curved plate surfaces, geometrically decorated cones and clocks with flower-like cogs on their faces. And we, the readers, are as bemused as the travellers, who have no language to explain what we see.

Resonances of horrors that we know from our own history are referred to in the imagery of nightmare. Various tales from different arrivals show child labour in an infinity of chimney stacks;

oppression evoked through huge spiked dragon tail shadows over rows of houses; racial cleansing with giant vacuum cleaners. And all this is created with just a graphite pencil and digitalised colour washes to emphasise mood. The grey of the lead is rarely left untouched. Instead, Tan has chosen to work with the palest of tints in tobacco, leather brown, faded sienna, a steely purplish sheen or a faint wintry blue. Rather than overwork his paper, Tan has allowed light to fall upon faces and objects through deft restraint of his media and an eloquent allowance of pinks and golds as hope gains a foothold, so subtle as to be nearly invisible.

Words are plainly inadequate to encapsulate the wonder and extraordinary power of this visual text. But reading it will take time and concentration – be warned, you cannot flip through it and 'get' it. Give it your full focus and you will be rewarded by finding your own nightmare and your own solace.

The Arrival has already won major international and Australian awards.

CONTRIBUTED BY LINNET HUNTER

The Astonishing Life of Octavian Nothing: Traitor to the Nation: Volume One: The Pox Party ➤ MT ANDERSON

YA/A USA 2006

Mr Sharpe stood above me, speaking in profile, declaring, oblivious to my convulsions, 'The world, Octavian – the real world of objects – and not the phantasies in which you have been indulged in the outrageous luxuries of your upbringing here – is engaged entirely in commerce. Make no mistake of this. Look everywhere, Octavian, and you shall see nothing but exchange and consumption.'

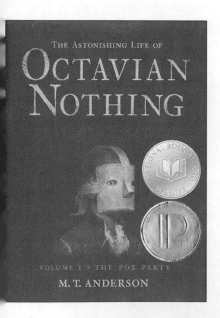

Set aside a weekend or a few days of a holiday to allow the time and mental space to absorb and relish this *tour de force* of language and invention. It is the mid-18th century: the period of the Enlightenment. New views of science and methods of scientific experimentation are emerging. Of course, these methods can be used for good purposes, or they can be abused.

From birth, Octavian has been the subject of a monstrous experiment at the Novanglian College of Lucidity. However, it takes time for him and the reader to understand what is happening and why. When we meet Octavian and his gorgeous mother, both are dressed in finery and being treated as nobility. Octavian is clever: he learns Greek and Latin and is particularly talented at playing the violin. But Octavian and his mother are black, so what are they doing in a grand American house at a time when slavery is still in full force? Then we realise that both *are* slaves and that Octavian's every move and bodily function is measured and noted and that only he and his mother have names. Everyone else, no matter their status, is known by a complicated series of numbers. Octavian becomes increasingly curious, especially about what is behind the one locked door. Once he penetrates this room he begins to understand that *he* is the experiment and that the college is being funded to produce results to prove that black people are inferior and cannot be 'civilised'.

But this is also a time of ferment in the USA as the War of Independence gathers pace. The second part of the book is full of action and drama as Octavian escapes, is caught, and suffers terrible hardship, torture and punishment. The fate of his mother, a victim of the 'Pox Party', is unbelievably cruel and horrific and almost destroys Octavian's sanity.

In a remarkable feat of imagination supported by prodigious erudition and research, Anderson, best known for his outstanding science fiction novels – **THIRSTY** (1997), **FEED** (2002) – and books for younger readers, creates a complex, hypnotic, almost gothic, tale that is as much a satire about contemporary American values and political and commercial practices as it is about 18th-century practices and pretentions. *Octavian Nothing* won the 2006 US National Book Award for Young People's Literature and the 2007 Boston Globe–Horn Book Award for fiction and poetry.

Here are opinions from two major US review journals:
'A historical novel of prodigious scope, power and insight . . .' *Kirkus Reviews*
'This is a brilliantly complex interrogation of our basic American assumptions. Anderson has created an alternative narrative of our national mythology, one that fascinates, appals, condemns – and enthrals.' *The Horn Book*

enduring international 'outside the square' books **for keen readers**

CRIME AND PUNISHMENT Fyodor Dostoyevsky,
translated by David Magarshack A/YA RUSSIA 1865–66
This is the first of Dostoevsky's great works to extend his
reputation beyond Russia. The protagonist, the student
Raskolnikov, murders a grasping old woman to try and escape
his debts and is then wracked with guilt. A long, complex and
demanding book, its continuing power and relevance come from
its forensic insight into the psychological plight and emotions of
Raskolnikov, its gallery of fascinating characters and portrayal
of the times.

THE HOUND OF THE BASKERVILLES Sir Arthur Conan Doyle
A/YA UK 1901
Described by the author as 'a real creeper', the story was inspired
by local legends of ghostly hounds that roamed Dartmoor. It
features Doyle's creations, master detective Sherlock Holmes and
his sidekick Doctor Watson, about whom Doyle wrote over sixty
enduring stories (see page 20). Walker Books has produced a
sumptuous illustrated edition.

ANNE OF GREEN GABLES LM Montgomery Y CANADA 1908
An eight-book series with a couple of spin-offs that feature a
feisty red-headed orphan girl from age eleven. Anne Shirley is
mistakenly sent to work on a farm on Prince Edward Island, but
allowed to stay. Now considered 'Canada's most lucrative literary
franchise' and a major tourist attraction. There is a museum and
several stage, musical, comic book, TV, animated movie and film
adaptations. There are also many Anne fan clubs, especially in
Japan, where cottages like the one Anne lived in have even been
built. The Anne industry flourishes but the books, originally not

specifically written for young people, are still much loved and avidly read by teenage girls. A timeless classic.

LE GRAND MEAULNES (THE LOST DOMAIN) Alain-Fournier, translated by Frank Davison A/YA FRANCE 1913

The sole novel by a brilliant young writer killed in action in 1914. The beauty of the rural setting and of the heroine are as spellbinding as the exploration of that elusive, magical time in a young man's life between boyhood and manhood.

THE OLD MAN AND THE SEA Ernest Hemingway A/YA USA 1952

This is the last significant work by Hemingway to be published in his lifetime, and it helped him win the Nobel Prize for Literature. A deceptively simple little story about an old Cuban fisherman desperate to regain his prowess. Santiago eventually manages to catch an enormous marlin and, in an epic struggle with the fish and against the Gulf Stream, he finally makes it home. But all he brings with him is an enormous skeleton stripped bare by sharks. Hemingway, himself a great sportsman, often wrote about men facing great physical and moral challenges in wars and against nature. Read also **A FAREWELL TO ARMS** (1929) and **FOR WHOM THE BELL TOLLS** (1940).

THE LORD OF THE RINGS TRILOGY JRR Tolkien A/YA UK 1954–5

Considered to be the first book to create a complete alternative world, including a language, The Lord of the Rings trilogy often tops lists of favourite books and is one of those books both adults and young people read over and over.

TO KILL A MOCKINGBIRD Harper Lee A/YA USA 1960

Set in the Deep South of the 1930s, the story is told from the point of view of Jem and his sister 'Scout' Finch, whose father is defending a black man charged with raping a white woman. This was Harper Lee's only novel and won her the Pulitzer Prize. It is an engrossing and deeply compassionate work and was unusual at the time for the way it deals with issues of race and class.

The Book of Everything ➤ GUUS KUIJER

Translated by John Nieuwenhuizen

Y/YA HOLLAND 2006

Thomas saw things no one else could see.

Thomas went up to his room and took out the book he was writing. The Book of Everything, it was called ... He looked out of the window to think, because without a window he couldn't think. Or maybe it was the other way round: when there was a window, he automatically started to think. Then he wrote, 'When I grow up, I am going to be happy.'

Only Thomas can see tropical fish swimming in canals, sparrows playing bright trumpets and frogs wriggling through the letterbox. It is Holland in 1951 and the echoes of World War II are still being heard. Thomas's father is a stern and angry man. He believes the Bible is the only book his family should read. He also expects complete obedience, otherwise he hits his children and his wife. When Thomas's father hits his mother, Thomas sees the angels cover their eyes and weep. Thomas is nine, and he is not happy, but help is at hand. Thomas chats with Jesus, who is surprisingly informal, saying, 'Just call me Jesus.' Thomas meets the gentle Eliza, and, most importantly, Mrs van Amersfoort, next door, hears what is going on. She invites Thomas in, plays him Beethoven, gives him *Emil and the Detectives* to read, and gets Thomas's mother, his sister and some local women together to challenge Thomas's father. But is she a witch as some locals think?

Guus Kuijer is one of Holland's best-loved and most distinguished writers, but this is his first English translation. It appeared, to considerable acclaim, simultaneously in the USA, the UK and Australia. It brings to English-speaking readers of any age a very special story with a distinctly European sensibility. It is sophisticated, simple, wise, subversive, magical and utterly real. It presents a unique take on the world though the eyes of an unusual and courageous boy. Thomas learns not to be afraid and we rejoice for him.

The Book Thief ➤ MARKUS ZUSAK

A/YA AUSTRALIA 2004

Once, words had rendered Liesel useless, but now . . . she felt an innate sense of power. It happened every time she deciphered a new word or pieced together a sentence.

She was a girl

In Nazi Germany

How fitting that she was discovering the power of words.

Zusak tells a gripping, devastating tale of death and survival in Munich during World War II. Liesel, nine, and her little brother are being brought to Munich to live with foster parents. Father has been taken away for being a 'Kommunist'. Little brother does not survive the cold, gruelling trip. But Liesel finds a book and this sets her off on a life and soul–saving journey. Liesel steals books and learns to read, helped by her accordion-playing foster father, whom she comes to love dearly. She is nourished and empowered by words and by the courage, love and tiny gifts from the Jewish fist-fighter hidden in their cellar; by her friend, Rudy; and by her foster family, including her rough-talking foster mother.

Told in short fragments with punchy, clever headings, *The Book Thief* is exceptional for its invention, storytelling, characterisation and observation, and is rich in vivid language, compassion and insight. The daring device of having Death as narrator gives the reader a wide perspective, and allows Zusak to show that the destruction is so great that ultimately even Death is sickened by the scope, randomness and futility of Hitler's carnage.

Readers will know Markus Zusak for his clever, funny books such as **WHEN DOGS CRY** (2001) and **THE MESSENGER** (2002). *The Book Thief*, published in Australia as an adult title, is a giant, imaginative leap forward in terms of subject matter and the brilliance and sophistication of its structure. A major novel, and widely recognised as such in the UK and the USA, where it topped bestseller lists.

Centre of my World ➤ ANDREAS STEINHÖFEL

Translated by Alisa Jaffa

YA/A GERMANY 1998/2005

I am so used to regarding the residents of the town with disdain, so utterly convinced that Visible [the family's decaying, rambling, house] turns Glass, Dianne, and me into something special, that up to now I have simply denied emotions such as love or affection to those out there, the Little People, those on the other side.

An enormous, discursive book that works like a complex jigsaw, where small fragments gradually fall into place. It meanders – exploring, behaviour, motives, ideas and the way society and families function. The key pieces of the jigsaw make up seventeen-year-old Phil's riveting coming of age story. He has felt like an outsider for as long as he can remember. His enigmatic, eccentric mother, Glass, has placed herself, and therefore Phil and his twin Dianne, apart from society and any sense of normal life. Glass is anything but transparent but the truth about her and her belated journey to maturity become important to the story. All Phil knows about his father is that he was Number Three on his mother's very long list of lovers. The story opens when seventeen-year-old Glass arrives from America to live with her sister. She is nine months pregnant and instantly gives birth to twins. She is rescued by the proudly gay lawyer Teresa, come to deal with the sudden death of Glass's only sister. Teresa is a stalwart friend to Phil, as he too starts life as a gay person. Dianne deals with her pain, anger and frustration in spine-chilling ways. When Phil starts a fraught affair with the beautiful, equally fragile Nicholas, it is not his homosexuality that is the focus but his need to escape and shape his own life. The book is determinedly sophisticated and literary but can absolutely hold a committed reader. In Germany one critic wrote: 'This book changed the landscape of juvenile literature' and it has duly brought its author international acclaim. The stylish translation maintains a European sensibility while being accessible and constantly engaging.

Clay ➤ DAVID ALMOND

Y/YA UK 2005

There I was, an ordinary kid. This was home, an ordinary town. I'd stolen the body and blood of Christ and I wouldn't give them back. I'd go further into the darkness with Stephen Rose. I'd make a monster if I could.

Felling-on-Tyne is a mid-20th-century former mining village in Almond's usual north-country England setting. When new boy Stephen Rose arrives, the lives of Davie and Geordie are seriously disrupted. Both are altar boys, inclined to minor mischief-making, like illicit smoking and drinking the altar wine. Davie is increasingly drawn into Stephen's mysterious, bizarre, tortured world.

Who is Stephen? Why was he ejected from his seminary and what impels him to make the increasingly large, life-like and menacing clay models? Almond creates a scary world that mirrors the horror of the world of the deeply damaged Stephen. Davie is unable to resist Stephen's snare; he doesn't understand what he is involved in and where it might lead, though he senses what he calls the 'craziness' of Stephen's monster creations. Yet he is drawn to the promise that one of the monsters could defeat Mouldy, the local bully.

The ensuing tragedy is no less horrifying for being an inevitable outcome of this craziness. *Clay* is a stunning, haunting, magical book, but it is not fantasy. Rather, it is located, as are most of Almond's books, in that strange place where children's vivid imaginations, fuelled by events and circumstances that are painful and often beyond their understanding, create bizarre, dangerous situations, and even monsters.

Having tried for years to get published as a writer for adults, Almond found his voice, an international audience and universal acclaim with **SKELLIG** (1998), his first book for young people.

The Curious Incident of the Dog in the Night-time ➤ MARK HADDON

YA/A UK 2003

It was 7 minutes after midnight. The dog was lying on the grass in the middle of the lawn in front of Mrs Shears' house. Its eyes were closed. It looked as if it was running on its side, the way dogs run when they think they are chasing a cat in a dream. But the dog was not running or asleep. The dog was dead. There was a garden fork sticking out of the dog . . .

My name is Christopher Francis Boone. I know all the countries of the world and their capital cities and every prime number up to 7,507.

Christopher Boone can do all the above but he has trouble interpreting facial expressions and he can't 'do chatting'. He knows adults 'do sex' but has no sense of what it means. Though we are never told it, we know Christopher suffers from Asperger's Syndrome, a form of autism.

Christopher is an intriguing and unusual narrator. As well as facts and numbers, he loves clues, so when he finds the dog with the fork sticking out of it, he is determined to work out 'who done it' just the way his favourite author, Sherlock Holmes, might. But Haddon does far more than produce a mystery story. As he plods after clues, Christopher finds out far more than he expected about his sad, mixed up family. In the process he moves well out of his comfort zone and undertakes bold journeys – both actual and emotional – including a long, gruelling train trip to find his mother.

In an astute bit of marketing, the book was simultaneously brought out for both adult and young adult audiences, by two different publishers. One of the reasons it has been a runaway success with adults and young people alike, is because Haddon, who up to this time had produced only picture books, has presented a unique and unerring view of the world through Christopher's eyes, and in his voice.

Another of Haddon's considerable achievements is to make us laugh and cry almost at the same time. Although we can't help laughing about Christopher's literal mindedness and odd take on things, we never laugh *at* him. Indeed, as his quest develops and becomes more puzzling and painful for him, we become increasingly keen for things to turn out okay. This boy needs affection and certainty and though his parents, particularly his long-suffering father, do try, we want them to try harder.

No wonder Haddon scooped international prizes and was besieged with invitations to festivals and conferences. We all want to know how he did it and let him know how much we enjoyed his very special book.

The Harry Potter series ➤ JK ROWLING

Y/YA/A UK 1997–2007

'I'm a what?' gasped Harry.

'A wizard, o' course,' said Hagrid, sitting back down on the sofa,
which groaned and sank even lower, 'an' a thumpin' good'un, I'd say,
once yeh've been trained up a bit.'

HARRY POTTER AND THE SORCERER'S STONE 1997
HARRY POTTER AND THE CHAMBER OF SECRETS 1998
HARRY POTTER AND THE PRISONER OF AZKABAN 1999
HARRY POTTER AND THE GOBLET OF FIRE 2000
HARRY POTTER AND THE ORDER OF THE PHOENIX 2003
HARRY POTTER AND THE HALF-BLOOD PRINCE 2005
HARRY POTTER AND THE DEATHLY HALLOWS 2007

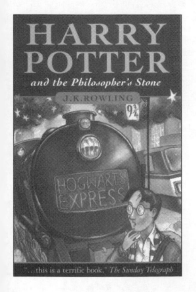

"...this is a terrific book." *The Sunday Telegraph*

What can you say about Harry Potter that hasn't already been said? In some ways, it doesn't really fit in 'Outside the Square', because it's about as inside the square as a fantasy book can be. Harry Potter covers all the bases – witches, wizards, dragons, elves, owls, broomsticks, potions, werewolves, unicorns; the list goes on. And perhaps its familiarity is part of the appeal: reading Harry Potter is like slipping into a comfortable old pair of pyjamas. They are a mix of old-school fantasy stories, boarding school tales, with a dash of Roald Dahl's humour and ickiness thrown in for good measure. Perhaps these qualities are what attract so many adult readers, a topic that is much debated. But Harry Potter *is* outside the square, and this is why: *Harry Potter and the Order of the Phoenix* sold 1.8 million copies in the first twenty-four hours of its release in the UK. That's one copy for every sixty people in the country – just in the first day. The series as a whole has sold well over 300 million copies in 200 countries in fifty-five languages – figures matched only by the Bible and the Book of Mormon. Harry Potter books are the seventh most challenged books in US libraries, and the Pope has declared that Harry bears 'the signature of the king of darkness, the devil'. But the news isn't all bad. The John Radcliffe Hospital in Oxford reported that on Harry Potter release weekends, an average of thirty-six children needed emergency medical care, as opposed to sixty-seven on other weekends. A 2006 US study found that 51 per cent of teenagers said they hadn't read for pleasure before Harry, and 65 per cent reported improved academic performance after reading about the boy wizard. It will be interesting to see what happens after the hype surrounding the final book dies down – will Harry Potter be ushered into the exclusive world of Children's Classics? Or will it just steadily fade from notice until it is nothing more than a nostalgic early 21st century fad?

CONTRIBUTED BY LILI WILKINSON

books on the big screen ➤➤➤

'outside the square' books
make **fabulous movies**

HARRY POTTER series JK Rowling

THE LORD OF THE RINGS trilogy JRR Tolkien

GONE WITH THE WIND Margaret Mitchell

LOOKING FOR ALIBRANDI Melina Marchetta

SCHINDLER'S ARK Thomas Keneally

TO KILL A MOCKINGBIRD Harper Lee

Holes ➤ LOUIS SACHAR

Y/YA USA 1998

Stanley Yelnats was given a choice. The judge said, 'You may go to jail, or you may go to Camp Green Lake.' Stanley was from a poor family. He had never been to camp before.

The palindrome that is Stanley's name should alert the reader that this story is not one to move straight ahead. Nothing in Stanley's life is straightforward either. Stanley knows this and knows that his family is cursed. He is resigned, but that doesn't stop his brain from busily ticking over. Of course, when Stanley arrives at his 'camp' he discovers it is neither a camp nor green nor anywhere near a lake. Stanley has been sent to a 'correction facility' for a minor crime he did not commit. He finds himself in a scorching desert in a bizarre situation among a bizarre collection of people, some with wonderful names such

as Kissing Kate Barlow and Madame Zeroni. All have secrets and great stories to tell. Most outrageous is the punishment devised for the inmates. Along with others, Stanley must dig a hole five feet wide by five feet deep every day. But Stanley's busy brain soon tells him that the aim of the digging is not merely to build character. The sadistic warden, 'Mr Sir', is looking for something. Against all odds in this parched, barren landscape, Stanley decides to escape and find the truth. His journey and courage are revelatory and gradually all is understood about Stanley and the others.

Sachar was not a new writer but hit the big-time with this surreal tale that is hugely inventive, deeply sad, profoundly wise and very funny all at once. Sadly, we have not had another book from Sachar to match *Holes*.

How I Live Now ➤ MEG ROSOFF

YA UK 2004

But the summer I went to England to stay with my cousins everything changed. Part of that was because of the war . . .

Mostly everything changed because of Edmond.

And so here's what happened.

To escape 'Davina the Diabolical' (stepmother) and 'Damien the Devil's spawn' (baby half-brother), Daisy (actually Elizabeth), is sent from New York to live with cousins in a ramshackle house in country England. Daisy is not happy and she doesn't like eating. She is picked up and driven to the farm by cigarette-puffing fourteen-year-old Edmond. This is an eccentric but socially engaged family. Soon Aunt Penn is off to Oslo to lecture on the 'Imminent Threat of War', and the five children are mostly left to fend for themselves. A bomb goes off in a London station, huge numbers are killed and, yes, England has been invaded. Little fighting is evident but the children's lives become tougher and bleaker as supplies and services run out. When the army requisitions the farmhouse, the children are separated. Daisy and Piper, the youngest, are taken to a far-off farmhouse.

The real heart of this story and what gives it its enormous force is Daisy's desperate and determined efforts to find Edmond, with whom she has started a loving sexual relationship. Rosoff perfectly captures Daisy's snappy, knowing, increasingly despairing voice. She also captures the concerns and anxieties of our times (this was written well before the London bombings of 2005). The ending is wrenching and terrible but the experience of reading this beautiful book is the consolation. The accolades that *How I Live Now* has gained worldwide are well deserved. It is a very special book. It's interesting to compare the tone, style and authorial intention with John Marsden's Tomorrow series, also about a nation invaded by an unnamed enemy. Rosoff hit the ground running as a young adult writer, so her second book, **JUST IN CASE** (2006), was eagerly awaited. It won the 2007 Carnegie Medal.

How to Make a Bird ➤ MARTINE MURRAY

YA AUSTRALIA 2003

'Well, what are you doing, Mannie? Where the hell are you going at this time? It's five o'clock in the morning. And why are you wearing that dress?'

I looked down at the dress, in a purposefully weary and innocent way, as if to ascertain what dress I was wearing.

It was the red one. We both knew it was.

'It's my mother's dress.'

Words such as 'whimsical', 'fey' and 'sensitive' are frequently used about Martine Murray's books. The characters and their worldview may be odd, but Murray is absolutely sure-footed in her writing – after all, she used to be a circus performer! Her prose is lyrical and luminous as it unhurriedly teases out her characters' feelings and their search for meaning. Mannie says about herself, 'I've simply come out of left field. I'm a stray . . .'

On her bicycle in her red dress, Mannie is heading for the train and escaping to the city. She's looking for someone, something, but the only clue she has is an address. She also thinks she needs to get away from small-town life and the pain of loss. It is her mother's ballgown she is wearing and this keeps her connected to the mother who has returned to France following a breakdown. There have also been tragic deaths in her family, and her grandmother is ageing and fading. Yet despite Mannie's apparent feyness, she is strong and resilient and purposeful, even if she may not be conscious of what her purpose and direction are. Over a period of two days Mannie finds out many unexpected things about her family and herself and this helps her decide how she feels about her father and the young man in her life.

One reviewer described this book as 'a truly breathtaking read'. Others found it slow and meandering. There are rich rewards if you allow yourself to be pulled into Martine Murray's unique way of seeing and constructing the world, and her fresh and special way of putting words together.

Nightjohn ➤ GARY PAULSEN

Y/YA USA 1993

'To know things, for us to know things, is bad for them. We get to wanting and when we get to wanting it's bad for them. They thinks we want what they got . . . That's why they don't want us reading.' (Nightjohn)

'I didn't know what letters was, not what they meant, but I thought it might be something I wanted to know. To learn.' (Sarny)

In the South of the USA in the 1850s, the penalty for a slave caught reading was dismemberment. Even so, the huge, badly scarred slave Nightjohn, who has managed to escape north, returns to teach the black children on the plantation to read. He knows it is their only hope for another life. Twelve-year-old Sarny is prepared to take the risk. In a tiny book of less than seventy pages, Paulsen creates a riveting story of unimaginable cruelty and inhumanity, but also of exceptional courage and beauty. This timeless, meticulously researched classic is clearly written from deep anger and the desire to immerse young readers in the realities of a grim period in America's past.

SARNY (1997), the sequel to *Nightjohn*, was apparently written because so many readers wanted to know about the future of this clever, brave little girl. Sarny's story has some resonances for Australia and its 'stolen generation' of Aboriginal children. A free woman after the Civil War, Sarny goes searching for her 'sold-away' children. Her story takes in the sweep of American history until her death in the1930s. The prolific Paulsen is best known for his action adventure stories, mostly notably the Hatchet series. But Paulsen is also a master storyteller and passionate about American history, injustice – and dog-sledding.

Northern Lights ➤ PHILIP PULLMAN

YA/A UK 1995

'What do you know about Dust, Lyra?'

'Oh, that it comes out of space, and it lights people up, if you have a special sort of camera to see it by. Except not children. It doesn't affect children.'

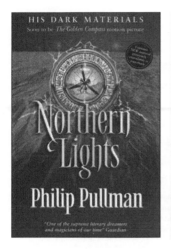  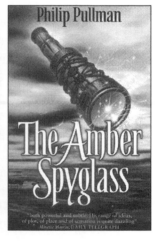

I have a theory that if the His Dark Materials trilogy had been released as adult fantasy, it wouldn't have been nearly as successful as it has been. It's less of a stigma to be seen reading a children's book than a fantasy book. But this series isn't really a series for young people. Pullman insists he does not write fantasy, and the series is, in fact, almost impossible to define, other than to say that it is possibly one of the most profound, terrifying and moving pieces of commentary on religion and the church that I have ever read.

Lyra Silvertongue lives in Oxford (not our Oxford, a different one). She overhears something she should not, and is catapulted into a strange series of adventures that take her to the icy lands to the north, and then out of her world entirely – to our world, to a strange world where creatures have wheels instead of legs, and then all the ▶▶▶

way to the Underworld. Lyra is accompanied by Pantalaimon, her dæmon. In Lyra's world, every human has a dæmon – an animal that is a sort of external representation of a person's soul. In childhood, the dæmon can change shape, being a moth one moment, a tiger the next. When a child hits puberty, the dæmon settles on a single form, and does not change again. The relationships between people and their dæmons are beautiful, perfectly captured and, at times, heartbreakingly poignant.

This is a change-your-life sort of series, and it must be read from *Northern Lights*, through **THE SUBTLE KNIFE** (1997) all the way to the stunning conclusion in **THE AMBER SPYGLASS** (2000). 'Historic first for author as judges shelve doubts', shouted *The Guardian*, as this final book in Pullman's epic trilogy was the first so-called children's book ever to win the overall Prize in the Whitbread (now Costa) Awards. In January 2007, Pullman was awarded the 'Keys to the City' of Oxford, where he lives. The Lord Mayor declared, 'His Dark Materials is one of the finest imaginative works in English. While it creates and explores new worlds and new systems, its roots are in Oxford and we are pleased to be able to confer the freedom of the city on someone who has given so much enjoyment to children, and adults, all over the world.'

In 2007, *Northern Lights* won the 'Carnegie of Carnegies' when it topped a poll to choose the favourite from seventy years of Carnegie Medal winners. The film adaptation of *Northern Lights* is due to be released in December 2007. It's called *The Golden Compass*, the title under which the book was published in the USA.

CONTRIBUTED BY LILI WILKINSON

Of a Boy ➤ SONYA HARTNETT

A/YA AUSTRALIA 2002

Three children bought no ice-cream, did not return home.

. . .

He doesn't like or hate school: his nine years have been lived doing what older people have told him to do . . . This isn't his first school – he'd been coming here only as long as he'd been living with his grandma and uncle, which is almost a year. Before then, while he'd lived with his mother, he'd gone to a school so close to home that he'd walked there and back alone every day; living with his father, he'd caught the school's trundly bus.

Sonya Hartnett often writes about children or young people lost in various ways. Adrian feels lost, lonely and abandoned. At school he is aware of his tenuous social situation, having only one friend. He also observes without any real understanding another lost soul, 'horsegirl', losing her grip, and the horrific way children become a mob and exploit her fragility – he takes part too. Adrian knows he doesn't belong anywhere or to anyone. He knows Grandma will care for him but that he is a burden. So when he hears about three children going missing, he empathises and is curious. (It was 1977, when the three Beaumont children disappeared in South Australia). Might these be the three children who move in across the road? Hartnett takes this desperately sad boy and sad story to one horrific, but logical, conclusion. Published as an adult book here, *Of A Boy* won major awards confirming Hartnett as one of Australia's most significant writers. Some critics, most notably Peter Craven, insist that Hartnett is 'too good' to be a writer for young people. Others feel her books are 'too dark'. These views seem to imply that young people don't deserve the best or are not 'up to' such fine literature. The comment below from a teenager seems to challenge this view:

'The style of writing in this book is so exquisitely exact, with every sentence, phrase and paragraph formed so perfectly as to form a true page-turner.' (Jesse, Year 10) « www.goldcreek.act.edu. au/yara»

australian 'outside the square' books

SEVEN LITTLE AUSTRALIANS Ethel Turner Y/YA 1894
The story of these seven 'select spirits' has now been enjoyed
for a hundred years and has also been made into a successful
ABC miniseries.

THE HARP IN THE SOUTH Ruth Park A/YA 1948
Set in an inner-city Sydney slum in the aftermath of World
War II, this saga chronicles the life of the Irish Australian
Darcy family. The book was republished for young people by
Penguin Books in 1988. A classic storyteller, Ruth Park wrote
over forty books for adults and children, including **PLAYING
BEATIE BOW** (1980) and the adventures that became the
much-loved Muddleheaded Wombat radio series.

MY BROTHER JACK George Johnston A/YA 1964
The first in a trilogy about two brothers who grew up in
a patriotic, suburban Melbourne household during World
War I and then went in very different directions, it won the
Miles Franklin Award and is acknowledged as one of the true
Australian classics.

JOSH Ivan Southall YA 1971
Southall, arguably Australia's greatest writer and innovator
for teenagers, challenged accepted notions about books
for young people – what they might be like and what they
could be about. Josh is a classic Southall male protagonist:
introspective and sensitive. An outsider in a hostile country
environment, he feels lost and unappreciated, especially
by his stern Aunt Clara, so he decides to walk home to
Melbourne. Recently reprinted by UQP in their Children's

Classics series, *Josh* is still the only Australian book to have won the prestigious UK Carnegie Medal. Perhaps Southall's finest, most intense book is **THE MYSTERIOUS WORLD OF MARCUS LEADBEATER** (1990), also one of his last. Sadly, as is often the case in Australia, Southall has not been duly recognised or celebrated at home.

STRANGE OBJECTS Gary Crew YA 1991
Teenager Steven Messenger discovers gruesome relics from the 15th-century shipwreck, *Batavia*, and his life changes dramatically. A brilliant mélange of actual and invented clues and texts, this book startled many readers and won many major awards. Crew's abiding interest is to research historical events and then transpose them into challenging fiction.

NJUNJUL THE SUN Boori Monty Pryor and Meme McDonald YA 2002
The conclusion to the award-winning trilogy, which begins with **MY GIRRAGUNDJI** (1998) and **THE BINNA BINNA MAN** (1999), *Njunjul the Sun* is told through the same innovative combination of text, photographs and illustrations. The young boy, now sixteen, leaves his close-knit Aboriginal family up north to stay with his uncle Garth and Garth's white girlfriend in the huge, complex city of Sydney. He has been in trouble, has a lot of sorting out to do, but, with support, comes to understand that this process must include gaining knowledge about his own people and culture.

The Red Shoe ➤ URSULA DUBOSARSKY

Y/YA AUSTRALIA 2006

The earth smelt strong to Matilda and full of things growing and dying all at the same time. She stood up against the fence between the two houses. She had many thoughts in her head.

As always, Ursula Dubosarsky has many thoughts in her head, too, and wild and wonderful ways of linking them. As we learn from the many real newspaper articles scattered through the book, it is April 1954, less than ten years since the end of World War II. The Cold War and the prospect of the hydrogen bomb are scaring people. The 'Communist Threat' is everywhere. (Sound familiar? Substitute 'Terrorist Threat' and this is a book for our times.) People fear 'reds (communists) under the bed'. Matilda is spooked by the classic fairytale *The Red Shoes* that Frances reads her. Mother has a pair of gorgeous red shoes. And in Australia the papers are full of our very own international spy scandal, the Petrov Affair. Is it possible that the silent, mysterious men coming and going from the house next door are connected to the Petrov story? Are the Petrov's 'reds'?

Matilda is only six, and one of Dubosarsky's great achievements is that she conveys the complexities and subtleties of the story mostly through Matilda's often uncomprehending eyes. The dramatic story plays out on a domestic level. There are two older sisters, Frances, twelve, and Elizabeth, fifteen. Something terrible happened one day on a family picnic at the Basin on a Sydney beach. So terrible that Elizabeth has had a nervous breakdown and can't or won't go to school. Father, a merchant seaman, is away. He appears to be missing. Mother makes many mysterious phone calls. Uncle Paul seems to be around more than he should. But, as so often, life has a way of sorting itself out, and in the end 'Matilda was not afraid at all'.

A story for readers of any age to savour and ponder, and one that has garnered several prizes. Also a story where we have to accept that not all mysteries can be fully solved. Read also Dubosarsky's equally enigmatic and enchanting **ABYSSINIA** (2003).

Red Spikes ➤ MARGO LANAGAN

A/YA AUSTRALIA 2006

'She was real. Jibber jabbers were real too, but they were somewhere else closed off from him now, while this soft harmless baby was here, drawing the pain out of his welted cheek, smoothing the welts flat by contact with her freshness and newness.'

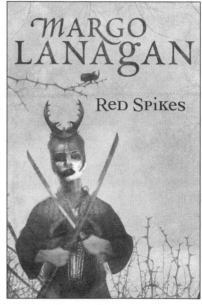

Red Spikes, the third of Margo Lanagan's short-story collections, is a *tour de force* in which ten stories tantalisingly traverse time, place, character and genre, evoking worlds that are startling in their originality and inventiveness, and yet immediately real and credible. They force readers out of their comfort zones, introduce new ways of looking at religion, culture and family, and are written in a style that expects the reader to decipher language, setting and characterisation in an often unsettling manner. Lanagan says they're, 'very dark and there's a lot of goddishness and religion in them. And a lot of death. But they're full of beautiful things too. The central characters (mostly quite young) are all earnest and curious people (or monkeys, or budgerigars) who intend no one any harm, and some are actively trying to improve the world.'

Several stories suggest the theme of parenting – birth, the demands and responsibilities of parenthood, the pain of separation or maturation, loss, rebirth or renewal. In 'Baby Jane' Dylan delivers a baby and becomes its carer, which entails losing his childhood; baby Jane loses her mother too.

These stories also suggest the qualities that distinguish human beings as they mature, such as bravery, fealty, kindness, honesty, ▶▶▶

jealousy and betrayal. According to the author, 'they're about people waking up to the world, to its mysteries and its horrible parts but also to its kindness . . . They're about life, bright and quick; and death, fast and dark.' Each is set in a seemingly familiar locale, which also seems strange. In skilfully colloquial language a distinctive 'voice' takes the reader directly into each character's world, traversing the boundary between the fantastic and the real. Everyday life throws up things which can tease the imagination. 'Monkey's Paternoster' asks 'How do monkeys think and communicate?' 'A Feather in the Breast of God' asks 'What is it like to be a caged bird? How do human beings look to a bird?'

Each story deals with elemental themes such as fear, anxiety, and abandonment; each contains archetypal symbols and metaphors which resonate in the reader's mind. Fairy tale and fable underpin stories peopled by characters such as Wee Willie Winkie and clay people who live in Fairyland; black humour and brutal honesty are their hallmarks. Each contains an epiphany – a moment when everything changes in both the character's and the reader's perspectives. Each is grim and yet hopeful, horrifying and yet uplifting in its respect for the power of love, life and honesty; each is a hymn to a life lived well.

These stories are hybrids, defying classification or explanation. Described as 'cross genre' and 'crossover', they might be defined both as science fantasy or realism, and are marketed for both a teenage and adult readership. An extraordinarily dense compilation of philosophical ideas and meditations on the precarious act of living, and the dark beauty of dying with dignity, they thrill with the epiphanies we have when life suddenly reveals its grandeur. They offer astounding insights into worlds just beyond our line of vision – the worlds conjured up in dreams that reflect our real lives so devastatingly. Greg Bear says they are like 'a memory of the real'. See the world through Lanagan's eyes and it will never look quite the same again. Read also **WHITE TIME** (2002) and **BLACK JUICE** (2004).

CONTRIBUTED BY ROBYN SHEAHAN-BRIGHT

This Is All: The Pillow Book of Cordelia Kenn

> **AIDAN CHAMBERS**

YA/A UK 2005

Pregnant.

What silly phrases people use: in the club, up the duff, a bun in the oven.

This one is better and is true: heavy with child.

I swell with you. I hunger for you. I'm so besotted with you I want you out of me. I want to see you and hold you skin-to-skin right now.

At the beginning of this book Cordelia is twenty and pregnant. (There are many homages to Shakespeare in this book – Cordelia's true love is called Will.) In a beautiful, heartrending love story, Chambers compellingly inhabits his female protagonist and her world. He also tells a gripping story with many twists, including a truly shocking one at the end. For her unborn child, Cordelia writes about all she knows, all she's interested in (and, as for the author, this means almost everything), and all that has happened to her over the past five years. She models her book on the ancient Japanese Pillow Book, which she knows about from her best friend, a Japanese exchange student. The book is an extraordinary feat of memory, imagination, insight and writing for its protagonist, as well as for its highly acclaimed author. This is not a book for a lazy or impatient reader, but if you allow yourself to be totally immersed it could be a life-changing experience. In over 800 pages it meanders purposefully, musing about reading, poetry, the history

▶ ▶ ▶

and ecology of trees, breasts, periods, writing, love, sex, passion, sensuality, violence, music, pregnancy, meditation/religion/belief, families and loss.

This is All is the sixth and last novel (and the first with a female protagonist) in a loosely connected sequence that began in 1978 with **BREAKTIME** and was followed by **DANCE ON MY GRAVE** (1982), **NOW I KNOW** (1987), **THE TOLL BRIDGE** (1992) and **POSTCARDS FROM NO MAN'S LAND** (1999). This is how Chambers sums up what he was trying to do in the books he calls the Dance Sequence: 'Together they paint a portrait of a certain kind of youthful life, of becoming adult in the last years of the 20th century and the first of the new millennium. Each is especially concerned with particular kinds of experience.'

With the publication of *Postcards From No Man's Land*, Chambers finally received, in the English-speaking world, the accolades he long deserved (he had received many European awards), winning the British Carnegie Medal (1999), the US Michael Printz Award (2002) and, to cap these off, the international Hans Christian Andersen Award (2003). Chambers has also been a critic, editor and noted international speaker, and an advocate for the importance of reading in the lives of young people. Before all that he was an Anglican monk and a teacher.

recent australian YA books with
shakespeare connections

Like Aidan Chambers, authors often find inspiration in
Shakespeare's plays, as many of them are timeless in their
presentation of human emotions and behaviour. Some authors
incorporate a play to shadow, or reflect, the actions or situation
of their characters, and to give their story greater meaning.

MUCH ADO ABOUT NOTHING
FAKING SWEET JC Burke 2006

KING LEAR
ALIKI SAYS Irini Savvides 2006
See page 142.

TWELFTH NIGHT
MALVOLIO'S REVENGE Sophie Masson 2005

THE TEMPEST
MY BIG BIRKETT Lisa Shanahan 2006
See page 331.

MACBETH
THE WHOLE BUSINESS WITH KIFFO AND THE PITBULL
Barry Jonsberg 2004
See page 336.

A MIDSUMMER NIGHT'S DREAM
CUPID PAINTED BLIND Charlotte Calder 2002
THE BOY THE BEAR THE BARON THE BARD Gregory Rogers 2004
A wordless picture book. A boy's ball flies through a window
of the Globe Theatre and he finds himself having some rollicking
adventures in Shakespeare's times. He even meets the Bard.
Midsummer Knight (2006) continues the bear's adventures,
this time inspired by *A Midsummer Night's Dream*.

We Are the Weather Makers: The Story of Global Warming ➤ TIM FLANNERY

YA/A AUSTRALIA 2006

So is climate change a huge threat, or nothing to worry about? Or is it something in between – an issue that we must face, but not yet?

Most of the books featured in this guide are fiction, autobiography or biography. However, Tim Flannery's book seems so significant and contains such urgent information for today that it demanded to be included. This is a version of Flannery's *The Weather Makers* carefully edited for younger readers. However, it is no less challenging and retains all the crucial questions and material. Together with Al Gore's documentary, *An Inconvenient Truth* (to be supplied free to all Australian schools that want it), it makes an extremely strong case for taking global warming very seriously. Young people need to be well informed if they are to drive change. Dr Karl Kruszelnicki advised, 'If you want to save the world, read this book.'

Below are a few of the key questions, statements and proposals used by Flannery to build his argument for urgent action. But you need to read the whole 270-page book to fully understand Flannery's passionately argued case.

- Until a black mood takes her and she rages about our heads, most of us are unaware of our atmosphere.
- Today we face a rate of change thirty times faster – and because living things need time to adjust, speed is every bit as important as scale when it comes to climate change.
- Nine out of ten of the warmest years ever recorded have occurred since 1990.

- What will they tell their children if their air-conditioners and four-wheel-drives cost them the nation's natural jewels?

- We must remember this. If we act now we can save at least four out of every five species. Some things about climate change are certain.

- Australia has the highest per capita greenhouse emissions of any industrialised country – 25 per cent higher than the USA.

- This is the single most important thing I want to say: there is no need to wait for government to act. You can do it yourself. The technology exists to reduce the carbon emissions of almost every household on the planet.

Trained as a field zoologist, Tim Flannery is an internationally acclaimed scientist, explorer and conservationist. His earlier books include two ecological histories, **THE FUTURE EATERS** (1994), about Australia, and **THE ETERNAL FRONTIER** (2001), about North America. Most recently he has become one of the most outspoken advocates on issues related to climate change. Flannery was named the 2007 Australian of the Year.

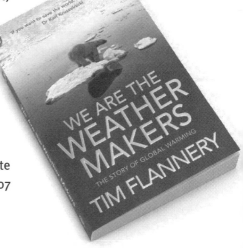

more about climate change ➤➤➤

climate change

People have been writing about it for years – not always with solid evidence, but sometimes with great foresight.

THE BURNING WORLD JG Ballard A/YA UK 1964
'The world, without rain, is drying up. Rivers are a trickle and we see the shrivelling of the species far from its sources and headed lemming-like for the sea.' *The Guardian* (Also published as *The Drought*.)

HEAT Arthur Herzog A/YA USA 1977
A fast-paced thriller based on the likely results of global warming. Herzog is known for his 'disaster' novels, some of which have been made into movies.

DROWNING TOWERS George Turner A/YA AUSTRALIA 1988
Soaring temperatures and rising ocean levels in Melbourne force nine-tenths of the population to live in high-rise towers.

WEATHER EYE Lesley Howarth Y/YA UK 1995
In the last year of the 20th century, weather conditions are weird, with huge floods, earthquakes and storms. Telly Craven lives on a windfarm. She is a Weather Eye, part of an international youth club who share information via computer about climatic conditions. But following a blow on the head Telly believes she is *the* Weather Eye with a huge task to accomplish. An exciting and prescient adventure book.

and a **documentary**

AN INCONVENIENT TRUTH 2006

Made and narrated by former US Vice President Al Gore. Gore is on a mission to get governments, businesses and ordinary people to understand the issue of global warming, look at the likely consequences, and effect change in policies and practices. Gore undertook an extensive tour of Australia to speak about the film and the issues it raises. He spoke to large gatherings, the media and politicians and, along with Tim Flannery and Sir Nicholas Stern (the Stern Report), seems to have put climate change on the political agenda. Appears in book-form for younger readers.

The White Darkness ➤ GERALDINE McCAUGHREAN

YA/A UK 2005

*I don't know if I'm stupid. I might as well be. When I open my mouth
nothing intelligent comes out. Inside my head I'm as articulate as anything,
look! But try and get a thought out and it's like pushing raw potatoes
through a sieve. There are things roaming around inside my head as clever as
Theseus in the Labyrinth. It's just that nobody ever gave them the necessary
piece of string, so they'll never find their way out.*

When Sym gets a seemingly extraordinary chance to go with her
Uncle Victor to the Antarctic, she is devastated to gradually discover
that Victor is far from the man she has believed him to be. Once
they reach Antarctica, the full scale of his delusions and madness is
exposed. Sym fights to survive in a terrifying, whirlwind adventure full
of crazy characters, gadgets and Antarctic lore in a landscape that is
at once alien and stunningly beautiful.

You need to be 'articulate as anything', at least inside your
head, to fully appreciate the layers, language and range of this
brilliant writer's brilliant book. You also need to understand the pain,
frustration and joys of largely living in your head. A lot of what goes
on in Sym's head is related to her passion for everything to do with
the Antarctic, and much of it is expressed in sophisticated, sparring
conversations with one Captain 'Titus' Oates, who walked out into
a blizzard almost a century ago in a heroic attempt to save Captain
Scott's doomed expedition. At one level this is a moving account of a
love affair with a long-dead man carried on entirely in a girl's head.

McCaughrean's weaves words together in dazzling ways. In a
review of *The White Darkness*, Adèle Geras wrote, 'Reading Geraldine
McCaughrean is like being on a spiral staircase. You move down and
down and it gets darker and darker, but somehow you're travelling
towards some kind of light. You surrender yourself to the writer, and
you are in the best of hands.'

McCaughrean is also famous for retelling the classics. In a much-
heralded feat, she was selected from 200 entrants to write **PETER
PAN IN SCARLET**, a sequel to the original.

robert ingpen
illustrated classics

Robert Ingpen is an Australian national treasure and his
books are read by people of all ages. They are wonderful for
sharing in families. Like Geraldine McCaughrean, he works
to keep the classics fresh for new generations of readers, in
his case through his luminous illustrations. He illustrates
many other types of books, too, and is often involved
in artistic projects with an environmental focus. So far,
Ingpen is the only Australian illustrator to win the Hans
Christian Andersen Award (1986). The five classics listed
here, re-imagined artistically by Ingpen, are for readers
of any age who appreciate beautiful, sumptuous books.
Ingpen has also illustrated two books by Michael Rosen,
one on Shakespeare and one on Dickens. All the books are
meticulously researched and the artworks often appear in
specially curated exhibitions.

TREASURE ISLAND Robert Louis Stevenson
1993 CENTENARY EDITION

AROUND THE WORLD IN EIGHTY DAYS Jules Verne 1999

PETER PAN AND WENDY JM Barrie 2004 CENTENARY EDITION

THE JUNGLE BOOK Rudyard Kipling 2006

THE WIND IN THE WILLOWS Kenneth Grahame
2007 CENTENARY EDITION

let your eyes dance –
the magic of comics and graphic novels
by Erica Wagner

Comics have had a hard time through the ages but they are fighting back! Bookshops have graphic novel sections and, for many young people, combining text and images in their own comics and zines is a powerful form of self-expression. People of all ages are discovering the joy of a new form of reading.

Frequently viewed as lower forms of literature, as crass, corrupting, stereotypical and ungrammatical, comics have nevertheless remained the preferred form of reading for many children, especially boys. Manga (comic books), anime (animation that is made in Japan, for example, Osamu Tezuka's **Astro Boy** and my childhood favourite, **Kimba the White Lion**), the cartoon creations of Hanna-Barbera, Disney and Pixar,

and series like **Superman**, **Tarzan**, **Wonder Woman**, **Asterix** and **Tintin**, have always had a passionate following. Now graphic novels (comics in book form) and manga of all varieties are making their presence felt in the mainstream – comics are cool, and a much wider audience than just young boys are reading them. Graphic novels, like Art Spiegelman's **Maus** books and Chris Ware's **Jimmy Corrigan, the Smartest Kid** on Earth have won major literary awards: Maus the Pulitzer Prize Special Award in 1992 – the judges couldn't decide whether it was fiction or biography – and Jimmy Corrigan the 2001 Guardian First Book Award.

Like film, graphic novels employ cinematic techniques to great effect. Picture the opening of your favourite film or graphic novel without the images. Then look at the images without sound or words. Drama is created by the interplay between words and images, the tone and mood of the text and pictures, the gaps between the panels. Graphic novels in black and white evoke the richness of colour; they often have stark tones, yet convey the most subtle characterisations; imagery is simplified, yet presented through a variety of sophisticated points of view.

Graphic novels can tell big stories in original and exciting ways. They can play with narrative in ways that are impossible in conventional novels. Concurrent, intricate storylines, shifts in time, place and mood, different voices and expressive artwork are all managed through the careful sequencing of words and pictures in panels. Graphic novels tackle big issues and are frequently autobiographical and political, like Marjane Satrapi's Persepolis books, which tell the story of her childhood and teenage years during the Islamic revolution in Iran; Joe Sacco's Palestine, an eye-witness account of the Palestinian experience, described as setting 'the benchmark for a new, uncharted genre of graphic reportage'; and David B's Epileptic, the powerful, impressionistic biography of the author's development as an artist, against the background of his brother's illness. Bruce Mutard's forthcoming The Sacrifice tells the story of a young man struggling with his socialist, pacifist ideals in World War II Melbourne and Nicki Greenberg's graphic adaptation of F Scott ▶▶▶

Fitzgerald's **The Great Gatsby**, while faithful to Fitzgerald's plot, mood and characterisation, surprises and delights the reader as familiar players are depicted as an array of fantastical creatures.

Graphic novels are a logical transition from picture books and many picture books appeal to older readers too. Raymond Briggs was one of the first to bring the genre of comics and children's books closer together. **Ethel and Ernest** is a perfect example of visual storytelling fusing in a tender, evocative memoir that is also a social history. Briggs's **When the Wind Blows** remains a potent and controversial study text in secondary schools. See also Neil Curtis's poignant memoir of his London childhood, **The Memory Book**.

Neil Gaiman, described by Stephen King as 'a treasure house of story . . . we are lucky to have him in any medium' is also a master of the genre and his books with Dave McKean – **Wolves in the Walls**, **The Comical Tragedy or the Tragical Comedy of Mr Punch** and **The Day I Swapped My Dad for Two Goldfish** all reward multiple readings and rely on a deep engagement with their images as well as the words. At the other end of the spectrum,

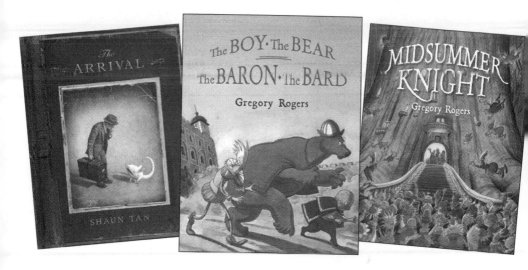

relying entirely on their images to carry the narrative, are Shaun Tan's masterpiece, **The Arrival** (see page 198), and Gregory Rogers's joyous and inventive **The Boy the Bear the Baron the Bard** and its sequel, **Midsummer Knight**.

To really appreciate the beauty of graphic novels you have to let yourself go, and allow words and images to fuse, as your eye dances over the page and takes in both together – even the gaps in the panels can supply sound effects, drama and movement. If you want to find out how they do it then Will Eisner's **Comics and Sequential Art** and Scott McCloud's **Understanding Comics, the Invisible Art** (a comic book about comics) are invaluable and enlightening.

this sporting life

What do they know of cricket, who only cricket know? It's the question asked in arguably the best book ever written about sport, *Beyond a Boundary*, by the historian CLR James. Books about sport can offer much much more than just the mechanics of the on-field contest. Like good books on any theme or topic, sports stories can, and do, offer the reader a window onto a larger world, a world where the game might be one part of a larger drama. 'Community theatre in the paddock' is how Bruce Pascoe described country football. Many of the books in this section offer more than a narrow view of sport. Sport is also an arena for wildly inventive language. Each sport, whether cricket, motor racing or rugby, comes ready-packed with its own metaphors and meanings. Many of the books in this section celebrate the language of the playing field. The way we talk about it, write about it and read about it is key to sport's essential beauty.

ENTRIES SELECTED AND WRITTEN BY MIKE SHUTTLEWORTH

Dairy Queen ➤ CATHERINE GILBERT MURDOCK

YA USA 2006

This whole enormous deal wouldn't have happened, none of it, if Dad hadn't messed up his hip moving the manure spreader. Some people laugh at that, like Brian did. The first time I said Manure Spreader he bent in half, he was laughing so hard. Which would have been hilariously funny except that it wasn't. I tried to explain how important a manure spreader is, but it only made him laugh harder, in this really obnoxious way he has sometimes, and besides, you're probably laughing now too.

Dairy Queen is alive and kicking with the same small-town humour that fired the popular film *Napoleon Dynamite*. Fifteen-year-old Amber Schwenk takes on the male world at its own game. Amber is struggling to keep the dairy farm going when her father breaks his hip. Her two older brothers have already fled farm and family for college football scholarships. Worse, Amber is saddled with Brian Nelson, a spoilt, good-looking rich kid who's a total stranger to hard work. Amber and Brian make the perfect odd couple, and Amber is quick to exploit his innocence about farm ways. Amber has learned about football from her brothers, and soon she is teaching Brian quarterback-for-the-rival-town Hawley, how to really throw a football. But what is a Red Bend girl doing perfecting the game of her town's biggest rival? It's a question that Amber asks herself, and the answer is a surprising one.

But *Dairy Queen* is much more than a story of conflicting loyalties. Amber's funny–sad tone makes this Pygmalion comedy work. She feels that her life is stuck, that she is, metaphorically speaking, a cow. The members of Amber's family (her father especially) are so uptight you could store milk in them. Why won't her brothers come home and why won't her parents talk about them? By contrast, Brian says his mother '*is* Oprah Winfrey', a relentless talker-through of family problems. How loyalties are affirmed and tables are turned, and how Amber pulls her life out of the mud, make *Dairy Queen* a page-turning pleasure.

Fighting Spirit ➤ LAUREN BURNS

YA AUSTRALIA 2003

The referee brought us together and we faced each other. I beat you, I'm going to smash you, I thought. We bowed and the referee gave the signal to start.

'Mental strength sets champions apart,' Lauren Burns observes, and there is no doubt that Australia's first tae kwon do Olympic gold medallist has it in bucket-loads. Broken bones, knee operations and an iron will are all part of the job description for a career in competitive sport. Burns tells her story with both candour and grace. What sets *Fighting Spirit* apart from so many autobiographies by successful athletes is Burns's way of showing the passion, the intensity and the vigour of competitive sport. You feel every crunching, stinging kick, whether given or received. And you are inside that strange bubble of the elite athlete where everything, *everything*, is about being your best on fight day. To get there, Burns overcomes setbacks, unexpected defeats and injuries. For the Olympic finals, she dieted hard for three months to bring her to fighting weight, all the time building the physical and mental strength needed to win. *Fighting Spirit* is virtually a handbook on what it takes to be the best. Burns teaches us that self-belief and the will to keep going are every bit as important as technique. There is also something strangely empowering in reading about an athlete whose primary goal is to kick other athletes in the face at full throttle. 'You're out there for one thing and that is to beat your opponent.'

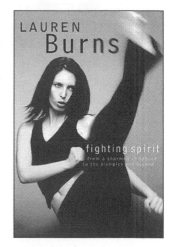

Goal! How football conquered the world ➤ CATHERINE CHAMBERS

Y/YA AUSTRALIA 2006

Football was reported in England's American settlement of Jamestown as early as 1609. But it was frowned upon as a bad influence and promptly banned. A local American ball game called Pahsaheman was also recorded at about this time. That was probably banned, too. But football gathered silent strength—often in the most unlikely places.

The word 'soccer' has been in use for little more than a hundred years, but the roots of the world game are amazingly deep. Evidence of athletes chasing a round object and controlling it with their feet is found in Mayan, Aztec and ancient-European civilisations. The game we see today came into view with the London Football Association codifying the rough rules of street and field in 1863. But what got the ball rolling globally for football was the spread of the British Empire. *Goal!* neatly explains the story of football's growth across the world without feeling too much like a history lesson. The narrative also touches on the world's most watched sporting event, the World Cup, and the emergence of FIFA. Australia's qualification for Germany 2006 is also covered, but this is, refreshingly, a book that pushes beyond the borders of the local to create a big picture. Adding to the story are brief portraits of the game's greats, including Diego Maradona, Johann Cruyff, George Best, Franz Beckenbauer and Pélé. And if all that seems a little too blokey, there is a chapter on women's football, and its late-blooming struggle against the odds. *Goal!* is a smart, lively and well-packaged tour of the world game, one that will take readers beyond the headlines and highlights of this week's game.

Half the Battle > DON HENDERSON

Y/YA AUSTRALIA 2006

*Footy was the glue that had kept Batty and me pasted together since
I had moved to Port Road High from the country at the beginning of
Year Eight. It was all we ever talked about. I was even starting to think
that occasionally it might be nice to have a crack at one or two other topics
of conversation.*

Don't let the Adelaide-centric guernseys on the cover deflect you:
this book is a hoot! *Half the Battle* is the laugh-out-loud story of one
season in the life of Sean Watson, who has come to the city – his
family has split up and the farm has been lost. The football team at
Port Road High is a lot like the school itself: a great bunch of people
but serial under-achievers and misfits all. Their sworn enemy is the
neighbouring St Gracious College, an upmarket private school where
the kids all 'looked like they could win a part in a breakfast cereal
commercial'. *Half the Battle* is unlikely to be pored over for a term
in high school English, but young readers should snap it up like Jeff
Farmer hunting a loose ball in the forward pocket. The sports book's
familiar narrative arc – the team's journey from stone-cold apathy
to busting down the door – is part of the charm. Somehow the story
never loses its bounce. Sean's observations about his team-mates,
his teachers and opponents have a comic flair and easy authenticity
that the audience will instantly recognise. The secondary plot line
about Sean's separated family never seriously threatens to derail
the main business. Which is, of course, getting the better of the
snobs from the school next door!

Keeper ➤ MAL PEET

YA UK 2003

El Gato put the tips of long fingers together and rested his hands on the table. 'Two years, Paul. Almost every afternoon for two years. And at the end of that time I knew pretty much everything I know now. OK, I have played professionally in Italy, and I am stronger and maybe a little faster than I was back then. But everything I know, really know about football and keeping goal I learnt in the forest.'

Goalkeepers are different. They stand apart, defending territory alone against the strength of ten. Paul Faustino has seen it all. As a South American sports writer his knowledge of the world game is intimate. But he has never heard anything like the true story of how a World Cup–winning goalkeeper got to be so great. *Keeper*, by Englishman Mal Peet, takes us deep into the Amazon jungles where El Gato, the goalie, learns the 'keeper's secrets' from a mysterious and haunting master. Along the way, we get a sense not just of the national passion for football, but of just how tough the lives of working men and their families are, struggling to survive on the edge of the Amazon rainforests. *Keeper* is a brilliant book on many levels. It is built upon the relationship between El Gato's incredible tale and Faustino's sceptical, probing search for the truth. This shadowplay of truth and doubt lends the book a powerful tension, while the passion and precision of football are portrayed as sharply as the wilderness, mud and sweat of the South American forests. A keeper indeed.

Another Mal Peet book, **THE PENALTY** (2007), features journalist Paul Faustino in even deeper trouble: mixing football, ancient magic and the legacy of the slave trade. Like *Keeper*, *The Penalty* powerfully evokes Latin American places and people. Peet has written mostly non-fiction but has leapt to prominence recently with these two books and by winning the 2006 Carnegie Medal for **TAMAR** (2005), a very different kind of book (see page 279).

published for adults
perfect for teens

**BROTHERBOYS: THE STORY OF JIM AND PHIL
KRAKOUER** Sean Gorman AUSTRALIA 2006
*Take the family to see some Aboriginal art this
weekend*, read the advertisement. The artists
were Jim and Phil Krakouer, two footballers from
Mt Barker. The venue: the MCG. A penetrating
and sympathetic portrait of indigenous brothers
in the years before Nicky Winmar and Michael
Long campaigned to stamp out racist sledging in the AFL.

FEVER PITCH Nick Hornby UK 1992
Fever Pitch changed the way we think and talk about sport.
Hornby's childhood and young-adult obsession with the dour
Arsenal FC (now a glamour club) legitimised the fans-eye-view of
big sport. Hornby reveals a lot about why sport plays such a big
part in his life. Truly a boy's own story.

MONGREL PUNTS AND HARD BALL GETS
Paula Hunt and Glenn Manton AUSTRALIA 2006
Footy as she is spoke. Hunt, a rabid Carlton fan, and Glenn
Manton, a former Blues backman, tease out the terminology that
makes the game unique. The book is beautifully designed, too.

REMEMBERING AMY Mike Safe AUSTRALIA 2006
Amy Gillett was an Australian road-racing cyclist who died in
Germany when she and four other riders were hit by an out-of-
control car. Journalist Mike Safe, who was also Amy's uncle, puts
together a rich portrait of a committed athlete.

TUMBLE TURNS Shane Gould AUSTRALIA 2003
At age fifteen, Shane Gould held every freestyle swimming world
record between 100 and 1500 metres. At sixteen, she retired.
Few autobiographies are this revealing – or this interesting.

The Line Formation > PAT FLYNN

YA AUSTRALIA 2006

IF YOU WANT SOMETHING BAD ENOUGH, YOU WILL BE DENIED BY NOTHING OR NOBODY.

That quote, from A Winning Focus, was taped to the locker room wall. It made Ozzie smile, recalling how the only thing ever taped to the wall before a Yuranigh game was the weekend racing guide.

So you think Australians are mad about their sport? Young Ozzie is in for a mighty education when he trades rugby league in south-west Queensland for a season of Texas high school football. Ozzie signs on to the Hope High School football team, the Shooters, but it's not just a matter of learning a new set of rules on the field. Indeed, it is Ozzie who teaches the locals some new tricks; his rugby league smarts become the key to Hope High's season. But for Ozzie, success on the field doesn't solve all of the questions life throws at him.

Author Pat Flynn spent time at the University of Texas on sports scholarships, providing a satisfying texture of realism and detail to events. In *The Line Formation* high school football becomes America writ large, where winning is everything and failure is absolute. The Shooters, including Ozzie, are worshipped by their peers, especially by the girls, and carry the hopes of the town on their shoulders as they try to overcome Denham, their more powerful neighbours. Ozzie's year away also poignantly tests his ties to his home, his girlfriend Jess, best mate Johnno, and his fragile family, as he tries to square the 'success above all' ethos of Hope, Texas. For eye-opening insights into the fanaticism of American sport, and an action-packed tale of success against all odds, *The Line Formation* is a sure-fire winner.

On the Mat ➤ ARCHIMEDE FUSILLO

Y/YA AUSTRALIA 2006

"So, you know much about wrestling, Big Fella?" the kid asked.

Let's face it, sport is not for everyone. So it's a very good thing that
we have wrestling. It's just choreographed acting between men in
tights, isn't it? Or is it? Claude is a boy who knows he will never
win a gold medal but that doesn't stop him trying. Not in running,
in football, in anything. He's too big, but he's not too fast. So when
Claude meets Mario, or Whitetail as Mario introduces himself, a new
and mysterious world of sport is gradually revealed. Here, at last, is
a game that might allow Claude to get the better of Tom De Silva, the
school poster boy for sport. But Mario, named after the great Italo-
Australian wrestler Mario Milano, has even bigger plans in mind. He
has the scripts of past bouts, and of one mythical encounter that
never took place. Now, with Claude renamed the Big Fella, Whitetail
is ready to rise again. But what kind of sport is it that needs a script,
Claude wonders.

In Mario, Archie Fusillo has created a lively, spirited character
whose energy and optimism help to carry this entertaining story. For
many years in Australia, wrestling occupied a place two rungs below
soccer; it was the obscure but passionate pastime of migrants. *On
the Mat* brings that strange, but hardly distant, world close to the
reader. It's a beguiling, touching and surprising story that younger
readers should find highly enjoyable.

Shakespeare Bats Cleanup ➤ RON KOERTGE

Y/YA USA 2003

Man, a good double play is beautiful.
That's mostly what I miss, being part of
something beautiful. I know, I know. Guys
don't talk about stuff like that. But this is
between me and my journal.

To 'bat cleanup' you need to be calm under pressure. The cleanup batter is the team's strongest hitter – the one relied on to bring home others who have made base. So when cleanup batter Kevin Boland goes down with 'mono' (glandular fever), his place in the team, and with his friends, takes a major dive. Kevin's forced to rest, rest and rest. But those hours on the couch are not filled with daytime television. His dad is a writer and he gives Kevin a writing journal to help pass the time before he can get back to the baseball field. *Shakespeare Bats Cleanup* is an unusual verse novel, drawing on both the language of sport and the many and varied forms of poetry. Kevin records his recovery, his thoughts about his friends, including girlfriends, and memories of his late mother in a range of poetic forms, from haiku to sonnet, to ballad and pastoral. Ironically it's Kevin's illness that allows him to see life from the outside, even when that isn't always a comfortable place to be. It is through poetry that Kevin meets Mira Hidalgo, who, while wary about baseball, shares Kevin's love of words. Mira's Spanish-language heritage offers a whole new slant on life and ultimately takes Kevin and the reader outside the diamond, to a wider, richer world. By turns thoughtful and playful, *Shakespeare Bats Cleanup* is all about grace under pressure. For a different kind of verse novel by Koertge see page 121.

lunchtime legends
aussie sports series
for younger readers

SPECKY MAGEE Felice Arena and Garry Lyon
The phenomenally successful series of five books (so far)
charts the rise of Simon 'Specky' Magee and his teammates
of Booyong High in pursuit of premiership glory and a
future in the AFL big league.

THE TOBY JONES SERIES Michael Panckridge with Brett Lee
An old Wisden cricket almanac provides the doorway for
a cricket-mad Melbourne boy's journey back to the great
cricket matches and moments. Australian fast bowler Brett
Lee provides special comments.

LEGENDS and **ANNIVERSARY LEGENDS** Michael Panckridge
Two outstanding series spanning a wide range of sports,
involving both boys and girls at Sandhurst School. Rivalries,
friendship, fair play: *Legends* is sport as a noble pursuit.
Includes, maps, quizzes and score tables.

LOTHIAN SPORTS FICTION various authors
Series for young readers covering a wide variety of sports
from some unusual perspectives: netball, a girl playing
footy, swimming, bodyboarding and wrestling.

ALL STARS various authors
Netball. Eight books in the series, but just seven players
make the team of netball.

Surfing Goliath ➤ MICHAEL HYDE

Y/YA AUSTRALIA 2006

They watched the dark green waves, which rose sharply on an underwater ledge a hundred metres from shore. The waves quickly became fast left-handed breaks speeding towards the rocks, crashing and surging, then sucking back into the sea in a whirlpool of madness . . .

Boogie boarding or 'bodyboarding' may not have quite the cachet of surfing, but there is no question of its enormous appeal. When you are in the water, bodyboarding makes the same demands as surfing: you need to know the ocean and respect its dangers in order to thrive. *Surfing Goliath* pulls together a strong cast in a tightly written story about facing danger to live life to the full. Better still, it has the salty tang of authenticity. Seal (aka Sam) and his mates Nuts, Dolphin (a girl Seal is keen on) and Angelo are out to catch the big one. Angelo is crazy about fishing and wants to hook a big bronze-whaler shark. Seal, Nuts and Dolphin dream of the monster waves that seem to arrive in a three-yearly cycle. But the waves and the shark are destined to share the same reef – and the group's courage and friendship are about to be tested to the max. Seal, the main character, is a grommet, pure and simple: he lives to surf. Nuts is instantly recognisable as one of those kids for whom danger is a meaningless notion. For Nuts it's always a case of 'act first, worry later'. Dolphin, like Seal, is here for the waves. But so too is a city TV film crew, which provides an oily town mayor with a chance to exploit, for financial gain, the town's reputation. The kids just want to face their fears and surf. *Surfing Goliath* is an old fashioned adventure with a strongly modern feel. It should score with grommets, shark biscuits and speed humps everywhere.

Taj Burrow's Book of Hot Surfing ➤ TAJ BURROW

YA/A AUSTRALIA 2003

I love surfing! . . . Yeah it's my job, but even if it wasn't I would do what I can to surf every day of my life. The only thing better than surfing is surfing well. And that's what this book is all about.

There are a lot of books on surfing out there full of beautiful photos: pros shredding their way through impossibly large waves at remote and often secret locations. 'Only a surfer knows the feeling', the saying goes. All well and good, but what are the steps that a young surfer can take – what does he or she need to know – to be able even to think about riding those monsters?

Young West Australian surfer Taj Burrow has never won a world title but is highly regarded for his passionate and creative styling. It shines through on every page of his book. Taj succinctly shows how to pull off several key moves, from basic turns to backside floaters, roundhouse cutbacks and big big airs. The chances of being hurt when beginning are very small. 'Water up your nose and sand in your tweeds is not pain,' he says. In a chapter on how to wipeout the right way, Taj recalls being pile-driven, head-first into the North Point reef. Now *that's* pain. But he shows how to surf safely too. The book is ingeniously designed, with detailed, precise layout. Every other page includes a very useful practical tip (with passing nods to cars and girls), and there's a handy glossary too. *Taj Burrow's Book of Hot Surfing* is a model of what a good book about sport can be. Read, look, learn and enjoy.

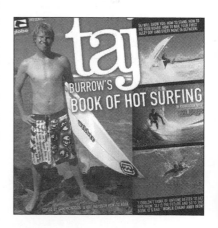

more action from the edge ➤➤➤

action from the edge

BETWEEN A ROCK AND A HARD PLACE Aron Ralston USA 2004
When rock climbing all went wrong for Ralston, he was faced
with a horrible choice: die in the desert or cut off his own arm
with his Swiss army knife. Hmmm. Extreme enough for you?

THE GIRLS' GUIDE TO SURFING Andrea McCloud USA 2005
Smart advice, cool design. There's something no-fuss about the
surfing smarts here – just what's needed when you're learning to
handle the ocean. Big brothers could learn something here, too.

INSIDER'S GUIDE TO ACTION SPORTS Matt Higgins USA 2006
You've always wanted to try a no-handed air on your motorbike,
right? Find out how in this crash course on the wild world of
extreme sports, including skateboarding, surfing, motocross
and snowboarding.

SKATEBOARDING IS NOT A CRIME: 50 YEARS OF STREET CULTURE
James Davis and Skin Phillips USA 2004
This book features the key people and key moments in the
history of American skateboarding. It's a well-packaged
document, backed up with sensational photographs. Twelve
million skaters can't be wrong.

TOUCHING THE VOID Joe Simpson USA 1988
21 000 feet up a mountain in the Andes
is a bad place for things to go wrong.
Joe Simpson's climbing partner was forced
to leave him for dead, but miraculously
Simpson survived.

Valentino Rossi: Legend ➤ FILIPPO FALSAPERLA

YA/A ITALY 2006

Valentino was always special, but just how special nobody knew back in 1997. The lanky boy with the long blond hair was just another promising kid.

Ten times in his first GP season Valentino Rossi hit the tarmac. What does it take to get back on the bike and become a world champion? The 26-year-old, seven-times world champion is truly something else, winning in all classes from 125cc to Moto GP. Valentino is a hero to millions and is one of the world's top ten earners as an athlete, banking around US$30 million  annually. His achievements are suitably reflected in this lavish visual documentary. It is exactly the kind of book that the difficult-to-reach teenage reader may just find irresistible. Why? For starters, Rossi has the look of a Year Nine boy who has just skipped double science and is on his way to do something far more exciting. An air of boyish fun surrounds him, but his peerless success is built upon outrageous skills. The 450 pages of colour-saturated photography are alive with action, tracing Valentino's rise, season by season, from childhood go-kart races to his first podium finish (when he was scarcely shaving) through the myriad of Grand Prix wins on a vast array of extremely fast machines. There is an extensive visual catalogue of all Rossi's bikes and racing leathers. And then there is the sequence of hilarious post-race celebratory dress-ups. This level of detail is a rev-head's dream. *Valentino Rossi: Legend* is a long and loving look at an athlete and a world that most people rarely even glimpse.

Why Dick Fosbury Flopped and answers to other big sporting questions

> ## DAMIAN FARROW AND JUSTIN KEMP

YA/A AUSTRALIA 2006

Approaching the crease at 6 metres per second or approximately 21 km/h, a fast bowler generates an average force of seven times his own body weight every time his front foot contacts the pitch at the point of delivery . . . Cricket may be considered a non-contact sport, but try telling that to the body of a fast bowler.

How is it that a ball kicked from thirty metres can travel smoothly on one path only to dip and swerve beyond the fingertips of the goalkeeper's outstretched arm? How *do* you bend it like Beckham? It's simple physics, Kemp and Farrow explain. The art is to make that ball slow down exactly where you want it to as it moves towards the net. As regular presenters of Melbourne radio station 3RRR's *Run Like You Stole Something*, Kemp and Farrow share the city's love of all things sporting. But as leading professional sports scientists they also have extraordinary knowledge and the curiosity to fuel their obsession.

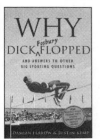

Why Dick Fosbury Flopped provides an entertaining, quirky and rewarding look at a wide range of issues and milestone moments. Tightly organised chapters cover the evolution of techniques, the science of sporting projectiles, changes to equipment, body types, drug cheats and testing, and how research is shaping sports. The authors shine a light on issues like 'chucking' in cricket, why drug cheats are so hard to detect, and how a winged keel works. This is sports science with the passion, wonder and humour left in. **IT'S TRUE! SPORT STINKS** covers much of the same material for younger readers.

And why did high-jumper Dick Fosbury flop? It's all to do with moving the centre of gravity outside the body in the leap. The discovery was enough for Fosbury to clinch an Olympic gold medal and revolutionise the high jump. Ah, sweet science!

Wondrous Oblivion ➤ PAUL MORRISON

Y/YA UK 2004

He lobbed a slow ball. David curled his body up and then unleashed an almighty swipe. Judy ducked as David's follow-through narrowly missed her head. The ball rolled gently onto the stumps, and the bails toppled to the ground.

Wondrous Oblivion is a story of family, friendship, racism and hope played out on a strip of grass 22 yards long. When Britain opened its doors to post-war West Indian migrants, they brought with them not just low-wage labour, but their enormous passion for cricket. It was one of the few things the two countries both held dear but England hardly embraced them for it. *Wondrous Oblivion*, set in south London in 1960, uses this historical moment to tell the story of David Wiseman, an eleven-year-old boy obsessed with cricket. David can hardly hold a bat let alone a catch, but he dreams brightly of one day making a name for himself as a cricketer. But good fortune is at hand when his new neighbours turn out to be cricket-loving migrants from Jamaica. And David has plenty of time on his hands: his father works long days as the owner of fabric shop so David spends many hours in the neighbour's backyard cricket net.

The arrival of new neighbours brings out an ugly and potentially violent racism in the suburbs. For David's family the growing tension carries with it memories of another past, when as Jewish refugees they fled from Nazi Germany. And of course there is a ready comparison today with the treatment of other refugees. But *Wondrous Oblivion* also fixes on young David's friendship with the young Jamaican girl Judi and the conflict with his own schoolmates from the grammar school.

war & conflicts

Stories of war and national and international conflicts continue to inspire writers. They include world wars and the horrors of the Holocaust, as well as conflicts in Vietnam, Afghanistan, Iraq, in other Middle-Eastern countries, and in other parts of the world. Such conflicts are generated by struggles between groups and nations, caused by religious, ethnic and racial differences and the cycle of hardship and cruelty in the name of revolution. Great writers and illustrators can transform such hot and heavy topics into enthralling stories that, when finely crafted and imagined, never go out of date.

Aleutian Sparrow ➤ KAREN HESSE

Y/YA/A USA 2003

THE JAPANESE

*They weren't always our enemy. There was a time when the
Japanese sailed in and their crews played baseball with
our Aleut teams.*

ATTACK

*Alfred's family was preparing to leave for their summer
fish camp.
I was going with them, leaving Pari, leaving my mother to
stay in Kashega and watch over Solomon's store
But in the endless light of June
The Japanese stung from the sky*

SIMPLE QUESTION

*The Japanese have been defeated on Attu,
They have retreated from Kiska,
We Americans have retaken the Aleutians as our own again.
May our people go home now?*

ON THE ISLAND OF UNALASKA

*The flowers have closed their mouths and begun their
descent into winter sleep.
Snow comforts the shoulders of Mount Newhall,
A brown jumble of chest-high grasses rasps and scrapes in the
williwaw winds.*

Seven months after the bombing of Pearl Harbor in 1941, the Japanese invaded Alaska's Aleutian Islands. The Aleutians were United States citizens, yet they were abused, hounded, herded and their numbers decimated over a period of time.

In tiny, spare, telling fragments Karen Hesse reveals a proud people struggling first to survive, then to maintain their heritage and communities. Below are a few other headings that, together with a few lines of verse for each, paint heartrending word pictures of children, parents, shopkeepers, the landscape and events, and the fight to keep going and keep up spirits:

Evacuation
attack
blanket
houses
keeping clean
finding work
rusting
seal
kill
fever
left behind
resettlment officer
growing wings

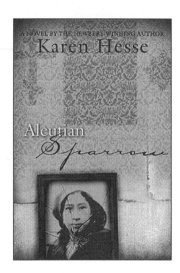

Angels of Kokoda ➤ DAVID MULLIGAN

Y/YA AUSTRALIA 2006

Everybody was in a terrible condition. Everybody was permanently tired – exhausted. Every day more Diggers came down with malaria. Nobody could wash and nearly everybody had some kind of disgusting skin disease.

There was no dry ground. There was only mud.

These were the conditions along the infamous Kokoda Track in New Guinea during World War II. Derek's father is a missionary doctor, his mother a teacher. They are strict and stern and their son Derek is alienated and unhappy. When the Japanese attack, all women and children are sent back to Australia. Derek refuses to go to boarding school and is determined to stay with his Papuan blood brother, Morso (their joint initiation is a fascinating vignette), so together they disappear into the jungle. As the situation deteriorates, the twelve-year-olds become indispensable, looking after artillery, the sick and the dead, and manning the radio. Forced to work together, Derek's relationship with his father improves, too.

Mulligan has placed the two boys in the midst of real life characters and situations to bring to life a grim but heroic episode in Australia's wartime history. Most of the soldiers were hardly more than boys and their ability to withstand and repel the Japanese is legendary – as is the contribution of the Papuans, known as the Fuzzy Wuzzy Angels. We see courage, mateship, suffering, deaths, racism, horrific conditions and the psychological damage that takes Derek a long time to overcome. Clearly Mulligan wants young Australians to know this story. As Derek writes in one of his many unsent letters to his sister, 'Everything must be known about these wonderful men who have saved Australia.'

Read another account of this important piece of Australian history in Tony Palmer's compelling new **BREAK OF DAY** (2007).

mixing fact & fiction
australian and nz war stories
for younger readers

THE BOMBING OF DARWIN: THE DIARY OF TOM TAYLOR, 1942
Alan Tucker 2002
Another in the excellent My Story series from Scholastic, in which
invented characters are placed in critical moments in Australian
history – here in the tense days leading up to the bombing of
Darwin by the Japanese.

SCARECROW ARMY: THE ANZACS AT GALLIPOLI 2005 and
RED HAZE: AUSTRALIANS & NEW ZEALANDERS IN VIETNAM 2006
Leon Davidson NEW ZEALAND
Both these books are from Black Dog Books' inventive, accessible
The Drum series, which interweaves authoritative historical detail,
expert commentary, eye-witness accounts, photos and newspaper
reports with fictional segments to involve readers and provide
substantial accounts of important events, times and lives.

SOLDIER BOY 2001 and **YOUNG DIGGER** 2002 Anthony Hill AUSTRALIA
Set during World War I, both novels are lovingly researched
and tell stories of the war-time experiences of boys involved in
fighting. In *Soldier Boy*, Jim Martin, at fourteen, may have been
the youngest enlisted soldier. He joins up early in the war and
endures the horrors of Gallipoli. In *Young Digger*, orphan Henri
Hemène attaches himself to Australian soldiers in France, becomes
a mascot, and is smuggled back to Australia after the signing of
the Armistice in 1918.

THE TRENCHES: BILLY STEVENS, THE WESTERN FRONT 1914–1918
Jim Eldrige 2002
Two fictitious sixteen-year-olds put their ages up to nineteen and
join the army. A realistic, factually accurate account of what Billy's
grim life would have been like in the trenches. This is also part of
the My Story series.

Boys of Blood and Bone ➤ DAVID METZENTHEN

YA/A AUSTRALIA 2003

Dedication: With admiration and gratitude I dedicate this book to the memory of the Australian men and women who served in the First World War, 1914–1918. In particular, I mention my grandfather, Private AJ Metzenthen . . . who fought with the Fourth Machine Gun Battalion in Belgium and France in 1916, 1917 and 1918.

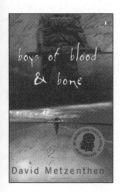

Wanting to know more about his grandfather's experiences, Metzenthen researched the period and visited many of the battlefields and cemeteries of World War I. The result is a gripping, thought-provoking read and an homage to a gallant, much-loved grandfather. Metzenthen brings the past and present together through the parallel lives of Andy Lansell, an Australian Digger, killed in the Somme in 1918, and Henry Lyon, about to begin university in the present. While Henry waits in a small country town for his car to be fixed, he is given Andy's diary, long held by his then fiancée. Henry is enthralled and touched by the story of the lost youth of someone of his own age. Henry can't fail to see how different, and perhaps banal, his life is in comparison to Andy's. He begins to see what was expected and given, sometimes unwittingly, by those innocent young men. Most believed they were going on an adventure, or getting a leg up in the world, while also making their contribution to beating the enemy. The battle scenes, the mud, fear and the courage of the Diggers are graphically presented, but there are also flashes of humour and some romantic interludes in the lives of both young men.

Metzenthen's next beautifully written book, **BLACK WATER** (2007), makes a fine companion piece, showing the impact of the war on those at home. Farren Fox's father is lost at sea, then his brother returns from Gallipoli damaged and changed. Set against the beauty of Swan Bay in Queenscliff the tragedies elicit personal courage, community warmth and laconic Aussie humour.

Dark Hours ➤ GUDRUN PAUSEWANG

Translated by John Brownjohn

YA GERMANY 2006

'The first World War was nothing compared to this . . .' That's what our neighbour, Grandpa Hausler, kept saying these last few months . . .

'We oughtn't to be surprised,' Granny grumbled yesterday while we were packing. 'We Germans started the war. Hitler was positively itching for it, and we gave him all the support he needed.'

As a gift for Stephanie's sixteenth birthday, her grandmother writes the story of what happened on her own sixteenth birthday. She writes, 'It's a true story. I lived it myself, sixty long years ago.' Granny's story opens as her family, made up of her heavily pregnant mother, four children – ranging in age from eighteen-month-old Wolfi to Gisel (Granny herself), very nearly sixteen – and their grandmother, are hastily packing a few essentials. Father is away fighting. The Russians are coming, so the family must evacuate. They are heading for their other grandparents' home in Dresden, but mother goes into labour and is left behind in a hospital in an unknown town. At the station the children are separated from Granny. When the air-raid siren sounds, Gisel must take charge. She hustles the children into an air-raid shelter. Then the shelter takes a direct hit and the children are trapped in the bathroom. For some days the children must survive in total darkness with a tiny bit of food and water from the one undamaged cistern. Gisel and Erwin, twelve, care for and entertain the little ones and eventually manage to attract attention. They are saved and find granny, only to discover that Dresden has been razed by the allies. What has happened to their grandparents and can they find mother and father . . . and the new baby?

Pausewang writes this as a breathtaking heroic adventure-survival story, but her serious purpose is never in doubt: to highlight the acquiescence of so many Germans to Hitler and to show that 'Every war is a crime'. An important book that is strengthened by the informative, hard-hitting afterword.

Ellen's People ➤ DENNIS HAMLEY

YA/A UK 2006

*'My dear young lady,' said the colonel. 'I never thought I would live
to see the world overtaken by such madness. Millions of young men
all over Europe looking for a little adventure to brighten up dull lives.
Their families sad to see them go, but proud as well. They are answering
their nation's call. That's not wrong. But what will these young men find on
their adventures? We've unleashed a monster that we can't stop.'*

The colonel, who lost an arm during the Boer War, is the wise man and the conscience of this tale. He is accused of being a traitor by some rabid village locals for pointing out that the enemy (the Germans) are also young men fighting for their country. Ellen recognises his wisdom and compassion. Her parents mistrust all 'toffs'. Yet when Jack, Ellen's brother, returns minus a leg, angry and despairing about the future, it is the colonel who sets him up in a bicycle repair business.

Against her parents' wishes, Ellen takes up nursing, and eventually goes to France to be part of Lavinia's Flying Circus, a field hospital run and funded by an enterprising woman. Here Ellen witnesses the day-to-day horror of thousands of damaged, dying and dead young men, including, as the war progresses, many ever-younger Germans. We see the war from the perspective of a feisty young woman who battles the prejudices, expectations and fears of her family and of society. Hamley has written non-fiction about the two world wars and crams much information into his lively family saga that shows the end of an era and of a sheltered way of life. Watch out for the sequel, **ELLEN'S CHILDREN**.

famous epic war stories

WAR AND PEACE Leo Tolstoy A/YA RUSSIA 1865–1869
War and Peace appeared in instalments between 1865 and
1869. So detailed and with such a huge canvas of events, at
first it was not considered a novel. This epic, with almost
600 characters, real and fictional, shows the impact on five
families of Napoleon's invasion of Russia, and sweeps from
family life to the battlefields of Austerlitz and Borodino.

THE RED BADGE OF COURAGE Stephen Crane A/YA USA 1895
This great novel of the American Civil War is given added
power and authenticity because Crane actually fought in
this war. It is considered Crane's masterwork and the first
modern war novel because it depicts the terrors and realities
of war from the point of view of an ordinary soldier. Henry
Fleming expects glorious battles but flees when reality hits.
He returns to fight with real courage, no illusions, and an
understanding of the injustice of war.

ALL QUIET ON THE WESTERN FRONT Erich Maria Remarque
A/YA GERMANY 1929
An epic classic, a worldwide bestseller and also a 1930
Oscar-winning movie. A World War I veteran, Remarque
wrote about the horrors of war, but also about the
disillusionment and inability of German men to fit into
civilian life when they returned from the war.

CATCH 22 Joseph Heller A/YA USA 1961
Everyone knows this phrase, signifying a no-win situation,
coined by Heller in his gritty, funny, horrific, satirical
anti-war novel set in World War II Italy.

▶▶▶

FALLEN ANGELS Walter Dean Myers YA/A USA 1988

A tough, uncompromising account of the Vietnam War seen through the eyes of a Harlem teenager during a year of combat duty. Like many young black men fighting in the Iraq war today, this soldier thought joining up would be a way out of a bleak life, but reality showed otherwise. Controversial for its anti-establishment line. Published as both a young adult and adult book.

BIRDSONG Sebastian Faulks A/YA UK 1993

In 1916, Stephen Wraysford returns to Amiens, where six years ago he had a passionate affair. Now a British Army officer, he endures unimaginably horrific conditions and survives some of the fiercest battles of the Western Front. Sixty years on, Elizabeth tries to understand the events that shaped her grandfather. A harrowing but intense reading experience.

THE GHOST ROAD Pat Barker A/YA UK 1995

The third in Pat Barker's deeply imagined, enthralling but devastating Regeneration trilogy. Barker places fictional characters like Lieutenant Billy Prior, a working class man elevated to the position of British officer, alongside historical characters like Dr Rivers, an eminent psychiatrist famous for treating shell-shocked soldiers, and the war poets Siegfried Sassoon and Wilfred Owen. A great feat of imagination and re-creation highlighting the futility of war.

Fireshadow ➤ ANTHONY EATON

YA AUSTRALIA 2005

*Old spirits walked here. Ghosts as old as time. Vinnie stepped into
the clearing. The leaves of the eucalypts trembled in the midday heat and
the occasional insect chirped. Otherwise the bush stood silent . . .*

Did you know that during World War II many German and Italian
prisoners of war worked in the farms and forests of south-west WA,
and that their labour often supplied Perth with fuel and food? Eaton
sets his moving story in POW Camp 16 in Marinup. (You can still see
the remains of the settlement.) At the heart of this big story is the
love between the granddaughter of the ageing Australian camp
doctor (a beautifully realised character) and the proud, defiant young
German POW, Erich. In an intricately plotted tale,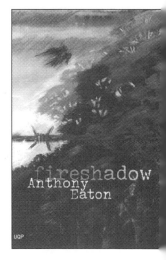
Eaton pieces together what happened to these
two and brings their stories up to the present
by intersecting Erich's story with that of Vinnie
– running, grieving, hiding, and damaged in the
car crash that killed his sister. It is a powerful tale
of war, guilt, disillusionment, loss and love. The
bush setting, so healing and welcome to Vinnie
and so alien to Erich, adds further texture and
meaning to the lives of these two confused and
grieving young men, both of whom find new ways
of living. *Fireshadow* would make a great movie.

major **australian war movies**

THE ODD ANGRY SHOT 1979

Focuses on the experiences of Australian soldiers in Vietnam, but avoids direct political comment on the involvement of Australia.

BREAKER MORANT 1980

Depicts three soldiers accused of killing Boer prisoners of war during the Boer War, and the court martial that results. The focus is on 'The Breaker', an Australian horse-breaker, and the lawyer asked to defend him at short notice. The riveting court scenes are at the heart of the story.

GALLIPOLI 1981

Two Australian sprinters face the brutal realities of war when they are sent to fight in the Gallipoli campaign in Turkey during World War I. About the illusions and realities of war.

LAND MINES: A LOVE STORY 2005

An award-winning anti-war documentary set in Afghanistan, made by the renowned Dennis O'Rourke.

KOKODA 2006

An action/adventure/drama set in modern-day Papua New Guinea, *Kokoda* looks at the horrific struggle to survive and defeat the Japanese, and the differences between two veterans of the Kokoda campaign fifty years on. An excellent companion to David Mulligan's **ANGELS OF KOKODA** (see page 260) and Tony Palmer's **BREAK OF DAY**.

Jacko Moran, Sniper ➤ KEN CATRAN

YA NEW ZEALAND 2003

*Going back to New Zealand didn't seem real. The trenches and the mud,
the bullets and stink of rotting bodies – they were real.*

*I don't remember much about the last years. Drinking, drunk and disorderly,
sleeping rough, in and out of jail. War couldn't kill me but the bloody peace
did. It just took a hell of a long time.*

Jacko Moran, Sniper is the first in an impressive, action-packed
quartet that places young people from subsequent generations of
a family at the centre of major wars and battles. Like many others,
Jacko, a slum kid given a rough time by his father, thinks war is a way
to move out of his situation and find glorious adventure, too. In France
and Gallipoli during World War I Jacko gains respect as a sniper. He
seems fearless and willing to go where others won't, including into
no-man's land to pick off the enemy. Catran doesn't mince words and
he keeps the reader turning pages. His research and carefully placed
detail bring characters, situations and periods to life. He reveals the
horrors and futility of war by showing us how it was and is.

In **ROBERT MORAN, PRIVATE** (2004), Jacko's son can't shake his
father's shadow while he fights in World War II, in battles in Greece,
North Africa and Italy.

JIMMY MORAN, REGULAR (2005) takes us to Vietnam – a
different kind of war, but one that is no less grim and gruesome. This
war divided nations and families, including Jimmy's. Jimmy's war
experiences are different as he is a professional soldier, who copes
well in the forces and ends up as a major general. The final book,
TERESA MORAN, SOLDIER (2007), is set in Iraq and Timor. Catran
has said, 'It's a very controversial subject and I wanted to show both
sides of the story – Muslim vs Christian, Iraq vs USA. So much of
what really happens never makes it into the newspapers and I want
to offer informed choices for young people to make up their own
minds. Again, soldiers involved in this war don't want to talk about
their experiences, but I've sourced some excellent information from
journalists and war artists.'

Lord of the Nutcracker Men ➤ IAIN LAWRENCE

Y/YA CANADA 2003

'My father made it,' I said.

'Did he? At the front?' Mr Tuttle let the figure stand on his palm, in his fingers. He studied poor Harry Black [the carving of a friend the father had made at the front] *from every angle. 'It's beyond words,' he muttered. 'It tells a whole story, doesn't it?'*

'What story?' I asked, desperate to know if he thought the man was dancing or dying.

'It scarcely needs saying. He's one of the fallen,' said Mr Tuttle . . .

'I don't know how, but your father's given a soul to this wooden soldier.' He closed his fingers round the man and lifted it up to his face. 'I can smell the mud on him, Johnny.'

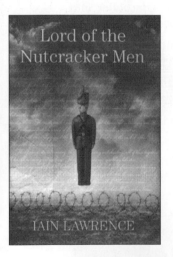

We too can smell the mud in this remarkable war story. Johnny's father is a quiet, gentle man and a highly skilled toymaker. But it is 1914. When his father goes to war, ten-year-old Johnny is sent for safety to an aunt in the country. The relentless, terrifying life in the trenches is hidden in the loving, careful letters from a father desperate to shield his son. However, with each letter comes a carved soldier or figure to add to Johnny's huge collection. As Johnny plays war games, he tries to make sense of what is happening and how he feels. It is through the changing stance and demeanour of the carved figurines that the father's experiences and emotions are revealed. There are brilliantly created layers upon layers, though the child's perspective and voice never waver. Lawrence is a notable writer of Canadian historical fiction. He also writes with verve about the sea and sailing. Here he couldn't be more English in tone and perspective.

Malka ➤ MIRJAM PRESSLER

Translated by Brian Murdoch

Y/YA GERMANY 2002

*[Hannah] wasn't frightened. Not really. She was needed, she was protected
by her profession ...*

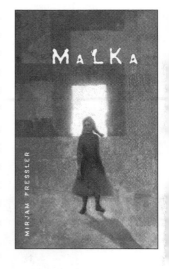

In Poland in 1943, Hannah, Malka's mother,
believes that despite being Jewish she is safe
from the Nazis because she is a doctor who
treats Germans. But no Jew is safe, and Hannah
must escape. She relies on friends and strangers
as she and her two daughters struggle over
mountains in the freezing cold. When Malka
gets ill, she is left behind for her own safety, but
in the chaos she ends up completely alone. The
drama and intensity of the book are at their best
when showing the physical realities of Malka's
experiences: sleeping in cellars, surviving the
cold and begging for food. Will her determined,
traumatised mother find her and forgive herself?
Can a small, spoilt girl survive, abandoned and starving? And if she
does, what sort of imprint will this leave on her? Will she ever re-
establish real contact with her mother or live a normal, happy life?

Malka existed and survived. In 1996, Pressler found her in
Israel, but Malka had suppressed much of her ordeal, so this is an
imaginative recreation. Of the thousands of Holocaust stories, what
makes some stand out? In this case it is the clarity of the voice, the
resilience of Malka, and the mind-stopping realisation that people
can perpetrate such horrors on others, especially children.

more about the holocaust ➤➤➤

important holocaust books for all ages

BEARING WITNESS: STORIES OF THE HOLOCAUST Hazel Rochman and Darlene Z McCampbell (eds) Y/YA USA 1995
An excellent compilation of memoirs, poems, stories and extracts from well-known contributors such as Elie Wiesel, Primo Levi and Art Spiegelman, with equally poignant and dramatic pieces from less well-known American writers.

The Boy in the Striped Pyjamas

JOHN BOYNE

THE BOY IN THE STRIPED PYJAMAS
John Boyne Y UK 2006
Boyne places a small, pampered, middle-class boy within sight of a concentration camp. Bruno fails to make any connection between what he sees or hears at home and from his window. (His father works for Hitler, who comes to dinner.) He misunderstands terms: 'outhwith' (Auschwitz) and 'the fury' (the Führer). Because of his innocence or ignorance, his friendship with starving little Shmuel on the 'other' side of the long fence, and finally because of his curiosity, he pays dearly. Perhaps a metaphor for all those adults who heard or saw no evil? A grim, haunting tale.

THE DIARY OF A YOUNG GIRL Anne Frank Y/YA/A HOLLAND 1947
See page 181.

THE FINAL JOURNEY Gudrun Pausewang,
translated by Patricia Crampton YA GERMANY 1992/1996
The powerful, heart-wrenching story of a Jewish girl and
her grandparents being 'relocated' to Auschwitz. Pausewang
combines compelling stories with strong political messages about
the past, the present and the future.

HANA'S SUITCASE Karen Levine
Y/YA CANADA 2002

Following pleas from young people, the
Director of the Tokyo Holocaust Education
Resource Center undertakes an exhaustive
search to find out what happened to
Hana Brady, the owner of a small suitcase
in their collection. Eventually Hana's
fate is discovered. The search leads to
Hana's brother, who is living in Canada.
Here, award-winning broadcaster Karen
Levine continued the quest and made this
remarkable story into a program for
radio. This beautiful, haunting book –
her first – followed, and it led Karen
Levine into what effectively became a
new career telling the story of Hana and
her suitcase.

MAUS: A SURVIVOR'S TALE and
**MAUS II: A SURVIVOR'S TALE: AND HERE
MY TROUBLES BEGAN** Art Spiegelman
A/YA USA 1972

Brilliant, classic graphic novels of Hitler's
Europe, surviving a concentration camp,
and of the cartoonist son trying to come
to terms with history and his father's story.

▶▶▶

NIGHT Elie Wiesel A/YA USA 1958

Having lost most of his family, Wiesel survived the concentration camp and was liberated by Allied troops. Like many Holocaust survivors, he was initially unable to discuss his ordeal. However, the great French writer François Mauriac persuaded Wiesel to document his experiences. After struggling to find a publisher, *Night* was released in 1958 and has become a classic. Wiesel went on to win the Nobel Prize for his tireless work to spread the message that the Holocaust must never be repeated.

NUMBER THE STARS Lois Lowry Y USA 1989

Set in Denmark during the Nazi occupation, this story explores a lesser known aspect of World War II. Like many children during the war, ten-year-old Anne Marie Johansen learns to keep secrets. Jewish Ellen Rosen is passed off as a member of their family, and a Christian, until safe passage can be arranged for the Rosens to Sweden.

ONCE Morris Gleitzman Y AUSTRALIA 2006

A lost, desperate little Jewish boy escapes from the convent where he has been placed for safety, and sets out to search for his parents. A devastating, fable-like tale of a trusting child who keeps hoping for the best in the face of contrary evidence that the reader can see, but the child can't or won't.

SCHINDLER'S ARK Thomas Keneally A/YA AUSTRALIA 1982

Keneally's best-selling 1982 fictionalised account of how Oskar Schindler, a German industrialist, risked his life and defied the SS to save many Jews in Nazi-occupied Poland. It is even better known as *Schindler's List*, the Oscar-winning movie.

Private Peaceful ➤ MICHAEL MORPURGO

YA/A UK 2003

I want to try to remember everything, just as it was, just as it happened. I've had nearly eighteen years of yesterdays and tomorrows, and tonight I must remember as many of them as I can. I want tonight to be long, as long as my life, not filled with fleeting dreams that rush me on towards dawn.

Tonight, more than any other night of my life, I want to feel alive.

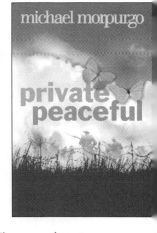

What a terrible irony that this is a night when Tommo wants to feel alive! Many books reveal the horrors of World Wars I and II, but Morpurgo manages to make these experiences new and intensely moving, partly through the honest, innocent voice and recollections of Thomas, one of the thousands whose illusions of glory during World War I have been shattered.

Life for the Peacefuls, in their small rural home, has not been easy since the death of Thomas's father. The opportunity to enlist seems a way of holding the family together. For Thomas, often bullied, it may also be a way to prove himself. Revered older brother Charlie helps by allowing Thomas, almost sixteen, to pass as his twin. But nothing has prepared the boys for the conditions and carnage they encounter. What are they fighting for? Will they ever get home? In the hands of this superb storyteller and former UK Children's Laureate, Tommo's story is achingly painful but never sentimental. Morpurgo said, 'I happened to interview three farm boy veterans, then well into their eighties, when I was researching my book *War Horse*. They told me something of what they had lived through. There was no poetry in their stories, only horror and regret and great sadness for the loss of good friends.'

more michael morpurgo ➤➤➤

michael morpurgo

WAR HORSE 1982

When war breaks out, Joey, a beautiful red-bay foal with a distinctive cross on his nose, is sold to the army where he, like the soldiers around him, must try to cope with the horrors of World War I. Involved in a cavalry charge, then captured by the Germans, Joey faces much danger and hardship before finding love and care.

WAITING FOR ANYA 1990

From a tiny village in the Pyrenees mountains on the French–Spanish border during the German occupation of France in World War II, Jo helps Benjamin smuggle Jewish children to safety in Spain. Benjamin is desperate to find his daughter, Anya, from whom he was separated when they fled Paris. Despite great danger the whole village becomes involved.

WAR: STORIES OF CONFLICT 2005

Compiled by Morpurgo on the sixtieth anniversary of the end of World War II, this is an outstanding collection exploring many wars in many countries, from the past to the present. Contributors include Geraldine McCaughrean, Elizabeth Laird, Margaret Mahy and Eva Ibbotson.

The Road of Bones ➤ ANNE FINE

YA UK 2006

We were all slaves, walking a road of bones. Like everyone else in our benighted country, I was a cog in the machine.

This is a grim, scary, but totally gripping book about the horrific things that leaders and people will do in the name of ideology, self-interest and survival. It is also unexpected subject matter from this author, mostly known for her humour and insight into family life (remember *Madame Doubtfire*?). Here Anne Fine (a former UK Children's Laureate) imagines a country very like Russia, at a time very like that of the infamous Revolution that ousted the corrupt Czar in the early 20th century and created the Russian Republic. We meet bright student Yuri at the age of twelve. Already he is trying to make sense of the poverty, cruelty and fear around him, generated by the supposedly 'Glorious Revolution', or, as his long-suffering grandmother prefers, 'The Glorious *Lie*'. Churches have been sacked and locked up, people disappear, starvation looms and propaganda is rife. One careless comment can result in death – or exile to a labour camp, which is Yuri's fate. He endures prison, starvation, and a gruelling train journey to the iciest regions of the country. He escapes and survives in the wild, is captured, then escapes again. Despite the extreme dangers, he becomes increasingly involved in the growing resistance.

In this angry and compelling story, described by the publishers as 'truly a novel of our times', Fine shows the horror and futility of this endless cycle of inhumanity, as the so-called freedom-fighters convince themselves that the end justifies the means. Yuri, brutalised by his experiences, is also trapped in this cycle. An important book, which is frighteningly relevant in the context of today's Russia.

The Running Man ➤ MICHAEL GERARD BAUER

YA AUSTRALIA 2004

Joseph fixed his eyes on the coffin and thought of silkworms. Before him the honey-coloured casket lay still and silent like a cocoon, and for a moment he was in another time, another place. Each ripple of sound . . . reminded him of where he was, and then the sickly ache of regret and loss lurched inside him once more. 'It's my fault,' Joseph thought . . .

Joseph's love of drawing gradually leads the quiet fourteen-year-old into the sad, silent life of his neighbour, Tom Leyton. Leyton lives with his sister, Caroline, who entices Joseph to draw a portrait of her brother. Tom seldom emerges from his house. For some time he has seemed a looming, scary figure to Joseph, almost as scary as the Running Man who shambled and loped around the neighbourhood, haunting Joseph's childhood and dreams, and generating much gossip. Tom's past also encourages tongues to wag. Has he been dismissed from teaching? For what? And should Joseph be allowed near him? But Tom's demons stem from his experiences in the Vietnam War. Joseph himself is struggling with confused emotions towards his father. Tom and Joseph gain confidence around each other through art and by sharing Tom's interest in silkworms. But there is too much pain and guilt swirling about to allow an easy resolution.

Not directly a 'war story', but rather about the endless circles of pain that wars and other catastrophes can cause in people's lives. Bauer created his wonderful first book from many strands and images, but cocoons and silkworms recur in varied ways. One inspiration was a favourite poem, *The Silkworms*, by the great Australian poet Douglas Stewart. Another was a mulberry tree in the young Bauer's garden, and yet another, Bauer says cryptically, was 'my own Running Man'.

Tamar ➤ MAL PEET

YA/A UK 2005

In the end, it was her grandfather, William Hyde, who gave the unborn child her name. He was serious about names; he'd had several himself.

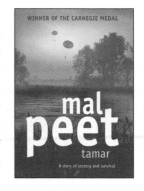

For many years nobody understood why the baby girl had been named Tamar. When her grandfather jumps to his death from his balcony, Tamar, now a teenager, is bequeathed a box full of possible clues. With the help of her Dutch cousin, Johannes (Yoyo), she embarks on a journey that takes her to the mouth of the Tamar River in Cornwall. Gradually they uncover the secretive and terrifyingly dangerous wartime existence of William Hyde and his beloved Marijke. They also begin to understand why Tamar's father disappeared.

Codenamed 'Tamar' and 'Dart', two very young Dutchmen, trained in England, parachute into freezing, starving Holland during the final winter of World War II. One is to coordinate the resistance, the other is to maintain secret wireless contact with London. Isolated, bored and in constant fear, Dart becomes addicted to the amphetamines he takes to keep himself awake and functioning. Tamar is constantly on the move and in danger, but is sustained by his passionate relationship with Marijke, in whom Dart is also interested. Inevitably, terrible choices have to be made.

Peet shows that horror and survival guilt reverberate down generations, and are not only felt by those who braved the battlefields. We also see the courage and resilience of civilians. 'This sombre and distinguished book is as fine a piece of storytelling as you are likely to read this year,' wrote Jan Mark in *The Guardian*. *Tamar* won Peet the 2006 Carnegie Medal. (For another aspect of Peet's writing, see page 244.)

the great **robert westall**

Robert Westall (1929–1993), wrote his first book, *The Machine Gunners*, to tell his twelve-year-old son about his own childhood during World War II. It won the Carnegie Medal and led to a career in writing and a life-time of exploring wartime experiences. As well as war stories, Westall wrote exciting tales of the supernatural. He was also a teacher and art critic, and wrote non-fiction, picture books and adult books.

THE MACHINE GUNNERS 1975
When Chas, a passionate collector of war memorabilia, finds a machine gun in a crashed German plane, he adds it to his collection. Little does he realise he will be putting many people's lives in danger. Westall presents a thrilling adventure and a picture of life during World War II: blackouts, food shortages, terrifying bombing raids and people pulling together.

BLITZCAT 1989
A World War II adventure that features Lord Gort, a courageous black cat, searching for her beloved master using 'Psi trailing', a documented phenomenon whereby animals track their owners. Lord Gort's travels allow many affecting glimpses into life in war-torn England, and an unusual perspective on the horrific bombing of Coventry Cathedral and its impact on people already struggling to survive.

GULF 1992
Here Westall brings war and the supernatural together in an intense, hugely imaginative gem. Tom's brother, Figgis (really Andy), suddenly thinks he is someone called Latif. So an English boy is somehow connected to an Iraqi one during the first Gulf War in a terrifying ordeal that can only end in death. But whose?

FALLING INTO GLORY 1993
In the 1950s, after World War II, men were scarce. Emma Harrison is seventeen-year-old Robbie's teacher. She is lovely and lonely. Robbie 'falls into glory' with Emma. Robbie is inarticulate and rough, but also enraptured. His other great love is football. He juggles both passions. A bold and beautiful book, it shows that relationships between students and teachers are always highly dangerous, but not a new phenomenon.

war books with pictures
as well as stories

LET THE CELEBRATIONS BEGIN Margaret Wild and Julie Vivas AUSTRALIA 1991
Children and women in a concentration camp find scraps to make
toys for other children in anticipation of the celebration when they are
liberated. Some objected to this book because of its focus on celebration
rather than suffering.

ROSE BLANCHE Roberto Innocenti USA 1985
A young German girl discovers a concentration camp near her home
and takes food to the children there, with devastating consequences.
A beautifully realised but explicit work that shows how children may be
affected by the inhuman and random acts of others.

THE TIN POT GENERAL AND THE IRON LADY Raymond Briggs UK 1984
A vicious and harrowing graphic novel about the Falklands War.
WHEN THE WIND BLOWS (1986) is another graphic novel in which Briggs
imagines a nuclear holocaust in England with a couple, based on his own
parents, obeying futile regulations until they succumb to the fallout.

weird & wonderful stuff

by Kevin Steinberger

Consider the average teenager's lot – a tightly scheduled routine of school, and work at the local fast-food franchise. Week in week out, year after year. It's enough to stir up longings for rebellion or escape. Anything for a bit of colour and excitement. Non-fiction provides examples of how to be different, to challenge orthodoxy and have a laugh at the world.

It is an established fact that many boys prefer non-fiction. Unlike girls, these boys seem less willing to become absorbed in narrative fiction. They are more inclined to read sporadically, dipping into a book at whim. Their reading experience is substantially influenced by peer recommendations. So it is a very eclectic experience that often draws from the mainstream of publishing, titles such as the spoof Jetlag Travel Guides by Tom Gleisner et al which include **San Sombrero: a Land of Carnivals, Cocktails and Coups**. Humour is the hook that draws boys to reading – laconic wit, wry observation, puns, black humour, parody, belly laughs, the politically incorrect; the Jet Lag Travel Guides have it all by the truckload.

Similar humour is found in **Dude, Where's My Country?** by Michael Moore, of **Bowling For Columbine** fame. Moore is an unashamed polemicist but he does show some balance in his darkly humorous examination of post-9/11 USA. Another exposé which is a little closer to home for many teenagers is the juvenile edition of Eric Schlosser's **Fast Food Nation – Chew on This: Everything You Don't Want to Know About Fast Food**. Teenagers do not readily accept the status quo, rumours and urban myths are their currency and there is plenty in this book to feed that appetite.

Graham Seal's **Great Australian Urban Myths: Granny on the Roof Rack and Other Tales of Modern Horror** indulges teenage suspicion, debunking an amusing catalogue of myths which have reached into every high school in the country. Everyone loves a conspiracy theory, and they don't come much weirder than in **The Men Who Stare at Goats**, a mainstream book by Jon Ronson. This is a hilarious but purportedly true account of the Pentagon's hopeless foray into parapsychology-based warfare, like staring at your enemies until they drop dead. Just another insight into the crazy world in which we live.

However, there is a rational explanation for everything and Karl Kruszelnicki is just the man to provide the answers. **It Ain't Necessarily So ... Bro** is the latest in a long line of science compendiums which have been very popular with teenagers, just the right kind of book for the odd half hour of reading. Leaving the magazine style aside, Tim Flannery in **We Are the Weather Makers** (see page 228) explains the dominant issue of the moment – global warming.

More personal is the examination of adolescent growth. Jesse Martin's **Kijana** reflects many of the issues that teenagers will work through on their road to maturity. The clash between youthful idealism and pragmatism saw his ambitious voyage of young adventurers drift to an unhappy, premature end. Away from the troubles of group dynamics, the kitchen has become a site of solace and pleasure, and many teenagers are enjoying the challenges laid before them by the likes of fellow-teenager Sam Stern in **Cooking Up a Storm** and **Real Food, Real Fast**.

Serious or amusing, true or dubious, pictorial or wordy, informative or entertaining, there's a lot of weird and wonderful non-fiction around to satisfy any teenager.

what if . . . ?

'The finest writers for children deal in cause and consequence.'

—Boyd Tonkin, *The Independent*, August 2005

The question *What if...* allows writers to explore BIG QUESTIONS and BIG IDEAS. It also allows writers to have fun and entertain their readers by turning upside down the way we expect things to work.

What if... books don't have to be science fiction. They may consider an aspect of society, such as racism, and ask: What if blacks were in charge and whites were virtual slaves – as Malorie Blackman imagines in her Noughts and Crosses trilogy? *What if...* books often extrapolate or stretch a real issue – global warming, for example – out to a likely scenario. This is what Julie Bertagna achieves in *Exodus*. Businesses and governments may be reluctant to confront big issues and this makes many writers even keener to 'talk' to their readers in challenging, inventive ways.

Some other current hot topics are cloning and creating designer humans, as in *Sharp North* and *The Lab*. In *Genesis*, Bernard Beckett considers the potential of artificial intelligence. Some other intriguing ▶▶▶

questions explored here are: What if a teenager ran for US President or took on the US President on national TV about the right to birth control? What if Australia was invaded? What if ADS R US? What if we die and wake up Elsewhere? *What if* . . . books can be hugely entertaining as well as excellent for getting us thinking and talking.

Ads R Us ➤ CLAIRE CARMICHAEL

YA AUSTRALIA 2006

*'That's not all,' said Taylor, clearly enjoying my bemused expression.
'Once the system is activated, your pillow will talk to you all night long.
The moment its sensors feel the weight of your head, it starts off with
lullabies. Then, when it detects you're asleep, soft little voices will start
planting ideas about products you should buy.'*

**What if everyone is duped into being an active participant in the
push to increase the dominance and control of advertisers?**

Barrett, sixteen and an orphan, has been living free of ads and
'products' on a remote farm called Simplicity. When his uncle dies,
Barrett is brought to town by his aunt – the ruthless Kara Trent,
who heads the Ads-4-Life Council. Barrett, she figures, will prove
excellent for testing the impact of ads. Kara enlists her spoilt, bratty
product and status obsessed daughter, Taylor, in this project. They
assume Barrett, being a 'farm boy', is stupid and gullible. In fact he
is charming, highly educated, intelligent and alert, though shell-
shocked by the noise, consumerism and brashness he encounters.
Ads flash up on his desk in each class, and the school itself is
sponsored. Every aspect of life is permeated by ads.

Carmichael has fun inventing all this but is serious and astute
in her predictions and intentions. Kara is in league with the suave,
power-hungry tycoon Maynard Rox who even engineers panic about
an AIDS-like 'plague' so his company can sell masses of drugs. (For
more about the corrupt multi-national drug industry, read John Le
Carré's **THE CONSTANT GARDENER** (2001).) Eventually, even Taylor
realises she is being duped and, with the help of her father and the
underground protest group ADA (Against Deceit in Advertising),
there is a tense, action-packed race to reveal all to the brainwashed
populace.

All American Girl: Ready or Not ➤ MEG CABOT

YA USA 2005

Why were people clapping? Didn't they understand what David's dad was saying?

And why had none of this stuff been in the literature the White House Press Secretary had given me? There'd been nothing about requiring clinics and pharmacists to notify parents if teenagers came to them for birth control.

What if a US teenager took on the President on national TV about girls' rights to birth control without their parents' permission?

In **ALL AMERICAN GIRL** (2002), Sam saved the President's life and scored his son as a boyfriend. In this sequel, Meg Cabot places Sam in a much more complex situation. David invites Sam to stay at Camp David, the President's country 'estate'. What kind of invitation is this, wonders Sam. She and David have a subtle, warm, mature relationship. Should they now move on to sex? The confused messages about expectations and about who sleeps where provide a beguiling subplot. The front story is that Sam is asked to speak on MTV for the President's 'Return to Family' campaign. However, when the President announces that, as part of this campaign, he wants legislation that requires teens seeking prescription contraception at family planning clinics to have parental consent or to have clinics notify parents five business days in advance of providing such services to teens, Sam is so outraged that she presents a brave, articulate rebuttal, live to millions of people. Yes, it's far fetched, but its also a fresh and pointed comment on US politics and social conservatism. Fighting words from an author best known for her mega-bestselling **PRINCESS DIARIES** (see In Praise of Pink Books, page 138). Entertaining, thought-provoking and informative.

Box ➤ PENELOPE TODD

YA NEW ZEALAND 2005

Marti: *'Yes, it serves anyone right who doesn't think about what they're letting other people put on them. Serves my parents right too . . . Why won't they fight it? Why have they left it up to us?'*

What if chemical feeds make it rapidly possible for a government to gain almost total control of all citizens?

Penelope Todd: 'I think that any society finds a certain level of conformity in its citizens more convenient than free-thinking and acting out.'

In this fast-paced, thought-provoking – but at times very funny – story for our times, it has indeed been left up to New Zealand teenagers to take a stand against the government and their sudden sinister policy of 'Endorsement'. The whole population is being forced to have 'wands' implanted, so that substances (chemicals) can be automatically 'calibrated' and released into their bodies. The supposed aim is to control recent mega-viral illnesses (such as bird flu and a virulent type of head lice), but some are sceptical about the motives of the authorities, and of Pharmix, the pharmaceutical company with much to gain. A feeding network is rapidly established because 'people who refuse to get endorsed can't have the new Scope-card so they can't buy food.' Very soon, communication is also being controlled. Life for abstainers gets really tough and scary. Friends Marti, Derik and Disco are on the run. Big risks are taken – by some brave adults, and by the bold, wild, beautiful Becka. Will they defeat Pharmix and the authorities? Will the outside world intervene?

Elsewhere ➤ GABRIELLE ZEVIN

YA/A UK 2005

I am dead, Liz thinks. And then she says it aloud to hear how it sounds. 'I am dead. Dead.'

It is a strange thing being dead, because her body doesn't feel dead at all. Her body feels the same it always has.

What if you wake up 'elsewhere' and realise you are dead?

Having arrived in Elsewhere on a cruise ship mostly full of old people, Liz is introduced to a comfortable life. She even gets to live with her warm, loving grandmother, Betty, who died before she was born. She volunteers as a counsellor for the Division of Domestic Animals, and finds she's really good at it. Liz is able to watch her family and friends through special binoculars, and she meets some kind and interesting people (also dead, of course). But Liz despairs because, as she yells in frustration one day: 'I'LL NEVER GO TO COLLEGE OR GET MARRIED OR GET BIG BOOBS OR LIVE ON MY OWN OR FALL IN LOVE OR GET MY DRIVER'S LICENSE OR ANYTHING'. There are ways of getting back to one's previous life, but these are tricky to manage. Grandma Betty tries to convince Liz there is a lot to do and enjoy in Elsewhere, and even teaches her to drive her little red convertible. But what happened to Liz? And why did she die so young?

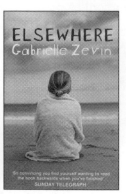

Those in Elsewhere gradually become younger and eventually return to Earth, to start a new life as a baby. This is a curious and painful process, and we see Liz at four suddenly being unable even to read. In this ingenious, gentle, sad, clever and philosophical book, Liz comes to understand what makes life worthwhile. A charming and impressive first novel.

There have been a few 'life after death' books lately. See **JACOB'S LADDER**, page 301, for a quite different view of what this might be all about.

Exodus ➤ JULIE BERTAGNA

YA UK 2002

Mara forces herself to look and see how far the ocean has now risen
A lot, she concludes. The storm season has made a wreckage of the fields of
windmills and the solar panels . . .

And this storm season has been the longest, fiercest she has ever known.

What if the earth was drowning because people had ignored climate change for so long?

I am writing this entry on September 12, 2006, the day after watching an extended interview with Al Gore, former US Vice President. He has been in Australia to promote his documentary, *An Inconvenient Truth*. For almost 30 years, Gore has been warning about climate change. His country and Australia are, at this point, the only two developed countries not to have signed the Kyoto Protocol. Gore insists that, contrary to what our Prime Minister, John Howard, has been saying, *not* reducing the use of fossil fuels and carbon dioxide emissions significantly – and soon – will greatly harm the economy and endanger lifestyles *and* lives. He also challenged the climate change skeptics by reminding us that, so far that year, Australia had already experienced two category 5 cyclones, and water is becoming increasingly scarce on this, the driest inhabited continent. Ironically, the greatest threat from climate change is the melting of polar ice caps and the consequent rise of sea levels (too much water!).

All this links neatly to Julie Bertagna, an exciting new Scottish writer whose book *Exodus* presents a powerfully imagined scenario of what the Earth might look like in 2099. The world is gradually ▶▶▶

drowning as the Arctic icefloes melt. Mara and her family eke out a precarious existence, perched on the rapidly disappearing island of Wing, buffeted by mighty storms. Mara thinks she has found a solution to her tiny community's immediate plight from a search of Weave (a version of the World Wide Web) on her portable cyberwizz. She persuades her sceptical father, and others, to leave in their tiny boats for the new city built on the remains of Glasgow. But this new breed of asylum-seekers find themselves locked out of the high towers inhabited by those with power. So, in the ultimate exodus, they must seek yet another new home and, hopefully, a better future. Described in *The Guardian* as '. . . a miracle of a novel [that] is written in stark, simple prose and uses an imaginatively created world to look at our own problems', *Exodus* unexpectedly sold over 10 000 copies in the first week of publication. So perhaps there is hope for the world yet, especially if young people are interested in tough, unsentimental books like this. (For more global warming books see page 230.)

imagining the future

TWENTY THOUSAND LEAGUES UNDER THE SEA

Jules Verne A/YA/Y FRANCE 1870

Considered by many to be the father of science fiction, Verne wrote many adventurous *What if . . .* stories that imagined the future in extraordinary ways – and that have often come to pass! Here he explores the possibilities of life deep beneath the sea.

THE WAR OF THE WORLDS H G Wells A/YA UK 1898

This book depicted an alien invasion of the world. When director Orson Welles adapted it for radio in 1938, the broadcast caused panic, as many thought it was a real invasion. The book became the basis and inspiration for many films and other alien invasion stories.

BRAVE NEW WORLD Aldous Huxley A/YA UK 1932

Huxley boldly, but satirically, imagines London in the 26th century – a world without warfare and poverty where new inventions in reproductive technology allow people to live without illnesses, defects or cares. Life is enhanced by free sex and lots of drugs. But the arts, family and any differences have been eliminated.

NINETEEN EIGHTY-FOUR George Orwell A/YA UK 1949

It is intriguing to see how much of what Orwell imagined and feared has or has not come to pass. Orwell invented the term 'Big Brother' in his scary, angry book showing one man's fight against the totalitarian state in which he lives. This is how the book was summed up in *The Guardian* when it was published: 'Orwell's *Nineteen Eighty-Four* speaks of the psychological breaking-in process to which an up-to-date dictatorship can subject non-cooperators.'

▶▶▶

THE DAY OF THE TRIFFIDS John Wyndham A/YA UK 1951
What if most people in the world were blinded by a
strange meteor shower and the planet was overrun by huge
poisonous plants?

2001: A SPACE ODYSSEY Arthur C Clarke A/YA USA 1968
When film director Stanley Kubrick asked Clarke to write
a film script, they eventually decided Clarke needed to
write the book first. Written before the first landing on
the moon, *2001* still presents a grand vision of man's place
in the universe. An enigma is discovered on the moon.
Men are sent into the solar system to investigate, but things
go very wrong. Clarke was prolific, and long considered
'the presiding genius of science fiction'. This is his most
famous and influential creation.

THE LEFT HAND OF DARKNESS Ursula K Le Guin A/YA USA 1969
On Winter – a freezing world – the people of Gethen are
androgynes: they can function as both male and female to
create and bear children. They were biologically engineered
this way long ago. In this complex world, and even
more complex novel, Le Guin explores the notion that
gender struggles lead to nationalism and wars. Le Guin is
considered one of the greatest and most sophisticated
writers of fantasy and science fiction, and also one of the
first to weave in feminist and gender issues. Le Guin writes
for young people and adults, and created the much-loved
Earthsea fantasy series, which begins with the **WIZARD OF
EARTHSEA** (1968).

Z FOR ZACHARIAH Robert O'Brien YA USA 1974
What if you were the last girl on earth? A gripping,
thought-provoking story of the power of the human spirit
in the heroic struggle to survive after a nuclear holocaust.

EVA Peter Dickinson YA UK 1988

Dickinson has been writing varied, award-winning books –
including historical fiction   for almost forty years. He has
also written crime fiction for adults under another name
and he also writes speculative fiction. *Eva* is one of his most
compelling and challenging books. On his comprehensive
website he summarises *Eva* thus: 'Future world, grossly
overpopulated. A girl, horrendously injured in a road
accident, is given the body of a chimpanzee to replace her
human body and let her continue living. But her new body
brings with it elements of the chimpanzee nature to which
she then has to adjust, and at the same time cope with the
attempts of powerful commercial interests to exploit her
unique status.'

DAZ FOR ZOE Robert Swindells YA UK 1990

Margaret Thatcher was prime minister of England from
1979 to 1990. Her tough policies angered many, including
some writers, who believed she set out to create a divided
society. It is 2051 and the population is indeed divided.
The privileged half lives in fortified suburbs, and the other
half ekes out an existence in ghettoes. When rich Zoe meets
destitute, uneducated, unemployed Daz and they fall in
love, there is bound to be trouble. Writing in alternating
voices, Swindells convincingly presents Daz's sections in the
barely literate language of those locked out of even basic
schooling. In 1985, Swindells wrote the award-winning
BROTHER IN THE LAND (1984), which asks, *If there is
a nuclear attack would it be better to perish or survive?*
(See page 77 for Swindells's **STONE COLD**.)

Genesis ➤ BERNARD BECKETT

YA NEW ZEALAND 2006

The surprise on the Examiners' faces was nothing compared to what Anax herself felt. She had contradicted the panel . . . The panel were waiting for an apology. She offered nothing.

What if the distinction between being human and being a robot became blurred?

Genesis, which originated during a year Beckett spent studying DNA evolution on a Royal Society Fellowship, is strikingly original. Its format is simply (or not so simply) the record of a five-hour interview. Candidate Anax faces impassive Examiners as she presents her chosen subject, *The life and times of Adam Forde, 2058–2077*. This academic inquisition is deliberately dehumanising in structure, but Beckett's characters and ideas rapidly transcend it. We learn that Anax's republic sealed itself off from the world during a conflict known ominously as The Last War. Decades on, the barriers against refugees and plague are still maintained. Any who approach are destroyed on sight by an overlapping system of sentries, mines and electronic devices. Anax has been studying the surviving records of how Adam helped a refugee to enter. Adam risked the lives of everyone in his society, murdered his fellow sentry and caused another dozen deaths, all to save a child. It is clear that Adam's empathy for a drifting stranger had important consequences, but only a few hints are given. Instead, Anax's re-creation of Adam's prison cell conversations with a robot, Art, becomes a disquisition on artificial intelligence, ethics, free will, and the nature of the mind and the soul.

Every aspect of this story involves interpretation: how Anax sees Adam, how Adam sees Art, and how the examiners see Anax. For Anax, this interrogation is no mere academic exercise; it carries far deeper significance. She is forced to re-examine everything she has believed up to this point. And so is the reader.

The ending is a surprise and a triumph of writing skill, but it's also logical. Its implications are so great that I turned straight back to the beginning and started reading again, searching for the subtle clues I had missed. Beckett plays fair with his readers, and all the information is there. While this novel will not appeal to all, it will encourage brighter readers to look into the ideas of Greek philosophers like Anaximander (Anax's full name), who pondered the beginnings of life. They will also encounter Plato's idea of a just society, the Turing Test for artificial intelligence, and John Searle's Chinese Room thought-experiment. In fact they will realise that this science fiction novel is also a carefully planned thought experiment.

In 2007, *Genesis* won New Zealand's major young adult fiction award.

CONTRIBUTED BY TREVOR AGNEW. THIS IS A VERSION OF A REVIEW ORIGINALLY PUBLISHED IN *Magpies*.

The Gospel According to Larry ➤ JANET TASHJIAN

YA USA 2001

My best friend, Beth, was trying to talk me into forming a Larry study group with her. His Web site – www.thegospelaccordingtolarry.com – received hundreds of hits a day, mostly from teens and college students.

What if a teenager mobilises thousands of young people through a website to fight for political and social change?

How easily even simple projects can spin out of control! Josh Swensen is longing to get together with Beth. He's secretly admired her since sixth grade, and wants to impress her. He's also very bright (with a very high IQ), well read (he really knows his Thoreau and his Bible), is passionate about the evils of consumerism, and plans never to own more than seventy-five items. As Larry, he starts posting photos of his possessions, together with mini-sermons, on a website. There are sermons about 'Phonies', about 'The people we surround ourselves with', asking 'those out there' if they have 'ever tried to jump off the consumer carousel?' To his amazement, he gets thousands of hits a day. Larry clubs start springing up. Even Beth starts one, but Josh is determined to maintain his anonymity. Then, when Bono, the anti-globalisation rock star from U2, decides to support Larry with 'Larryfest', a Woodstock-like festival, and the mysterious emailer 'betagold' gets on his case, Josh's life threatens to implode. Can anyone today escape the media?

The probing of contemporary materialistic culture is timely and must hit home with idealistic teenagers. The writing and events speed along with verve and humour. Tashjian does stretch credibility, especially in the sequel where Josh/Larry succeeds in changing the laws to allow a teenager to stand for President. At the time of writing the final book in the **CHANGE THE WORLD** trilogy was in the pipeline.

The House of the Scorpion ➤ NANCY FARMER

YA USA 2002

'Matt's a clone,' said Steven.

Emilia gasped. He can't be! He doesn't – I've seen clones. They're horrible!
They drool and mess their pants . . .

'This one's different . . . El Patrón wanted his to grow up like a real boy.
He's so rich he can break any law he wants.'

What if people's DNA was harvested to produce clones so rich
people can have docile, cheap labour and spare body organs?

Sometime in the future, a strip of land between Mexico and the USA, known as Aztlan, is owned and controlled by drug barons. Nancy Farmer knows the landscape well. She grew up there. Many readers will be aware that for years the USA has been struggling to stem the flow of both illegal immigrants and drugs from Mexico into the USA.

In Farmer's complex, provocative story the two countries agree that if they both 'set aside land along their common border, the dealers could establish farms and stop the flow of illegals. In return the dealers would promise not to sell drugs to the citizens of the United States and Mexico. They would peddle their wares in Europe, Asia and Africa instead.' The Alacrán family exploits this situation, partly by using thousands of clones, including Safe Horses, to do most of the hard work. The ruthless family Patriarch, El Patrón, wields absolute power. However, despite advanced medical techniques and a ready supply of 'spare parts', at 140 he is frail and failing. His one real weakness is Matt (Matteo), who is his son and clone. Matt has been hidden for years, living with the faithful, loving servant, Celia.   ▶▶▶

Of course, things go wrong. Matt is discovered and starts seeing what is happening around him. He gets deeply embroiled in the struggle to find out who and what he really is, and to expose the way things work around him. He is helped by Celia, the mysterious fugitive Tam Lin, and the gorgeous, kind Maria.

Some of the big questions powering this book are: What does it mean to be human? What are the ethics of cloning? Should body parts ever be harvested? How can people's greed and power be limited? How honest and real is the 'War on Drugs'? And do even the vilest people need love?

Farmer takes her story in many convoluted directions, but never fails to keep up the tension and action. Yet what really keeps us turning the almost-400 pages is our strong empathy for Matt and also for Maria, Celia and Tam Lin, and our hope that they will come through and might even be able to change their world for the better.

Jacob's Ladder ➤ BRIAN KEANEY

YA UK 2005

Then he woke up.

The sense of loss that he felt on waking and realising he was lying in bed in the dormitory in Locus was overwhelming. The song of the bird and the understanding it had brought drained away from him, like water spilled upon sand. In their place he was left with a deep feeling of emptiness.

What if you woke up one day in the middle of a vast, barren field and could remember nothing but your name?

Where is Jacob? What has happened to him? Why can't he remember anything? And who are the hundreds of other similarly aged young people who, day in day out, sleep in the huge dormitories, wear identical clothing, eat the same weird food and collect and pile up stones from the seemingly endless field? Why is everyone so docile? And apart from Virgil, who only appears when necessary, why are there hardly any adults except for the almost robot-like few who carry out basic tasks?

Unlike the others, Jacob can't just accept the situation and fall in with the routine. He is befriended by Toby and then Aysha. Eventually the three escape. They struggle for miles in desolate country, go hungry and thirsty, and even meet the colourful, wandering, Dedanim, and then the evil Moloch. But do these creatures really exist? Or are they a mirage or figments of their imagination? And what is their purpose?

In this eerie, mesmerising story Keaney builds up tension and constantly challenges the reader to ask the same questions that besiege Jacob. A compelling allegory about having the courage to make choices.

The Lab ➤ JACK HEATH

YA AUSTRALIA 2006

[Few] really knew what had made Six the way he was. Most people, of course, did not know he was a Code-breaking genetic experiment.

What if sometime in the future genetic engineering leads to the creation of 'people' like Six, who have extraordinary physical and intellectual capabilities?

Move over James Bond and Indiana Jones! *The Lab* is high-octane, action adventure speculative fiction. With lots of guns and hardware too. You just have to keep reading. Our protagonist, Six, or rather Agent Six, 'could lift more, run faster, and jump higher than any other agent at the Deck . . . At sixteen years old, he was the youngest agent too. He had been there since he was only thirteen, when the Deck had been founded. Although ChaoSonic now controlled most of the organisations and facilities in the City, there were still vigilante groups like the Deck who had pledged to uphold moral and social values: the Code.'

Sometime in the future the forces of good and evil are battling it out. This is after 'Takeover', and, because of rising seawater, there is apparently only one continent left, protected by a huge seawall. Some of the characters – dodging bullets, jumping off buildings, climbing up cranes, battling helicopters and running incredibly fast – are after power and money, but others do care about people, the survival of the human race, justice and what is left of the planet. A great read and an impressive first novel that's asking to be made into an action movie. **REMOTE CONTROL** (2007) is the sequel.

Noughts and Crosses ➤ MALORIE BLACKMAN

YA/A UK 2001

'Those bleeding heart liberals in the Pangaean Economic Community make me sick! They said we in this country had to open our schools to noughts, so we did. They said we had to open our doors to recruiting noughts into our police and armed forces, so we did. And they're still not satisfied. And as for the Liberation Militia, I thought letting a few blankers into our schools would spike their guns . . .'

I froze on the bottom step at the sound of Dad's bitterly angry voice.

What if racial prejudice was reversed so that blacks (the Crosses) are in charge and whites (the Noughts) are locked out of power and treated almost like slaves?

'Children's fiction has long been the repository of great satirical writing, but Blackman's trilogy takes it to levels unseen since Orwell's *1984*.' – Amanda Craig, *The Times*

Words and phrases used to describe Malorie Blackman's Noughts & Crosses trilogy include remarkable, dramatic, moving, brave, sad, bleak, brutal, original, deeply disturbing, totally absorbing, thought-provoking and challenging. Perhaps part of what creates these strong, positive responses is that the books are fuelled by the author's own experiences and anger. Blackman is black. She reports having been called a 'jungle bunny' and feels that in the UK, 'things have got worse' regarding race relations. The trilogy is partly a Romeo and Juliet story set in a hard-edged political and social context. The ingenuity is in the clever and convincing way Blackman has turned the black vs white issue on its head. Sephy is black, living in a world of wealth and privilege where her father aims to become the next Prime Minister. Callum is poor and white, a 'nought' or 'blanker'. Circumstances have meant that Sephy and Callum have been best friends since childhood, but now, as near-adults, their feelings for each other change and deepen. In their ▶▶▶

brutally segregated world they are inevitably heading for tragedy, particularly as Callum's brother and father are increasingly involved in activities that move beyond protest to terrorism.

The second book, **KNIFE EDGE** (2004), cranks up the pace, action and passions. The third book, **CHECKMATE** (2005), created a furor because in it Sephy's mixed-race daughter, Callie Rose, is groomed to be a suicide bomber. Yet its focus is more on redemption than violence. In *The Independent*, Boyd Tonkin asked, 'Should parents and teachers be concerned? Only, I suggest, if children refuse to read the book.' Clearly young people were not refusing to read the book, which nudged at Harry Potter on the UK bestseller lists.

Sharp North ➤ PATRICK CAVE

YA/A UK 2004

Nothing changed! You needed information to change things, didn't you? Real information, the sort kept for Families themselves and the richer Visions, able to perpetuate themselves indefinitely with the expensive Fertility Board 'enhancement' licences. Vision numbers in proportion to the Scroats were slowly rising: 'second child' permits were also out of reach of the poor.

What if you discoverd that you were a cloned 'spare' for use by the ruling 'Families'?

Patrick Cave said, '*Sharp North* deals with one of the possible future scripts for our children's children – a script that is being prepared right now, with reckless abandon.'

Sometime in the future, global warming is causing huge floods in England and the country is 'drowning'. The 'Great Families' control everything, including the media, politics and fertility. To ensure their survival and dominance the Families have been cloning themselves for centuries. They have also been creating 'Spares'. Each Spare has its own sinister 'watcher'. *Sharp North* is big and complex, but also full of action and suspense. Here, global warming meets cloning meets murder in a scary society.

One day Mira sees a woman – who seems familiar – shot and killed. The body is quickly removed, but Mira finds a scrap of paper containing her own name, among others. Next to another name is the word 'watcher'. As she tries to understand, Mira begins to suspect that her life in the remote community in the frozen north of Scotland is not what it seems. She undertakes a dangerous escape to London. The physical challenges facing her are grippingly portrayed. To survive in the city, she disguises herself as a 'scroat', one of the many street people in this divided police state. From here she continues her brave quest in a bold, bleak story that does have glimmers of love, hope and even some answers. **BLOWN AWAY** (2006), the sequel, is equally eerie and compelling, and has received high praise.

Siberia ➤ ANN HALAM

YA UK 2005

She didn't tell me where my mother was. I didn't ask.

She's been taken away –

She's been taken away –

Taken away like my Dadda, and hung, or shot –

And I know who was to blame. Not the police, or the Settlement Commission, or Madam Principal: it was me. I was eleven years old, I had killed my mother. She was dead for two pieces of cake, and a taste of fake berry-jam.

What if the environment has been degraded so far that the world is mostly freezing, and there are no more animals?

Rosita was four when she and her mother arrived in the prison camp in the freezing, snowbound north. Her Dadda has disappeared, and all Rosita understands is that she must not disturb her mother while she makes nails. Their meagre shelter and food depend on her mother's productivity and unquestioning obedience. What softens this bleak existence is the intense love between mother and daughter. Gradually, we come to understand that in this future the rich live in warm, domed cities, while others eke out a precarious existence in the cold. The damage to the environment has been so great that there are no longer any animals, except some that have been horrifically genetically modified to be harvested for food and fur.

Rosita's mother has a dangerous secret: a kit carrying the DNA of several species of animals. Bit by bit she teaches Rosita how to activate these kits. Rosita thinks it's magic but understands the need for secrecy. Being clever, but also rash and opinionated, she is sent to a prison boarding school where she inadvertently betrays her mother. Has Rosita sent her beloved mother to her death?

Rosita decides to escape, find out the truth about her mother and father, and keep the Lindquists (the embryonic creatures) safe. She undertakes an epic journey, constantly tracked by the mysterious, threatening Yagin. Who is he and what does he really want?

A detailed, engrossing, brilliantly imagined story that is as disturbing as it is intriguing. The frozen landscape provides another dimension to a world of terrible beauty. Hallam also writes award-winning science fiction and fantasy for adults under the name of Gwyneth Jones.

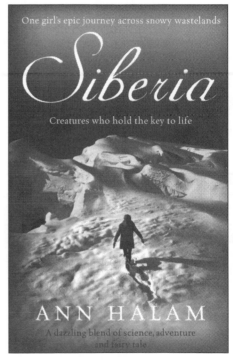

So Yesterday ➤ SCOTT WESTERFELD

YA USA/AUSTRALIA 2004

Definitely an innovator, I thought. They tend to specialize, looking like Logo Exiles until you get close, until you see that one flourish. All their energies focused on a single element.

Like shoelaces.

I pulled out my phone and pointed it at her foot.

What if trend-spotting and trend-setting become so competitive that they become dangerous?

Jen is the 'innovator', starting trends like lacing her sneakers in a quirky new way. Hunter is just what his name suggests, but a special kind: a 'cool hunter'. He is paid to spot brand new trends, photograph them, and send the photos on to his focus group to consider.

This is not science fiction but a recognisable world of pop culture, advertising, fashion and the need to be ahead of the pack at almost any cost. Westerfeld comes from New York (he is now living part-time in Australia) and makes good use of his Manhattan territory. *So Yesterday* buries its penetrating, serious social comment just beneath an exciting, fast-paced story of the players who want a piece of the cut-throat and hugely lucrative sneaker market action.

Despite being all about brands and brand recognition, Westerfeld manages not to mention a single brand (not hard to guess the shoe brand, though). Soon Hunter and Jen, now quite involved, find themselves embroiled in some nasty business that includes the 'Jammers', who ostensibly aim to sabotage all this consumerism. When Hunter's boss, Mandy, disappears, there is a lively chase that ends at a wild, drunken party at the Museum of Natural History, where people are viewing advertisements for a new shampoo.

Having written a lot of science fiction for adults, Scott Westerfeld is now making up for lost time in the young adult field, and making sure he packs in as much arcane knowledge, demanding ideas and sneaky plotting as he can, without slowing for breath.

scott westerfeld

UGLIES 2005
PRETTIES 2005
SPECIALS 2006
EXTRAS 2007

Fast becoming a cult writer, Westerfeld taps into the obsessions and anxieties of societies, and teenagers in particular, in the developed and wealthy world. The Uglies trilogy is set some time in the future, following a global catastrophe. Westerfeld's lively, action-packed, intensely imagined series again explores rampant consumerism, vanity and the desire for the perfect body and face. He's also interested in the environment, free will, the possibilities of totalitarian power and the addiction to speed, power and violence.

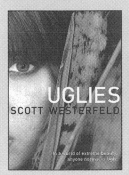 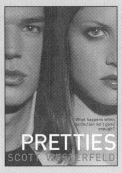 

Tally, almost sixteen, would be a good match for Jack Heath's hero Six (see page 302) as she moves, through extreme cosmetic surgery, from being an 'Ugly' to being a 'Pretty' and then on to becoming a 'Special'. But she and the story become complex and unpredictable. After meeting Shay, Tally is presented with an alternative to being a party-going air-head. Should she join Shay in The Smoke and challenge the status quo? Dangerous stuff! Big *What if* . . . questions here – and plenty of twists and surprises. Speculative fiction at its best.

The Sterkarm Handshake ➤ SUSAN PRICE

YA UK 1998

There were four members of the Geological Survey Team: Malc, Tim, Dave and Caro. They'd left the 21st that morning at eight, coming through the Tube to the 16th, where the plan was to spend four days. None of them had ever been so far from home before, and they often looked back at the Tube. It was their only way back.

What if scientists managed to connect the 21st century to the 16th century, intent on exploiting the latter's plentiful resources and pristine landscape?

What is a Sterkarm handshake worth? An ingenious, inventive take on colonial aspirations, this is time travel with a twist. FUP, a British corporation, uses state-of-the-art technology to get back to the 16th century. There is a lot of gold and oil in them there hills, and wouldn't wealthy tourists love to escape their polluted environment and visit a resort in the gorgeous, unspoilt landscape beside clear, babbling brooks? The Tube has been constructed to allow the crossing over. But the arrogant 21st-century types have not counted on the cunning, war-like Sterkarms, one of the proud ancient families inhabiting the land around the Scottish–English border. They are not about to cave in to the marauders. In fact, the Sterkarms do quite some marauding of their own – stealing from the FUP survey team and causing as much trouble as possible.

Adding spice and punch to this huge rollicking adventure, Price makes serious comment on our Western 21st-century culture and values. There's lots of action, detail about the way the Sterkarms live, and even a Romeo and Juliet love story. When Windsor, the power-hungry FUP boss, realises that the 'savages' will not be subdued or bought off with trinkets – or even the simple, but great, benefits of aspirin (a lovely, clever touch this) – he rages, 'Offer them all the benefits of the 21st century and, because they were too ignorant to appreciate them, they flung them back in your teeth and spat in your face too. Wipe them out, the lot of them.' Will the Tube and our heroes survive?

A STERKARM KISS (2003) continues the tale but in a slightly different dimension. Price's latest, **ODIN'S VOICE** (2005), the first in a trilogy, is a thriller that mixes Greek and Norse gods, girl prophets, electronically tagged 'Bonders', 'designed' rich people, and a pioneering journey to Mars. Price is a dazzler!

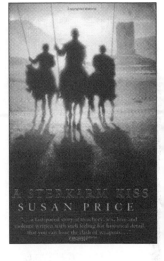

Thieves ➤ ELLA WEST

YA NEW ZEALAND 2006

'Blink and you miss me. Was I ever there?'

What if some people had the ability to disappear by 'teleportation', and this skill was abused by those in power?

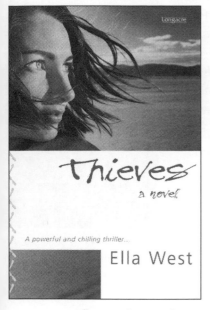

The rule for science fiction stories is that you're allowed one 'lie' (or imaginative creation), but that everything else has to develop logically from that single 'lie'. Ella West has followed that rule perfectly. In *Thieves*, Nicky has a unique ability: she can move instantly from one place to another. In 1950s science fiction this ability to teleport was a common human mutation. In one story, teleporters had to hire themselves out as instant-delivery taxis. West has taken a much more imaginative and plausible approach to this rogue talent.

When we first meet Nicky she has just travelled into her closet as a nervous reflex against embarrassment at school – the ultimate 'fight or flight' response. Soon she finds herself in a very special institution with four other teenagers who share the same wild talent. Nicky's first-person account tells about life in 'The Project': the training and the secrecy. Why are they locked away? Is it to protect them, or to protect society from them? Where are they? Tension increases as Nicky is told that her parents are dead. She suspects that they may have been murdered, but answers are hard to find. After training, Nicky is sent out on highly organised missions, most of which involve taking and returning office files and disks. Things change after Nicky and Paul are sent out to locate two children lost in a forest. Nicky realises she will never be allowed to leave The Project alive. She and Paul, both loners, become emotionally linked. The five travellers suffer emotional and physical exhaustion as they are sent out on repeated missions. Given no information, cut off from news, not even allowed to know the date, they doubt the purpose of The Project and the morality of their work. Yet they know there is no way out for them: 'We're not from anywhere. We don't exist.' The mood is chilling and tense but the travellers emerge as interesting and sympathetically drawn teenagers, trapped in an inhuman system. The conclusion is unexpected but logical and satisfying. *Thieves* is a remarkable debut novel, fresh and readable, with skilled, confident writing and clear characterisation.

CONTRIBUTED BY TREVOR AGNEW. THIS IS A VERSION OF A REVIEW ORIGINALLY PUBLISHED IN *Magpies*.

pictures tell stories too

by Linnet Hunter

THE RABBiTS
John Marsden & Shaun Tan

Turning symbols into meaning, remembering what happened in earlier episodes, finding cross-links between texts, recognising themes, predicting the next phase of the story. Sure, we all do this when we read novels, but this is actually a description of some of the intense thinking processes needed to decode a picture book, too!

No longer for those who 'haven't learnt to read words yet' the picture book for teenagers breaks every boring boundary and charts new territory – threatening the dominance of the written word.

Gary Crew is one author who uses his background in visual arts to challenge and inspire many illustrators in collaboration. **Watertower,** and more recently its sequel BENEATH THE SURFACE (illustrated by Steven Woolman), are intriguing, with their mood of brooding menace and conspiracy, just like **The X-Files**. And they play with conventions. Just which way is up?

Text and image collide and collude, impinge and seamlessly melt to create more effects. These books are more film than novel. Once they know how to handle them, teenagers revel in the search for intricate and eccentric details in Colin Thompson's surrealities. They puzzle over the gentle mix of genres, which shift our perceptions in Tohby Riddle's luminous cityscapes, or respond to the subversive messages about powerlessness to be found in Raymond Briggs and Anthony Browne. Only someone over the age of twelve would truly get the OTT references to other texts in the warped works of Jon Sciezska and Lane Smith.

Image eaters since birth, this generation are no strangers to multiple narratives occurring on the same screen/page, whether created by Quentin Tarantino or David Macauley. They thrive on the interplay of word and picture to be found in graffiti, music clips, advertising, billboards and DVDs made to be watched a hundred times. Shaun Tan's intricate layers of dark meaning entwined with symbols of measurement and ownership in **The Rabbits** and his other works where technical brilliance is subservient to the narrative power it carries, are grist to their mill. (See page 198 for Tan's **The Arrival**.)

The complex relationships in **Fox** (Wild and Brooks) are told through the richness of texture, colour and framing. The words needed to describe what is occurring come from the disciplines of art, media and politics. History and its value as cultural capital can be observed in a close reading of Alan Tucker's series on the history of Australia. Simple stick figure drawings? Look more closely!

Close observation is the key. Once you start looking you'll see many things you never noticed before. I promise!

when you want to laugh

Sometimes you want to be taken to another world by a book or you want to cry or be frightened. Sometimes you want to laugh and laugh (but maybe cry a little also). Writing funny books, and even creating cartoons, is a serious and tricky business because we all laugh about different things. Apart from being subjective, humour can also be regionally and culturally specific. The best humorous books often have serious undertones. Some can even be sad, gritty and funny almost at the same time – like *My Big Birkett*, *Notes from the Teenage Underground* and *Henry Tumour*. The edginess and sophistication of books like these are further reasons why they should not be considered for awards under the umbrella of the Children's Book Council of Australia. The creators of the US Michael Printz awards and the UK Booktrust Teenage Prize have recognised the need for stand-alone young adult awards.

Do the stories in this section make you smile or even laugh out loud? See if you can put your finger on what made you laugh (or not) in each of these books. But above all, enjoy them.

48 Shades of Brown ➤ NICK EARLS

YA/A AUSTRALIA 1999

And what a week my first week is. TV in a deliberately darkened room, and far more. Never have I eaten more pizza (twice in a row), been woken by rhythmic bed noises (Sunday, Tuesday and Wednesday, and all from Naomi's room), worked my way slowly through a beer on a weeknight (Thursday, after shopping).

Back from a visit to Geneva, Dan, almost seventeen, observes, 'Life in Geneva is spent putting on and taking off coats.' Dan is like that. He carefully observes and examines everything around him. Up to now he has been used to a highly ordered and unsophisticated life, and a mother who kept his socks neatly sorted. He brings this rather obsessive introspection and examination of details, of motives and of himself to his first highly tentative fumblings with girls and sex. Dan decides not to move to Geneva with his parents. Instead, he moves in with his older cousin, university student Jacq, and instantly falls for Jacq's beautiful housemate, Naomi. Sadly for Dan, Naomi already has an active love and sex life, which Dan is forced to listen to through their apartment's thin walls. Dan is a thoughtful, serious student trying to focus on calculus in his final year at school – and on the confusing possibilities of his future. But he also wants to learn how to live life to the fullest. All this leads to many hilarious and complicated situations.

Nick Earls is wonderful at capturing the voices, foibles and awkwardness of young people on the cusp of adulthood. He does not shy away from messiness, occasional crudity, or the complexities of contemporary life. His humour is sharp, but never cruel. *48 Shades of Brown* continues to be popular and also slightly controversial because of its honesty. Just as Nick Earls would like it, one suspects. Earls also writes wry, funny books for older (but not much) adults and has a big following in the US and Europe. (See page 128, for Earl's latest, more serious young adult title, **MONICA BLOOM**.)

Alice, I Think ➤ SUSAN JUBY

YA CANADA 2003

My parents didn't send me to kindergarten, because they said they didn't feel ready yet. But then my brother, MacGregor, was born, and they had to spread around their urge to overprotect. So off I went for the first day of first grade, where I quickly discovered that everyone else had bonded at kindergarten . . . My next discovery was that kids don't like other kids who think they are hobbits, especially kids who break into song and dance without any warning.

Alice, fifteen, lives in the tiny town of Smithers, and life is not getting easier. Since her bad experience in first grade she has been home-schooled. This has not given her what is considered to be 'age-appropriate real-life experience'. She now attends the 'Smithers Teens in Transition (Not in Trouble) Center'. Juby has fun with her characters and situations in this very assured and sad but funny first novel of a trilogy. Alice's experiences and aspirations are documented in her diary and include endlessly changing lists of goals, using the jargon of her many counsellors. Here is one set:

Decide on a unique and innovative career path.

Increase contact with people outside of immediate family.

Learn to drive a car.

Some sort of boy–girl interaction? (Possibly best left until after high school. Maybe best left until middle age.)

Publish paper comparing teenagers and chicken peer groups.

Read entire Lord of the Rings series.

What hope does Alice have with a flaky hippie mother; a father who aspires to be a romance writer but gets distracted by games of poker; a brother who is mad about fish; and Linda, her so-called (and only) friend, who wants to kill her. Read also the sequels, **MISS SMITHERS** (2004) and **ALICE MACLEOD, REALIST AT LAST** (2005).

The Betrayal of Bindy Mackenzie

➤ JACLYN MORIARTY

YA AUSTRALIA 2006

Bindy, you have to try to learn that you're not superior to every other person in the room.

Bindy, I'm not sure if you realise it but today you've upset almost every single person in the FAD group including Try! Have you ever considered USING that huge brain of yours?

These are anonymous contributions to the NAME GAME in a FAD (Friendship and Development) group. Here is Bindy herself:

DIARY ENTRY

BEST DAY EVER!! Won the School Spelling Bee. It is the first time anyone from Year 3 has ever won it. The Year 6 girl who was runner-up ran out of the room crying. Also discovered William Faulkner. Such haunting prose.

Something I enjoy doing is . . .

Eavesdropping on strangers. I do this on the bus, around school, in shopping centres, and in libraries. I type up transcripts of their conversations . . .

Bindy is hard to love, or even to like. Super-bright, opinionated, self-absorbed, she has little sense of how others feel or how they see her. We follow her innermost thoughts and feelings through diary entries, emails, cringe-making letters to officials, a 'Special Clippings File' and other musings.

It all adds up to a portrait of a sad, lost girl: a nerd and misfit. But gradually Bindy becomes more self-aware and realises that her so-called perfect life is far from it. She even finds friends and learns empathy and compassion. It is no mean feat to make us care about this infuriating girl and to stay with her through this long, hugely detailed book. Moriarty conjures a strong, compelling voice and a terrific insight into life as an outsider in an anti-intellectual culture that values conformity.

Black Taxi ➤ JAMES MOLONEY

YA AUSTRALIA 2003

Paddy Larkin is just a little bent. I don't mean he's one of those wrinklies you see walking along the street all doubled over like an upside down 'L'. I mean he doesn't always stick to the straight and narrow. To put it bluntly, Patrick Larkin is a crook.

But he's a nice crook . . . He also happens to be my grandfather. He likes me and I like him.

It's great to see an author trying something new. James Moloney has written a number of highly serious and successful books for teenagers, as well as some lighter works for younger readers. *Black Taxi* is a delightful and funny crime/adventure romp.

Rosie's grandfather is a small time crim. Now he has run out of lives and can no longer avoid a stretch inside. Rosie is the only one Paddy Larkin will trust with his beloved black Merc. Unfortunately, with the car comes Paddy's mobile and calls to do a few odd jobs, such as ferrying elderly people to what Rosie thinks is Bingo but turns out to be assignations! Who is making all those sinister phone calls? And what is the real story behind that missing diamond ring? A lot for a 'Prestie [Prestwick] chick' to handle. But Rosie is bright and resourceful, even as she juggles the attentions of two local hunks, the demands of her friend Glenda – who pays her way through Uni by being an 'exotic dancer' – and worries about her wardrobe and the size of her bum. Great fun!

Henry Tumour ➤ ANTHONY McGOWAN

YA UK 2006

'Thou whoreson obscene greasy tallow-catch!' *Whoooa! What the hell was that?*

It wasn't in my head. I mean it was in my head, but it was also in my mouth. I mean screamed at full volume, all decibels blazing . . .

Tierney and his stooges turned round.

'What did you say?'

I genuinely had no idea . . .

Numbers were my thing, or one of my things . . .

All the gang had a thing. Gonad's thing was history. He knew everything that had ever happened . . .

Stanislaw's thing was chess . . .

Simon Murphy, usually called Smurf for obvious reasons, was best at English . . .

I went to sleep that night thinking about many things. I thought quite a lot of Henry Tumour. I'd gone past the point of being gobsmacked by the mere fact of having a dirty-minded brain tumour that chatted away to me like he was some kind of friend or brother, or even sometimes in a kind of warped-dad way.

You need to hear Hector's voice, that of his gang, and of the loquacious Henry Tumour, to get a sense of just how sad, black, hilarious and clever this book is. *Henry Tumour* deservedly won the 2006 UK Booktrust Teenage Prize. **ANGEL BLOOD** (see page 197) was also on the shortlist, and these two books alone give us an idea of the brilliance and innovative edginess of some recent British writing for teenagers.

Hector, with his vague, hippie mum and absent dad, is gloomy enough. But as Hector's growing brain tumour begins to talk to him, and cajoles and almost bullies him to behave in increasingly bizarre ways, we see just how inventive and ingenious McGowan is to find concrete ways of showing us the likely impact of an aggressively growing tumour.

Hector's illness heightens the situation facing a group of bright and eccentric friends among a generally anti-intellectual, grubby bunch of schoolboys. The language dazzles, as the boys spar and grapple with big ideas and subjects – science, religion, philosophy and poetry. Despite all the mayhem, our sympathies are firmly with the desperately ill Hector as he makes his way, largely unsupported, through a battery of medical tests. We hold our breath as we read on. Will Hector survive major surgery?

If you weren't a hedgehog . . . If I weren't a haemophiliac . . . ➤ ANDREW WELDON

A/YA AUSTRALIA 2006

The 250 cartoons in this collection might make you laugh or cringe or frown or grind your teeth in your sleep. Andrew Weldon is a widely published cartoonist whose work appears in many major daily papers as well as in *The Chaser*, *The Bulletin*, *Punch* and *Private Eye*. His biting political cartoons were featured almost daily on the Opinion page of *The Age* in the summer of 2007. He has also been published in *The New Yorker*. According to an article by Weldon in *The Age* (2 December 2006) on the publication of this latest collection, 'The New Yorker is undoubtedly the most revered publisher of 'gag' cartoons – single-panel jokes – in the world, and a great many cartoonists dream of being published in it'. Weldon has also published two illustrated storybooks, **THE KID WITH THE AMAZING HEAD** (1998) and **CLEVER TREVOR'S STUPENDOUS INVENTIONS** (1999). His first book of cartoons was **I'M SORRY LITTLE MAN,**

I THOUGHT YOU WERE A HAND PUPPET (2000). It's best to look at a few of Weldon's zany, funny, witty, sharp cartoons from his new book to appreciate his talent and penetrating insights.

andrew weldon's
favourite funny books

NEVER EAT ANYTHING BIGGER THAN YOUR HEAD AND OTHER DRAWINGS B Kliban A/YA USA 1976
The cartoon book that made me want to be a cartoonist, and still one of my favourites – fabulous line drawings, and jokes that range from straight-up funny to bafflingly bizarre.

UNDER THE FROG Tibor Fischer A/YA UK/HUNGARY 1992
Before I read it I wouldn't have expected a novel about life under the Communist dictatorship in Hungary in the 1950s to be one of the funniest (and most moving) things I've ever read, but there you go.

▶▶▶

▶▶▶

THE HITCHHIKER'S GUIDE TO THE GALAXY (AND SEQUELS)
Douglas Adams A/YA/Y UK 1979
Everybody knows this is one of the funniest books ever.
I agree.

THE PRINCESS BRIDE William Goldman A/YA/Y USA 1973
They made a great film out of this, but the book is even
better. A rollicking tale of romance (eeeew!) and adventure,
with lots of hilarious tangents.

THE THIRD POLICEMAN Flann O'Brien A/YA IRELAND 1967
Absurdist, philosophical weirdness involving bicycles.

LAKE WOBEGON DAYS (AND SEQUELS) Garrison Keillor
A/YA USA 1985
Keillor is a wonderful rambling storyteller, with a warm
and gentle sense of humour that I've always loved.

THE GREATEST OF MARLYS Lynda Barry A/YA/Y USA 2002
Lynda Barry's comics capture the horror of teenagerdom
brilliantly and hilariously.

SCHOOL IS HELL Matt Groening A/YA USA 1987
When Matt Groening isn't inventing *The Simpsons* he
does cartoons like these. Angry, cute, subversive, funny.

DEEP THOUGHTS Jack Handey A/YA/Y 1992 USA
Word for word this little book has made me laugh more
than anything in print. Google it to get a taste.

IN ME OWN WORDS: THE AUTOBIOGRAPHY OF BIGFOOT
Graham Roumieu A/YA CANADA 2003
Absolutely hilarious story of Chewbacca-hating, sensitive,
misunderstood, homeboy Bigfoot, full of beautiful cartoon
illustrations – a twisted picture story book.

I'm Being Stalked by a Moonshadow

> DOUG MACLEOD

YA AUSTRALIA 2006

According to the local paper, Mr Raven (41) was well on the way to
tracking down the cyber-terrorist, 'following an anonymous tip-off'.
The letters page had a rather odd letter from an anthropologist.

Doug Macleod has a sharp eye for humour in the obvious and ordinary, and he creates running gags out of his observations. Why, for example, do journalists and the police always consider it relevant to put the age of a suspect or witness in brackets in a report?

When lonely, carrot-haired, nerdy Seth meets the rising kick-boxing star, Miranda, he admires her various well-developed muscles, and charms her by telling her so, using the correct names for each muscle. This romance flourishes and we cheer for Seth. Why should all the girls fall for his too-handsome younger brother Jack? Too bad that Miranda turns out to be the motherless daughter of the over-zealous, aptly named local environment officer, the black-hearted Mr Raven. A rapidly escalating feud develops between Seth's dad, Eric Parrot (is he the cyber-terrorist?), and Mr Raven – much to the chagrin of Eric's long-suffering wife, Zilla. Seth worries that his mother and dad seem disinclined to share a bed. Zilla runs the local neighborhood centre and the feud puts this and the classes there (including the kick-boxing classes) in jeopardy. For a while everyone becomes increasingly unhappy.

Macleod draws wonderfully eccentric characters and gives them great lines to create a light-hearted confection, poking gentle fun at their somewhat precious attitudes and predilections, such as Zilla's preference for wheatgerm drinks. Each chapter is headed by one of Eric's vast dictionary of essential animal behaviour facts (or are they?). Did you know that a giraffe's tongue is fifty-five centimetres long or that penguins love bananas or that the longest recorded flight of a chicken is thirteen seconds? A hilarious gem.

Jetty Rats ➤ PHILLIP GWYNNE

Y/YA AUSTRALIA 2004

Then, all of a sudden, the Photocopies [the twins] *started telling me these secrets . . .'*

'Jasmine isn't my real name,' blurted Jasmine . . . Storm gave her a real dirty look, but Jasmine continued. 'We changed them after we left the commune.'

'So, what's your real name/' I asked.

'Promise not to laugh?'

'Promise,' I said.

'Platypus Billabong,' she said quickly.

'What about you, Storm?'

'Gum –' Jasmine started, but Storm cut her off.

'Gumnut Waterfall, but if you tell anybody else, Fishface, I'll break every rod you've got!'

It was real hard not to laugh . . . So I thought of serious things, like the ozone layer, and testicular cancer and my missing dad.

Even if you have never caught a fish and don't yearn to do so, this book about a boy whose father's passion for fishing cost the father his life, but who still wants to catch the elusive giant mulloway, should grab you. *Jetty Rats* should make you laugh and laugh, but it is serious and a bit tragic too.

Dogleg Bay is full of retirees (and while Gwynne has fun with these, he does tend to stereotype 'seniors'), so there is nothing much for Hunter Vettori to do except chase dreams and escape his flaky mum (she spends a lot of time psyching herself up to get a tattoo). Hunter, the Photocopies and sundry other eccentric local youths – and some not-so young (including a paleoichthyologist) – eventually do conspire to make things happen in Dogleg Bay. But will Hunter catch *that* fish? An entertaining gem for every kind of reader.

The King of Whatever ➤ KIRSTEN MURPHY

YA AUSTRALIA 2005

'I like you, Claud, and I think we should go out some time.'

'You and me? Like on a date?'

Claudia paused for a moment and then began to giggle . . .

*She looked at him more closely. 'You're serious . . . I'm so sorry.
I really thought you were joking'.*

*He hadn't been joking, but he was Joe King, and it was obvious, as far as
he was concerned, that that was where all his troubles had begun. It could
have been worse. He could have been called Wayne.*

Joe is smart but always feels second best. After all, his brother is studying medicine and his best friend is school captain. All his attempts to take control or shine or be happy seem to fail. Despite his frequent despair, Joe always seems to be the one to help out or to step in; for example, when deb partners fall ill. When Joe discovers that his best friend is going out with the girl he loves there seems no way but up, and up Joe climbs.

Attuned to the voices and vicissitudes of teenagers – and with her customary compassion laced with liberal doses of wry humour – Murphy has created another deeply engaging book. For her insight and attitudes, she won the 2006 Australian Psychological Society Psychologists for Peace Biennial Children's Peace Literature Award. An admirable and well-deserved award, but one that again reinforces the 'educational' rather than literary value of young people's literature. Here is some of Murphy's acceptance speech: 'I wrote this novel for a few reasons. One reason was that I was inspired by the Ralph Waldo Emerson quote that appears at the front of the book: "What lies behind us and what lies before us are little matters compared to what

lies within us". I wanted to communicate to a young adult audience that ordinary is okay. We will not all be rock stars or famous sports people or geniuses at the age of seventeen; most of us will lead a relatively ordinary existence, but one we can be proud of. For it's the relationships we have with others that matter . . . I want to explore typical teenage issues and adult issues for that matter, with humour and in a way that is accessible to teenagers . . . I try to write the kinds of books that I would have loved to read as a teenager. They were books with humour, and above all, hope . . . What a great world we would live in if all our leaders looked for constructive, non-violent approaches towards the resolution of conflicts.'

My Big Birkett ➤ LISA SHANAHAN

YA AUSTRALIA 2006

On Saturday morning, Debbie dragged the whole of her bridal party to the annual Buranderry Bridal Fair . . . When they had finished their makeovers, we moved on to fake nails, push-up bras, lingerie, stationery, bridal registry lists, honeymoon packages and breast implants.

Preparing for Debbie's sudden wedding to Brian (a Chinese theme for the engagement party, as he proposed beside the five spice shelf in the supermarket), is only one strand in this rich and complex tapestry, threaded with laughs. At fourteen, Jemma, our protagonist, is ten years younger then Debbie. She is a reluctant flower girl. The groom's family is of a military bent, a family predilection also taken to extremes and milked for humour. Their garden is, of course, set up as a military obstacle training course. The wedding preparations provide many opportunities for 'birketts' – major tantrums, where 'the emotion has the necessary power to drive out all your common sense.'

The other main players are the De Head family, with sons named after birds (Raven, Maggie, Crow, Sparrow, Robin). The De Heads are poor, and in and out of jail. Mother holds the family together. Dad is given to acts of random violence. They are despised and stereotyped by the townspeople. Jemma and Raven are drawn together, particularly when both are cast in the school production of *The Tempest*. The parallels with Shakespeare, the description of the rehearsals, and the portrayal of the De Head family are dramatic and often heart-rending. There is tragedy but also a grand wedding. Shanahan can make the reader laugh helplessly and then cry in almost the same breath. A writer to watch!

Notes from the Teenage Underground ➤ SIMMONE HOWELL

YA AUSTRALIA 2006

Lo started slowly. 'Flyers are easy. Dad just bought a monster photocopier. What if . . .' she was getting warmer, ' . . . we make a film and screen it at an underground party . . .'

Suddenly I got it. 'A Happening!' I almost shouted.

'Huh?' That was Mira.

'A Happening. A cool artist thing. It would be totally Ug. Andy Warhol used to have them.'

Gem and her hippie mum, Bev, share a love of movies. So, quite obviously, does first-time-author-with-loads-of-talent Simmone Howell. Gem works at the local 'Video Nasty', where business is so slack she and Dodgy (Roger actually, and the two may or may not have something brewing) spend most of their time watching movies. Bev is an artist, an unreconstructed feminist, and she and her daughter are, inevitably, vegetarians. They get along really well. Gem's father took off many years ago, but sends increasingly frequent postcards with Haiku messages. As the school year draws to a close, Gem, Lo and Mira are getting restless and edgy. Being seventeen is a tricky, in-between time. So they plan the 'Happening', but soon the cracks in their relationships begin to show. Gem, inspired by Andy Warhol, wants to make a film ('really UG', short for Underground), but who is going to take control? Gem is serious about the project, and one of the many appealing aspects of this lovely, very funny, witty, gritty and at times unhappy novel is that Howell assumes her readers (like her characters) are able to be sassy, cool, crazy teenagers at the same time as being bright, curious and mentally agile. Gem seeks information about heroic women about whom films have been made, or who were, well, just heroic. This includes Joan of Arc, Cleopatra, Delilah, Mary Magdalene, Boadicea and even Brigitte Bardot (who became an animal rights activist) and Françoise Sagan (who wrote a bestselling novel at eighteen). If you can't enjoy the erudition and intellectual high jinks, the truly wild party that goes wrong; the unravelling of the friendships; the painful story of Lo, who cuts herself; and Mira who goes in for pranks in the nude; together with the story behind Gem and her dad, AND the story of how her film-making aspirations pan out, the loss will be yours! A truly young adult book to admire and celebrate.

Suburban Freak Show ➤ JULIA LAWRINSON

YA AUSTRALIA 2006

It was only because of hyperactivity, irritability, sleeplessness, short-temperedness and emotional outbursts occasioned by giving up smoking that . . . I decided to assist Christie's Hepburn Heights campaign.

I wish to make clear that I still have no vestige of interest in bushland, no matter how remnant . . .

In her first year of university, Jay just wants to study. She is clever, anti-social and loves research and writing essays, even when she realises that much of what is offered in English is meaningless and hard to justify. She escapes from the student village to a share-house, because the other village inhabitants seem to only want to party, take drugs and engage in immoral activities, if possible with the two large-breasted, party-loving Danish Lottes, who are especially enticing to the likes of Wheatbelt Wayne.

In the rundown house at Buckingham Place, Jay finds herself amid fanatical greenies and the totally laidback DJ, Ben. Jay is drawn into Christie's campaign to save Hepburn Heights. She is persuaded to relax a little, and even make time for Ben.

Lawrinson writes a witty, funny book and invents a wonderful set of characters. She manages simultaneously to support the aims of the Greenies, and send up their extreme, chaotic and often confused members and tactics. Poor Christie is desperately trying to escape her rich, suburban parents, while really needing their money for her campaign.

Lawrinson is known for her tough books about teenagers in tough situations (**OBSESSION** (2001), **SKATING THE EDGE** (2002) and **BYE, BEAUTIFUL** (2006)). *Suburban Freak Show* is a lively, clever, often laugh-aloud departure from a talented writer.

Turbulence ➤ JAN MARK

YA UK 2005

Eat your heart out, Wyatt Earp, Clay Winchester was there first blowing smoke from her pearl-handled Colts ... Clay rides shotgun on the Deadwood Stage ...

Somewhere in the upper branches of the family tree sits a gorilla, that's my theory. Most of the relatives are clearly descended from lemurs and marmosets, but now and again one of us turns out heavy and big-boned and powerful. In this generation I got the gorilla gene.

On her paper rounds Clay (Clare) often goes into Western mode. She and her dad watch a lot of Westerns and other movies in his studio/shed (he is a graphic designer). To get the full flavour of this lively, witty book it helps to get the references to books such as *The Great Gatsby*, and to movies including *Nosferatu*, *Casablanca* and some Hitchcock greats. They provide a brisk shorthand commentary on the goings on.

'Reliable Clay the Gorilla' lives in a happy, if chaotic, family with parents, no-nonsense Gran, grunting Jamze (cooler than James!) and walking tantrum Rosie. They love having people over for dinner. However, when Sandor and his fragile, much younger wife are invited, the domestic life of several families is seriously disrupted. Clay's self-deprecating voice and observations, sometimes in imagined conversations or in Western-movie style, provide the sharp humour in this quite blistering insight into how one dysfunctional person can manipulate and cause chaos in ordinary lives. For sophisticated readers, this is a light but thought-provoking look at how families tick. Jan Mark, a great writer and wordsmith, sadly died suddenly before *Turbulence* was short-listed for the Carnegie Medal, which she had won twice previously.

The Whole Business with Kiffo and the Pitbull ➤ BARRY JONSBERG

YA AUSTRALIA 2004

Our teacher told us to write a diary entry from the point of view of Lady Macbeth after the murder of the old king . . . So this is what I [Calma] wrote:

'Dear Diary . . . It's been a few nights since I've written to you. I hope I'm not getting lax, but I've been pretty busy recently, what with entertaining the King of Scotland and his three thousand hangers on. I was all for ordering takeaway, but Macbeth wouldn't have it. He reckons the local Thai restaurant is over-priced and he's been wary of the pizza place ever since he had the seafood thick crust and got crook with food poisoning. So I was up to my elbows in pie-floaters for everyone, while Macbeth and old Duncan were watching the Footy Show and getting a few VBs down them . . .

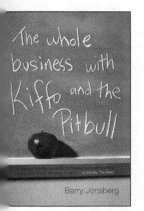

Kiffo has an unusual attitude to the world and to school in particular. He is unused to doing any work and used to wreaking havoc in any classroom – and getting away with it. That is, until the Pitbull arrives to restore order. Kiffo has one unlikely friend, the tough-talking, big-boobed Calma, our narrator. She knows that Kiffo is loyal, understanding and very bright, although he hides all this very efficiently. Kiffo and Calma are both neglected and confused. When Kiffo sets out in a rage to 'do' the Pitbull, he uncovers and takes on more than he can manage, or even understand. Is he about to uncover local heroin dealers? Mayhem ensues.

This first novel from a Darwin teacher is hilarious, serious and brilliant. Read also the sequel, **IT'S NOT ALL ABOUT YOU, CALMA** (2005). Jonsberg's latest book, **DREAMRIDER** (2006), is tough and spooky, rather than tough and funny.

THE END

about the author

Agnes Nieuwenhuizen was born in Iran to Hungarian parents and immigrated to Australia in 1949. By the age of 10, Agnes read in three languages and spoke another two. Books and reading were her main means of contact with her father, who introduced her to major British, American and European writers, whom she read avidly throughout high school. But she often struggled to finish class novels – not the right books at the right time and not chosen freely.

As a teacher, Agnes realised that even the most alienated and reluctant young people responded to story, so she read aloud to students of all ages and abilities and encouraged them to choose what to read. Books continue to feature in family dinner table discussions and to be shared and given as gifts. Agnes's immediate family are all readers and include a translator, two editors, a former publisher and Writers' Festival director, and six book-loving grandsons.

After many years of teaching, Agnes undertook Graduate Studies in children's literature, and in 1991 she established the Youth Literature Project to promote books and reading to and for teenagers, through a wide range of innovative, events based programs. In 1999 this program relocated to the State Library of Victoria, in a significantly enhanced form, as the Centre for Youth Literature. She retired from this work in 2005, but the Centre continues to evolve and flourish. In 1994 Agnes established the Youth Literature Days of the Melbourne Writers' Festival. She continued to devise and co-ordinate this program until 1998, by which time audiences of teenagers had increased to 3000.

Agnes has written and reviewed widely in the field, including two previous good book guides for teenagers. She edited the ground-breaking collection of essays, *The Written World: youth and literature* (DW Thorpe, 1994). In 1995, Agnes received the Dromkeen Medal for services to youth literature.

contributors

Trevor Agnew, a former History and English teacher, is now a freelance writer. He contributes to the Continuum Encyclopaedia of Young Adult Literature (USA) and writes for *The Press*, *Magpies* and *The Literature Base*. Trevor's interest in science fiction and fantasy began with Dr Doolittle's flight to the moon and continues to the present. His home groans under the weight of SF from Aldiss to Gibson, Asimov to Zelazny. Currently, he is excited by the resurgence of SF for teenagers at home in New Zealand.

Linnet Hunter is passionate about visual narrative and approaches picture books as an art form closer to film than any other. She has a particular interest in sophisticated picture books for older readers. Linnet reviews picture books, contributes to the *Education Age*, delivers talks and workshops on 'Reading the Picture book', and is a judge for the CBC Crichton Award, an award for first time illustrators.

John Nieuwenhuizen immigrated to Australia, from Holland, in 1955. At school he studied six languages and enjoyed translating from Latin and Ancient Greek. He worked as a teacher and later as a librarian. He began translating from Dutch into English to re-establish contact for himself and his children with his language and culture of origin. Also published in USA and UK, John has been short-listed for translation prizes in Victoria, NSW and the UK and his translation of *The Baboon King* won the prestigious US Mildred Batchelder Award.

Robyn Sheahan-Bright operates justified text writing and publishing consultancy services, teaches writing for children and young adults for Griffith University, and has published widely on teenage literature. Co-editor of *Paper Empires: A History of the Book in Australia (1946–2005)* (2006), she is also a judge for the Qld Premier's Literary Awards (YA category). Robyn greatly admires the richly intriguing intensity of Margo Lanagan's short stories, and has written Reading Group notes on *Red Spikes*.

Mike Shuttleworth's passion for reading when he was a teenager grew in proportion to his increasing awareness that he would not (a) play first ruck for South Fremantle and (b) replace Dennis Lillee as Western Australia's opening bowler. As an adult he is Program Coordinator at the Centre for Youth Literature, State Library of Victoria but retains a watching brief on many sports.

Kevin Steinberger is a former judge of the Children's Book Council Awards including the Eve Pownall Award for Information Books. He also reviews for a number of children's literature journals. As a teacher-librarian he is intrigued by the appeal of non-fiction to boys, especially books of unusual content and quirky presentation.

Erica Wagner has spent most of her life so far working with books, first as a bookseller, then as an editor and publisher. She was with Penguin Books Australia for ten years, before starting a children's list for Duffy & Snellgrove. In 1999 she was awarded the Beatrice Davis Editorial Fellowship and in 2000 she moved to Allen & Unwin where she continues to publish a range of picture books, fiction and non-fiction for children and teenagers. Illustrated books and graphic novels are a particular passion.

Lili Wilkinson reads a lot of teenage fiction. She seems to have become a resident expert on YA fantasy but also has a particular interest in popular culture and how people respond to this. Lili works at the Centre for Youth Literature, State Library of Victoria, managing Australia's first website about books for young people. Her YA books include *Joan of Arc* and *Scatterheart*, a novel about convicts, fairy tales and a giant white Bear.

acknowledgements

Thanks to the State Library of Victoria for permission to reproduce some sections of reviews I wrote for the newsletters of the Centre for Youth Literature (CYL) during my seven lively and productive years there. Special thanks to Mike Shuttleworth and Lili Wilkinson, my colleagues during the latter half of this period and contributors to this book. Their enthusiasm for books and promoting reading to teenagers enhanced my work and that of the CYL. Ray Turton provided invaluable suggestions and generously read much of RBRT when I needed encouragement. As always thanks to my ever present husband John, who gave me heart to finish this project during particularly difficult times. Our children, their partners and our six grandsons, all great book lovers, also constantly remind me of the joys and solace of reading. And all at Allen & Unwin have, as always, been kind, warm, highly professional – and patient.

The publishers would like to thank Meme McDonald for the photo on page 168, and istockphoto.com and the following photographers for photos used in the text: i Izabela Habur (girl reading), iv Nick Schlax (typewriter/Once upon a time), xii Anne Clark (man), 24 Andrew Dernie (knight), 50 Henk Badenhorst (boxer), 82 Stan Rippel (dragon), 110 Raveto07 (heart), 115 doodlemachine (game players), 140 Brian Chase (veiled girl), 181 Jaap2 (Anne Frank stamp), 192 Galina Barskaya (flying men), 238 Robert Churchill (playing volleyball), 256 Joseph Justice (statue of soldier), 284 Christine Balderas (question marks), 316 Michael Valdez (bubblegum girl), 337 Nick Schlax (typewriter/THE END).

Thanks also to the publishers of the titles mentioned in this book, for access to proof copies, cover images and extracts.

index

343